D0875283

DUTY OR PLEASURE?

*A New Appraisal of
Christian Ethics*

DUTY OR PLEASURE?

A New Appraisal of Christian Ethics

by Albert Plé, O.P.

Translated by
Matthew J. O'Connell

 Paragon House Publishers
New York

Published in the United States by
Paragon House Publishers
2 Hammarskjöld Plaza
New York, New York 10017

English translation copyright 1987 by Paragon House Publishers

Originally published as *Par Devoir ou par Plaisir?* copyright Les
Editions du Cerf, 1980

Library of Congress Cataloging in Publication Data

Plé, Albert, 1909–
    Duty or pleasure?

    Translation of: Par devoir ou par plaisir?
    Includes index.
    1. Christian ethics.   2. Pleasure.   I. Title.
BJ1252.P5713   1986   241   86–16986
ISBN 0–913729–24–8
ISBN 0–913729–25–6 (pbk.)

Contents

Part II

Introduction

"Having recovered two cents' worth of reason—it is soon gone!—I see that my disquietudes come from having understood too late that we are in the Occident—Occidental swamps!" This diagnosis by Arthur Rimbaud in his *A Season in Hell*[1] has long been for me a tiny light in the mist.

With Freud we may ask whether "under the influence of cultural urges, some civilizations, or some epochs of civilization—possibly the whole of mankind—have become 'neurotic.' "[2] If so, might it not also be possible and enlightening to diagnose the neurosis that affects Western civilization?

Such a diagnosis might throw some light on what it has become customary to call the "crisis of ethics." As a science and wisdom that has human moral attitudes and behaviors for its subject, ethics is lived (and turned into theory) within the framework of knowledge that is historically and geographically situated, within a concrete civilization. This is true of the "traditional" moral thinking that is associated with Christendom. Will not a neurotic civilization have a neurotic morality?

My intention in this book is to attempt a diagnosis of the neurosis affecting the West and especially of its morality. But I must immediately add (I shall return to the point later on) that in my opinion this neurosis acquired its structure and became widespread during the great fear which marked the fourteenth and fifteenth centuries[3] and not, as many believe, two centuries later.

The neurosis of the West may be characterized as a schizophrenia[4] accompanied by related symptoms of paranoia and obsessional neurosis.

A collective neurosis is, of course, not identical with a neurosis suffered by an individual. "The disorders of society bear some resemblance to individual disorders, but to go any further . . . is sheer word-play."[5] Nonetheless I think it useful to recall the psychiatric symptoms of schizophrenia; they will be a source of light in making my diagnosis of the collective level.

Schizein means to "divide by splitting" or simply to "cut." The schizophrenic is divided both within himself and in his relation to external reality. While it is true that the loss of reality is common to all mental illnesses,[6] this is especially true of the schizophrenic: his fear of reality is such that he flees from it to the point of being divided within himself. His illness is marked by *Spaltung*: dissociation, fragmentation. "Two mental attitudes have been formed instead of a single one—one, the normal one, which takes account of reality, and another which under the influence of the instincts detaches the ego from reality. The two exist alongside each other."[7]

Finding itself "in the position of warding off some claim from the external world which it feels as painful," the ego reacts "by denying the perceptions that bring to knowledge such a demand on the part of reality." The negative procedures, however, "turn out to be half-measures, incomplete attempts at detachment from reality. The rejection is always supplemented by an acceptance; two contrary and independent attitudes always arise and this produces the fact of a split in the ego."[8]

Schizophrenia seems to be connected with an inadequate response to the stimulus-response process, with a diffuse anxiety,[9] a fear of reality and of relationships with others, a self-doubt[10] that can reach the point of autism, or, in any case, with a predominant withdrawal into the self which gives itself over to productions marked by fantasy,[11] rationalism, excessive logic, and the geometrical spirit.

The reason for this is that when the intellectual life is more or less cut off from reality, it operates in a world of verbal magic, systematism, and idealism. The schizophrenic "treats concrete things as though they were abstract"[12] and refuses even to think about any reality that causes anxiety.

> Inasmuch as anything contrary to the affect is repressed to a greater than normal degree while everything consonant with the affect is favored in an equally abnormal way, the end result is that the subject is no longer capable of thinking of anything which contradicts an affect-laden idea. In his delusion the schizophrenic dreams only of his desires; anything that might prevent the fulfillment of these desires does not exist for him.[13]

The partial or total loss of investment of the affect in objects[14] locks the schizophrenic into an affectivity that is closed, hypersensitive yet not communicable, apparently cold, tending toward inhibition and stereotyped behavior, but also bursting out in impulsive[15] and compulsive discharges, obsessions, phobias, and so on.

All of these symptoms are more or less marked and extensive depending on whether the person is psychotic or neurotic. They may also be found in what is called the "schizoid character.[16] In this case they are to be interpreted as defenses against anxiety. Here we see the superego acting destructively at the expense of the ego, a poor self-image, a keen sense of duty, a stern self-discipline, a perfectionism, a dominant fanaticism, a propensity to defend God against his enemies. There is also a difficulty in communicating with others (such a person lives *beside* others but not *with* them; there is a wall of separation between him and the rest of the human race, a conviction that no one can love him), an absence of joy (the person is detached, cold, empty), a systematic relationalizing of feelings and behavior, and finally a lack of effectiveness in action.

If these traits are observable in a civilization, then the latter too can be called schizophrenic, although we are dealing, of course, only with an analogy. Such is the approach George Devereux takes when he says that modern civilization is suffering "from socio-politico-economic schizophrenia."[17]

Devereux sees as one proof of this the fact that schizophrenic psychoses and neuroses are becoming increasingly common in the West and that they resist any and every treatment. "The underlying conflict of the psychosis or neurosis is also present in the majority of the normal people. The conflict in the neurotic or the psychotic is simply *more* intense than it is in other people. In short, the patient is *like* everyone else, but more intensely so than anyone else."[18]

In Devereux's view, schizophrenic psychoses and neuroses are "strong indications of disorientation in a changing environment."[19] A disoriented society[20] disorients the individuals who make it up, and their efforts to orient themselves cannot shake off the influence of the surrounding schizophrenia or of what Maurice Bellet calls "the englobing."[21]

This widespread neurosis of the West shows itself in symptoms which Devereux has analyzed: the childishness of parents, the refusal of children to grow up, destructiveness, a fascination with death and the return to the inorganic, depersonalization, affective and intellectual (systematism) impoverishment, unrealism, idealism, blurring of the difference between imaginary and real, fixation and regression of the instincts (hallucinations, "commands coming from outside"), ambivalence (obedience—disobedience), loneliness, rejection of differences, fragmentation (inability to apprehend a person in his or her totality), discordances, and so on.[22]

I am convinced that Western civilization, especially since the fourteenth century, has been showing most of the symptoms of a collective schizophrenia. This is due in large measure to the social, political, and economic disorientation which Europe experienced at the end of the Middle Ages and to the resultant insecurity and anxiety among the people.[23]

The people tried to protect themselves by seeking security in "order," both in the street and in the mind, both in institutions and in morals. This defense against anxiety itself reflects a schizophrenia in its denial of the intolerable aspects of reality and in the "excisions" that are typical of this pathological condition. My interpretation makes possible a degree of understanding of the greatnesses and weaknesses of Western civilization. Here are some concrete applications of the interpretation.

The human person is interiorly divided. The ancient dualism of soul and body which comes to us from Platonism, gnosticism, and Mazdeism (all of them so alien to biblical anthropology[24]) increasingly leaves its mark on the habits of people (they stop bathing; the body is a "sewer of impurities," and so on) and is systematized in Cartesian philosophy. According to the latter, the soul is thought (*res cogitans*) and the body only a machine that is external to the soul, an extended thing (*res extensa*) that is subject to measurement and number.

The processes of understanding also show a break with reality outside the subject, as the nominalism of Abelard (eleventh century) is taken over by William Occam (first half of the fourteenth century) and then spreads throughout the Western world. According to the Nominalists we know only words, concepts, and the individual knower. A concept is simply an "image," a nonreal object of intellection or a "natural sign which is a real quality of the soul."[25] Reality outside the subject is unknown and denied. Individuals know only their thoughts. Western idealist philosophies, from Descartes to Kant and Hegel, will suffer from the same eclipse of reality, which remains beyond the grasp of the thinking subject.

It is true that "reality will always remain 'unknowable' "[26] and that this fact is a cause of insecurity and anxiety. This means, however, that reality will be experienced after the manner of schizophrenics: being compelled to renounce the "path to the object . . . by way of the word belonging to it, they then have . . . to content themselves with words in the place of things."[27] Schizophrenics "treat concrete things as though they were abstract."[28]

According to Freud, this approach to reality also shows certain traits proper to the world of animist thinking, such as "the overvaluation of the magic of words and the belief that the real events in the world take the course which our thinking seeks to impose on them."[29] There may also be a kinship here with the delusions of paranoiacs and their tendency to construct speculative systems.[30]

Thus cut off from the outside world are "thinkers who were for the most part turned away from the world"[31] and "philosophers, who know no kind of observation other than self-observation."[32] Such people tend to an "overvaluation of their own intellectual operations."[33] The criterion of truth then becomes the internal coherence of the discourse. The one discoursing is locked into his or her own autistic world.

Without going so far as this, we must indeed recognize some schizophrenic traits in the thinkers and philosophers of the West: the exaggeration of Aristotelian logic in decadent Scholasticism, the idealist philosophies, the fixism that characterizes essentialism, the rationalist dogmatism that leads to the cult of the goddess Reason in Robespierre and to the "God Logos" of Freud.[34]

In all this we are dealing not with isolated writers but with a prevalent mentality that is especially marked in "intellectuals," professors, engineers, jurists, technicians and administrators . . . and in moralists (nor should we overlook academicism in the world of art). "The intellectual has no direct contact with the raw material of life, but meets it in the synthetic form of it which is easiest to grasp: on the written page."[35]

More or less imprisoned, as they have been, in the autistic world of words and ideas, Westerners have lost the sense of the "relational" character of being and language. Words and concepts admittedly do not say everything there is to be said about the realities they express, but they do tell us something about them to the extent that they lead the mind beyond themselves to the realities which send out signals to us even if they do not make themselves known fully. However, for this very reason, reality is a source of anxiety, since it does not allow itself to be appropriated in a way that would bring a feeling of security.

Words and concepts establish a relation between the subject and that which is at once known and unknowable, present and absent. They lead the gaze to a void, a gaping emptiness, which the schizophrenic finds so intolerable that he reduces reality to ideas, to words that refer to nothing but the thinking subject himself. He uses them as a protective shell against the onslaught of reality.

"Words . . . are transformed from symbols into 'objects.' "[36] There is no longer any back-and-forth between symbol and reality.

A symbol is characterized by the fact that it is not a simple sign, because it shows a profound analogy with that to which it points, and by the fact that we cannot simply get rid of it after we have perceived that which it communicates. It cannot be replaced, and this distinguishes it from allegory. We must constantly return to it in order to feed and flesh out the meaning already discovered as well as in order to control, as it were, the extension and penetration of this meaning.[37]

The inability to utilize symbols properly is especially clear in the meaning that has been given to the word "mystery" since the fourteenth century. In the language of the Bible and the Fathers and as late as the thirteenth century,[38] "mystery" simultaneously embraces both "sign" and "signified reality" as a united pair. A mystery is a sign by which we understand in faith a reality that is both present and absent. Today, however, and for many centuries now, a mystery has been something obscure which we shall try in vain to understand: "you must not try to understand it."

There is thus a rupture between sign and signified reality. There is also a rupture in relations with other human beings; these are felt to threaten the subject with a loss of identity.[39] He therefore turns in on himself and falls into a certain autism such as is reflected, according to Occam, in the insularity of individuals, or in the monads of Leibnitz, or in the individualism that looks upon society as nothing more than a heap of individual persons.

There is a rupture within the human person as a result of Descartes' second precept in his *A Discourse on Method:* "To divide each of the difficulties under examination into as many parts as possible, and as might be necessary for its adequate solution."[40] When this principle is applied to human beings, they too are divided up into small parts and become an object of the knowledge and activity of a multitude of "specialists" (even within medicine) who have no connection with one another and no overall ("holistic") view of the person in its totality.

All these divisions or ruptures are of a schizophrenic kind, although they are happily offset by the inconsistencies that are habitually found in this pathological condition. There is one part of reality that the Western person has not refused to know. "The schizophrenic's fear of the world is proportioned to the attraction it holds for him."[41] In the Western world, knowledge of the real has made its way and prospered in the sciences based on observation and experimentation, in the application of mathematics and technical knowledge, and in the human sciences (history, sociology, ethnology, psychology, and so on). Westerners can thus acquire a control of the world and allay the fears they experience when faced with the forces of nature and social life.

The search for security above all else caused the merchants and bourgeoisie at the time of the fourteenth century crisis to focus their attention on the possession of goods and thus led to an extraordinary development of the economic side of life. The Western world has since been living under the tyranny of an endless and accelerating development of wealth; in the eyes of the far-sighted this phenomenon represents a grave threat to the human race.[42]

Schizophrenic ruptures and inconsistencies are also to be found in the affective life. Logical thinking, and especially thinking that is logical in a narrow and exclusive way, has no influence on what goes on in the id, the processes of which such thinking rejects in part: it "repudiates some of these processes and seeks to undo them."[43]

The most symptomatic example of this rejection is the elimination of all affectivity from the sphere of understanding. Since the fourteenth century, intellect has operated in a heaven rendered aseptically clean of all affectivity. In earlier times, intellect was recognized as having an affectivity; the human intellect was regarded as capable of love and other affects. This capacity was called "the will." The fact that the Western languages (except for Spanish) no longer have a word to express intellectual affectivity is in my view one of the specific symptoms of Western schizophrenia. We are forced to speak of "the understanding of the heart" because among "voluntarist" philosophers and theologians "will" now refers only to a predominance of volition over intellect in the determination of good and evil, and, in current usage, to contorted, tenacious, painful effort.

The affective life, when thus mutilated, is reduced to passions and feelings, and shares in a Manichean contempt for the body and especially for sexuality. Unable to rid themselves completely of affectivity and sexuality, people claim to "master" them by a will that is subject to law and authority, and not any longer by the ascendancy of the love-inspired intellect.

When repressed by prohibitions and taboos, the affective life finds a possible outlet in devotion (devotio moderna, the Sacred Heart, and so on) and in a mystical experience that draws little of its nourishment from scripture and the "mysteries of faith," but instead is immanentist or pantheistic (the Rhineland mystics), pessimistic about the human person, and individualistic (the Imitation of Christ). In the secular world we find a "faith" in the goodness of man and nature (J. J. Rousseau) or in humanity, reason, science, progress, and so on. We also see people attracted by the occult, [44] by astrology, clairvoyancy, witchcraft, and more or less freakish mysticisms. As Freud observed, these forms of mysticism are "the obscure self-perception of the realm outside the ego, of the id."[45]

The separation of affectivity from intellect is an obstacle to the successful control of the id by the ego and thus to reaching the decisive stage of maturity which Freud describes when he says: "Where id was, there ego shall be."[46] The repressed id then finds masked expression in irrational beliefs that are uncriticized and delusory or utopian but that also give security against social or individual anxiety. Security at any price is sought in dogmatism, ritualism, formalism, or blind submission to religious or political authority (the two forms of authority are closely tangled up with each other). Now that it has been decapitated and repressed, the affective life of the Western world is sick.

The same holds for morality, whether we mean by this word the actual behavior of people or the teaching of morality at the popular and university levels. It, too, looks for security above all else and, to get it, seeks the shelter provided by authority. Morality is based (to the exclusion of the invitations given in the gospel) on law (the commandments of God and the Church) that is promulgated by an absolute divine power which arbitrarily (voluntarism) issues its decrees on good and evil, these last being understood as what is permitted and what is forbidden. The West has thus opted for a juridicism in morality, for the obsessional refinements of casuistry, and for a confusion of the religious and political powers as guarantors of order and security.

Security is thus found in a moral fixism that is deduced from a human nature conceived, in essentialist fashion, as giving moral laws a universal and immutable character. Morality seeks to be "objective" to the extent of paying no heed to the subject and the relationships that make up his or her experience, or to his or her history and social, economic, and cultural environments. This is a morality that stands outside of time and the human milieu, an individualist morality. It is the morality of a mutilated subject whose relational being has been fragmented; the morality of a schizophrenic who finds an illusory soothing of his or her anxiety and doubts in the stern rigidity of laws. "The mind most prone to doubt always aspires to the greatest degree of Jansenism."[47] This morality based on public order seems to afford security because it allows, and even sets an excessive value on, the reassurance provided by a "good conscience" (which is confirmed by a good reputation), wealth, private property, income, and indefinite (and irreversible) growth in economic goods that are desired for their own sake and as end in themselves. The predominance in the West of the economic sphere is showing itself to be increasingly damaging to human beings, as well as idolatrous and demonic in character.

Here, at the beginning of this book, I want to say how angry it makes me to read and hear that this "traditional" morality is Christian and Catholic. In fact, it seems to me to be much closer to "the leaven of the Pharisees and the leaven of Herod" (Mk 8:15) than to the leaven of the gospel (Lk 13:21; 1 Cor 5:6–8).

And indeed this traditional morality perpetuates the attitudes that are typical of the Pharisees ("lovers of money": Lk 16:14) who were so harshly criticized by Christ beginning with the Sermon on the Mount: "Unless your righteousness exceeds that of the scribes and Pharisees, you will never enter the kingdom of heaven" (Mt 5:20). St. Paul, for his part, would constantly insist that the "practicers" of the Law are under God's curse (Gal 3:10). "You are severed from Christ, you who would be justified by the law" (Gal 5:14).

To the extent that Christians, led by the moralists, allow themselves to be locked into an idolatry of the law, they can no longer be disciples of Jesus Christ and in fact they bear witness against him. "Woe to you lawyers! for you have taken away the key of knowledge; you did not enter yourselves, and you hindered those who were entering" (Lk 11:52). The practice of the law has closed them to the gospel; those are not set free "who through fear of death were subject to lifelong bondage" (Heb 2:15).

This "abominable interpretation" of the gospel by human beings[48] has been traditional for centuries, but it is not Christian. This is not to deny, however, that the gospel has been heard despite the way in which Western culture has deformed and concealed it. As St. Paul said in other circumstances, "in every way, whether in pretense or in truth, Christ is proclaimed; and in that I rejoice" (Phil 1:18).

Regrettable though it is and harmful though it has been, this Western, somewhat schizophrenic way of hearing the word of God is to be understood as a result of the "mystery of the incarnation." As head of his mystical body, Christ is present in human time. The members of his body in this world live in a human environment; they think and act in accordance with a mentality which is that of their political, economic, and cultural milieu and which conditions their hearing of the gospel, allowing them to find in it only what they are looking for. "Misunderstandings" are inevitable, and they vary according to ages and individuals.

Two thousand years of history afford sufficient proof of all this. "The Son of man will be delivered into the hands of men" (Mk 9:31). He was delivered in his physical body, and they put him to death. He continues to be delivered into the hands of people who, if they can no longer kill him, can at least disfigure him, not only by their sins, but also by their "mentalities," which cause them to interpret, distort, and select from the inexhaustible ever new and ever relevant riches of the gospel. "Take heed then how you hear," said Christ to his listeners (Lk 8:18).

This has always been the case and will be to the end of time. As St. Thomas wrote, the ways in which the new law is lived "vary according to places, times, and persons inasmuch as the grace of the Holy Spirit is received more or less perfectly by different individuals."[49]

The way in which it has been received in the West, especially since the fourteenth century, is now a *fait accompli*. but it is not the only way either by right or in fact. Moreover, this Western way is showing itself in our time to be increasingly void and unacceptable. It has seen its day because the cultural "milieu" is no longer that of previous centuries.

In this book I want to explain my rejection of traditional morality and lay the basis for a morality that is as faithful as possible to the gospel and to contemporary human beings.

My study has been stimulated and my thinking marked by my personal and pastoral experience; it has drawn inspiration from scripture and support from moral thought prior to the fourteenth century (especially the morality of Aristotle, St. Augustine, and St. Thomas) and from the human sciences, especially psychoanalysis.

My appeal to these great masters does not mean that I am locking myself into their writings and systems. They have, however, confirmed me in thinking that a morality different from the traditional one is possible. Other ways may be travelled; those that I have taken have led me closer to the reality of human beings and the gospel. I hope that they will do the same for the reader.

Let me say it right off: I see this other morality as based on the fact and the laws of the quest for happiness and even for pleasure (in a sense which I shall define in due time). It is the task of morality to humanize and evangelize this pleasure.

PART
I

Chapter 1

The Moralities of Happiness

Until moralities based on law and duty became widespread in the fifteenth century, the various systems of morality, however different among themselves, had one thing in common: they were all grounded in the search for happiness. This is true of the Greek philosophers (except for the Stoics); it is true also of the gospel and the earliest Christian tradition.

These are statements that call for justification in terms of the facts. I shall, however, limit myself to a few essential "sources": the New Testament, the Greeks, and St. Augustine.

The Good News

We will search the New Testament in vain for a set of moral laws, a Decalogue, a list of duties. The New Testament is concerned with the good news of human liberation from judgment by a God who plays the spy.

The primary object of obedience to God is faith and the "gospel of Christ" (2 Cor 9:13); a Christian's obligations are those of charity. The "commandments" given are introduced not by a "Thou shalt" but by a descriptive adjective: "blessed" are you or will you be (or, conversely, "woe" to you).

I am not referring here solely to the beatitudes which form the prologue to the "programmatic discourse" with which Christ begins his three years of preaching.[1] As a matter of fact, the little word "blessed" occurs fifty-five times in the New Testament,[2] in passages where the moralists would have spoken rather of duties.

For example, after the washing of the feet, Christ urges his disciples to imitate him and be servants to their brethren; then he says: "If you know these things, blessed are you if you do them" (Jn 13: 17). He does not say: "You must. . . ."

In like manner, he says to a man who invites the poor to his table: "You will be blessed, because they cannot repay you" (Lk 14:14).

"Blessed are those servants whom the master finds awake when he comes" (Lk 12:37–46). The man who finds a treasure in a field "in his joy" sells all that he has in order to buy it (Mt 13:44). "It is more blessed to give than to receive" (Acts 20:35; cf. Rom 12:8; 2 Cor 9: 7).

The disciples of Christ have joy: the joy of faith,[3] the joy of Christ's presence,[4] the joy given by Christ[5] and by the Holy Spirit.[6] They have the joy of hope[7] and even more the joy of charity[8] which is to inspire the moral practices and thus the moral code of Christ's disciples.

After Pentecost the fervor of the apostles and their converts is marked by a joy[9] which is present as well in their eucharistic assemblies.[10]

How could the Good News fail to be a source of joy? It was this from the time when it was first proclaimed: for Mary[11] and for John the Baptist.[12] For it gives us access once again to God as he really is: a loving and merciful Father; it restores our pledge of a return to the lost Paradise which is loving intimacy with God.

As a result, our daily activity as adoptive children of God bears the stamp of the mercy which we have received from God and which we exercise in turn toward our fellow human beings. Now that we have been freed from "the curse of the Law" we have the happy experience of no longer being "judged" (Rom 4:6–9). The commandments of the new covenant urge us to make progress in love (and in the fruit of love, which is joy); they are no longer proposed to us as duties imposed by divine authority "under penalty of death."[13] He who puts into practice "the perfect law, the law of liberty . . . shall be blessed in his doing" (Jas 1:25).

This happiness—which does not exclude cares, sufferings, tribulations, and persecutions[14]—is also experienced in regard to "earthly" goods, including wealth: "God . . . richly furnishes us with everything to enjoy" (1 Tim 6:17).[15]

Conversely, "Woe!" is the judgment passed on those who refuse to believe in the one sent by the Father (Mt 11:21; Lk 10:13), on those who find their consolation in their wealth (Lk 6:24), and especially on the Pharisees and lawyers (Mt 23; Lk 11:52), to say nothing of Judas (Mk 14:21; Lk 22:22).

If, then, we are to highlight what is specific to an authentically Christian morality, we must say that it is not structured as a morality of duty, of law, or of blind and fearful obedience to authority. On the contrary, it is a morality based on faith in the mercy of a Father "who is Love." It is a morality of love, and its fruit is joy.

This joy, moreover, is not reserved for the next life. It is already present and experienced on earth, even though our joy here is only a foretaste of the blessedness of Paradise regained that will be ours on the day of the Parousia.

The morality of the gospel is a morality of happiness.

The Greeks

Greek moral philosophies (except for those of Zeno and Antisthenes[16]) have one thing in common: all of them make the search for happiness the focus of the moral life.

This happiness, or *eudaimonia*, includes a euphoria or sense of well-being, an absence of suffering and disturbances, a harmony, and, above all, measure.

The happy are those who have received a good share of luck from the gods and the goddess Fortune in particular; they are the fortunate people who have been able to profit by what has been given to them. It is through this happiness that they share the life of the gods: "The divine [*daimōn*] seeks in all things to attain to the blessed life," says Plato,[17] while Aristotle will observe: "It may be said that the happy person is the one whose *daimōn* is virtuous; as Xenocrates says: that person is happy who has a virtuous soul, for the soul is the *daimōn* of the whole person."[18]

This kind of *eudaimonia* is the happiness of the philosopher, for whom morality is normed by what is good, beautiful, and a source of pleasure. A. J. Festugière sums up as follows the typically Greek ideal embodied in this kind of morality:

> Here we meet again the basically Greek idea of *metriotēs* (measure), of what is good and wise and just, and therefore beautiful as well. In a final step—one that is likewise consistent with the most authentic traditions of the Greek mind—the beautiful and good is assimilated to the pleasurable and the useful. Right action is the necessary condition of euphoria, but euphoria in turn is the inseparable companion of virtuous action.[19]

If human beings act rightly, they bring their natural capacities to full development; they attain the end for which they were made:

> To a Greek the most important thing is not "You ought," but "You can." Existence has meaning for him only if it serves a specific purpose. Each plant and animal has within it an orientation which it brings to fulfillment when it develops fully its innate dispositions. Thus the human person need only develop his own essence fully and

he will reach the best possible state. He will then have attained his end
(telos) and with it his happiness (eudaimonia).[20]

I shall concern myself here only with the greatest of the Greek
philosophers, the ones who have left the deepest mark on the Western and Christian world. Specifically, I shall review the teaching of
Plato, Epicurus and Aristotle on pleasure and morality.

Plato

Like all the Greeks, Plato seeks the "happy life." He concerns
himself with this subject especially in the Philebus, the theme of
which is stated thus: "Each of us will endeavor to show what state
and disposition of soul is capable of leading every human being to
the happy life" (Philebus lld). The Symposium (205a) says: "It is
through the possession of goods that the happy possess happiness."

But there is a hierarchy of goods and pleasures, and Plato distinguishes pleasures which he calls "mixed" from those which are
"pure." Mixed pleasures are those that satisfy a need and a desire,
desire being the child of a paucity of resources, since "he who desires, desires what he lacks" (Symposium, Ch. 31). "That which a
person lacks is a source of suffering to him; the pure pleasures are
spared this suffering: the pleasures of agreeable perceptions, art, and
philosophical contemplation" (Philebus 51–53).

The contemplation in question has for its object the Good, in
which "beauty, proportion, and truth" are conjoined (Philebus 65a).
This Good resides in the world of the Ideas, of which the physical
universe and its goods are only images. This is why Plato urges the
soul to escape from this world of appearances and its pleasures:
"This is why those who seek to philosophize (in the true sense of the
term) abstain from all bodily desires without exception; they stand
firm and do not put themselves at the mercy of these desires"
(Phaedo 82c).

This escape from the world of the body, which will leave such a
deep mark on all of Greek thought and thereby on Christianity as
well, is accompanied by the persuasion that it is the passions and desires of the body that make us believe in the reality of the objects of
desire, whereas in fact these objects are only illusions and images of
the true Good, which is invisible:

> We are talking mainly of visible things, are we not?
>> Of course.
> But is it not through such affections that the soul becomes most
> fully the prisoner of the body?
>> What do you mean?

Let me explain: every pleasure and every pain has a kind of nail with which it fastens the soul to the body and pins it there, thus making the soul corporeal and causing it to judge things in accordance with what the body says of them. Since the soul thus conforms to the body in its judgment and takes pleasure in the objects which please the body, the inevitable result is, I think, to produce in the soul a conformity of tendencies and of training. The consequence is that it never reaches Hades in a state of purity but always as a soul that has been contaminated by the body which it has now left behind. And so it soon falls back into another body, where it seeds itself, so to speak, and takes root. As a result it is defrauded of all right to share in the life of what is divine and therefore pure and single in form (*Phaedo* 83d).

For Plato, then, true happiness consists in liberation from the body with its needs, sufferings, and pleasures, in order to contemplate the Idea-Forms in their purity. Thus love (*Eros*) gives complete happiness: "It is when he (Eros) seeks the good by following the paths of wisdom and justice, whether within us or in the heavens, that he possesses complete happiness and makes us able to live in society and be the friends even of the gods, far above us though these are" (*Symposium*, Ch. 13).

It is this "ordered Eros" (*Banquet*, Ch. 13) that inspires and determines the search for happiness.

The morality of Plato is thus a stranger to the idea of duty and of a law imposed from outside: "Good men spontaneously subject themselves to this law" (*Symposium*, Ch. 9).

This law of Eros bids human beings distinguish carefully among pleasures, give the privileged place to those of philosophical contemplation, and refuse to make pleasure the highest of goods. The most excellent of all goods is not pleasure but intellectual activity: "The intellect [*nous*] is far more excellent than pleasure, and a far greater source of benefit for the life of the human race" (*Philebus* 66e).

Plato connects what we nowadays call morality with the political sphere and is of the opinion that "anyone who would concern himself with laws should devote his attention almost wholly to the problem of pleasures and pains, in the individual and in cities" (*Laws* 636d–e).

In short, Platonic morality—if we may use this term—is not based on duty and law, but on the love-inspired passion for the Beautiful, for an "ordered" love, for a proper evaluation of pleasures, in the search for the happy life—which is located in the world of the Ideas, beyond bodies and their illusory and enslaving pleasures.

Need I remind the reader of the extent to which Platonism—and Neo-platonism,[21] which had a more direct impact during the first centuries of the Christian era—influenced the thinking and mental structures of Christianity: the Christianity of the Church Fathers,[22] of the Middle Ages,[23] and of the Renaissance?[24] Though the Platonic contempt for the body left an unfortunate mark on the Western world, it also left us the heritage of a morality that has its source of development within itself and not in something external, a morality inspired and ordered by love and the search for happiness.

Epicurus

The reputation inflicted on Epicurus, "the pig," especially by the Stoics, was false and even slanderous. The real Epicurus was quite different, if we may judge by the few writings, letters, and fragments that have survived from the three hundred scrolls he supposedly filled.[25]

Epicurus was first of all an observer of nature. We owe him a summary, remarkably acute for its times, of the atomic theory of Democritus. He was also an observer of human beings. He writes to Herodotus: "I . . . urge . . . the constant occupation in the study of nature, and find my own peace chiefly in a life so occupied."[26] He pursues this study of nature and of humanity even when he is ill:

> Epicurus says, In my sickness my conversation was not about my bodily sufferings, nor, says he, did I talk on such subjects to those who visited me; but I continued to discourse on the nature of things as before, keeping to this main point, how the mind, while participating in such movements as go on in the poor flesh, shall be free from perturbations and maintain its proper good.[27]

Epicurus—and this is the most remarkable thing about his thought—is not a philosopher in the Platonic mold; instead, he observes facts and tries to understand them. He regards perception as of fundamental importance and considers it to be the fourth element (which he declares to be "undefinable") of the soul, the other three being fire, air, and the breath of life.[28] "Epicurus used to say that all sensations are true and existent, for he made no distinction between saying that a thing is true and saying that it exists."[29] We are far removed here from Plato and "Truth as such."

It is in this realistic perspective that Epicurus takes note of the place pleasure has in human life: "Quite different is the opinion of Epicurus who posits as the basis of every judgment the senses, the ideas of things, and pleasure."[30]

He regards pleasure and pain as "primary affections,"[31] but he does not confuse pleasure with the happy life (*eudaimonia*). He does, however, think that the happy life begins and ends in pleasure: "For this cause we call pleasure the beginning and end of the blessed life. For we recognize pleasure as the first good innate in us."[32]

Being a realist, he supposedly said, to the great shock of the idealists, that "the source and root of all good is the pleasure of the stomach; even wisdom and culture must be referred to this."[33] This does not mean that he regards the pleasures of the stomach as the most important. He is simply observing a fact. In his view, the wise person is the one who passes judgment on pleasures and rejects those that are an obstacle to the happy life:

> From pleasure we begin every act of choice and avoidance, and to pleasure we return again, using the feeling as the standard by which we judge every good. And since pleasure is the first good and natural to us, for this very reason we do not choose every pleasure, but sometimes we pass over many pleasures, when greater discomfort accrues to us as the result of them: and similarly we think many pains better than pleasures, since a greater pleasure comes to us when we have endured pains for a long time. Every pleasure then because of its natural kinship to us is good, yet not every pleasure is to be chosen: even as every pain is also an evil, yet not all are always of a nature to be avoided. Yet, by a scale of comparison and by the consideration of advantages and disadvantages, we must form our judgment on all these matters. For the good on certain occasions we treat as bad, and conversely the bad as good.[34]

In this same letter to Menoecius, Epicurus draws conclusions from this differentiation of pleasures and from the search for the "greater pleasure," which in his view is the pleasure of wisdom and virtue:

> When, therefore, we maintain that pleasure is the end, we do not mean the pleasures of profligates and those that consist in sensuality, as is supposed by some who are either ignorant or disagree with us or do not understand, but freedom from pain in the body and from trouble in the mind. For it is not continuous drinkings and revellings, nor the satisfaction of lusts, nor the enjoyment of fish and other luxuries of the wealthy table, which produce a pleasant life, but sober reasoning, searching out the motives for all choice and avoidance, and banishing mere opinions, to which are due the greatest disturbance of the spirit.
>
> Of all this the beginning and the greatest good is prudence. Wherefore prudence is a more precious thing even than philosophy: for from prudence are sprung all the other virtues, and it teaches us that it is not possible to live pleasantly without living prudently and honourably and justly. . . . For the virtues are by nature bound up with the pleasant life, and the pleasant life is inseparable from them.[35]

Pleasure, then, while remaining the beginning and end of the happy life, is not identical with it. Epicurus looks for "static pleasures;" he puts it this way in his book *Concerning Choice and Avoidance*: "Freedom from trouble in the mind [ataraxia] and from pain in the body are static pleasures, but joy and exultation are considered as active pleasures involving motion."[36]

Epicurus aims at this *ataraxia* (which is the ancestor of, but also different from, the Stoic's *apatheia*) and in his search for pleasure makes it his primary concern to avoid pain and disturbance.[37] He looks to achieve this liberation by a certain detachment, which consists not in keeping reality at a distance, as Zeno thought, but in a careful observation of reality.

Observing, for example, that one of the greatest human fears springs from the prospect of death, Epicurus urges us to confront it: "Death is nothing to us: for that which is dissolved is without sensation; and that which lacks sensation is nothing to us."[38]

Epicurean *ataraxia* is the happy result of a "healing" of pains and anxieties. In the fragments of his book *On Nature*, which were discovered during the excavation at Herculanum, we find this wish: "Let us only keep at hand this fourfold remedy: God is not to be feared; in death there will be no sensation; the good is easy to obtain; suffering is easy to bear."[39]

This *ataraxia* of the happy life enables human beings to be self-sufficient: "And again independence of desire we think a great good —not that we may at all times enjoy but a few things, but that, if we do not possess many, we may enjoy the few in the genuine persuasion that those have the sweetest pleasure in luxury who least need it."[40]

It is in this way that the wise man is rich: "The wise man when he has accomodated himself to straits knows better how to give than to receive: so great is the treasure of self-sufficiency which he has discovered."[41] This leads him to freedom, because "the greatest fruit of self-sufficiency is freedom."[42]

We slander Epicurus, therefore, when we depict him as teaching people to be sensualists. In my opinin, he simply takes for his starting point as "scientific" a study of reality as was possible for him in his time. He does not turn to the world of the Ideas; instead, realizing the basic importance in human life of the search for pleasure and the flight from pain, he makes this the basis of a wisdom that does not preach the satisfaction of all desires but on the contrary distinguishes among desires. The purpose of this distinction is the attainment of the happy life, a life that is as free as possible thanks to the detachment attained through *ataraxia* (which, we repeat, is not the Stoic *apatheia*).

It is in this "realistic" outlook that he sees the outlook of the wise person in regard to desires: "We must not violate nature, but obey her; and we shall obey her if we fulfill the necessary desires and also the physical, if they bring no harm to us, but sternly reject the harmful."[43]

We will not find in Epicurus a morality based on duty or any reference to laws (except those that observation detects) or to a Good-in-itself of a Platonic kind. Here we have the unique originality of Epicurus, even though his thinking is controlled by the idea of the happy life, as is the thinking of all the Greeks.

In the face of human reality as it is Epicurus responds as a man of good sense. Consequently he is able to assign pleasure a place that is both basic and relative. In this respect he seems to me to be, along with Aristotle, one of the philosophers who have made an important contribution to the search for a morality in which pleasure has the place it deserves.

But whereas the Stoics, Plato and Plotinus, and then Aristotle, strongly influenced Christian and Western thought, Epicurus was unfortunately but little known and was even misrepresented and calumniated. As a result, he exerted hardly any influence on Christianity, even through his Latin disciple Lucretius.[44]

Aristotle

The *Nicomachean Ethics* begins with the observation that all beings aim at their proper good[45] and that "our actions are ordered to an end which we desire for its own sake" (1094a16-19). This end is the supreme good and, equivalently, happiness (*eudaimonia*). Both the good and the happiness are chosen for themselves and never for the sake of something else. In fact, the sovereign good is happiness. "Most people agree on the name: this good is happiness, according to men generally and cultured people alike, and the other names that might be given to this good: "good life," "doing well," are accepted as equivalent to happiness" (1095a16-19).

Happiness has something divine about it.[46] It is also an end: "Happiness is evidently, then, something final and self-sufficient,[47] for it is the end to which all the objectives of our activity are ordered" (1097b20).

In specifying the happiness proper to human beings, Aristotle rejects the Platonic notion of the Good-in-itself, on the grounds that this has no real existence (1096a11—1097b13) and that the moralist is looking for a good which human beings can take as the object of their action and which they can possess (1096b34). In keeping with his conception of ethics as a "practical science,"[48] he begins with facts and observes that "for all beings that have a task to accomplish and an activity to perform, it is in this task that the good and perfection of the being reside by general admission" (1097b25-26). Now the proper task of the human person is an "activity of the soul in accordance with virtue" (1098a16-17) and, among the virtues, "according to the best and most complete" of them. The activity that is best and most specific to human beings is the activity of the intellect (Logos), "contemplation,"[49] philosophy (1096a2; 117a).

For the majority of human beings, pleasure (*hēdonē*) constitutes happiness; "this is their way of saying that the life they prefer is the

life of enjoyment" (1095b14–16). But there are many other pleasures: "Happiness is at once the supreme good, supreme beauty, and
supreme pleasure, and these attributes must not be separated. . . .
The three attributes belong to the best activities" (1099a24–30).

Aristotle is faithful to the Greek idea of happiness, *eudaimonia*,
according to which the virtuous person and the wise person are
happy. This means for Aristotle that pleasure is "mixed" with happiness: "The whole world believes that the happy life is a pleasurable life, and considers pleasure to be a part of happiness" (1152b15).

Aristotle undertakes an analysis of pleasure which I am obliged to
present here in some detail, since the detail will be useful to me in
the study I have undertaken in this book.

Pleasure is an act (*ergon*). It is not a "movement," that is, a passage from potency to act (1174a14–b7), because every movement
unfolds in time, whereas pleasure is a "complete," "perfect"
whole,[50] as the act of seeing, for example, is complete for as long as it
lasts (1174a14). "Therefore, it is not accurate to say that pleasure is
a 'felt process,' but rather that it is 'an activity of a state which is in
accord with nature,' and that it is 'unhindered' rather than 'felt' "
(1153a12).

"Every pleasure is closely connected with the activity which it
completes" (1175a29), or, in other words, with life.

> If all beings desire pleasure, may we not think that this is because they
> aspire after life? Life, however, is an activity, and each being exercises
> its activity on those objects and with those faculties which it values
> most: the musician, for example, with hearing and melodies, the stu-
> dent with thinking about objects of contemplation, and so on. Pleasure
> completes the activities, and therefore the life, which all beings desire.
> It is to be expected, therefore, that all will aim at pleasure, since for
> each being pleasure completes the life that is precious to it. But do we
> value life for the pleasure it brings, or do we value pleasure because of
> the life it augments? We may leave this question aside for the moment.
> In any case, we see now that life and pleasure are inseparable, because
> without activity there is no pleasure, and pleasure completes activity
> (1175a10–20).

Pleasures and activities "are so closely and inseparably linked that
one might ask whether pleasure and activity are not identical. They
are not, or at least pleasure does not seem to be identical with
thought or sensation; an identification would not be in keeping with
the commonsense view. Yet, being inseparable they seem to some
people to be actually identical" (1175b33).

Aristotle distinguishes as many different pleasures as there are activities,[51] and classifies them according to the three manners of life
which he ranks in the following ascending order: the life of enjoyment, the political life, and the contemplative life (1095b17).

The life of enjoyment is governed by bodily pleasures. These "involve appetite and pain" (1153a3)[52] and lead to excess. Such are the pleasures of children and brutes (1152b15; 1153a27), of young people (1154b9), and of the mass of human beings: "The majority of people show themselves to be really slaves; they prefer the life proper to animals. We allow them only this, that the tastes of the majority are shared by men like Sardanapalus" (1095b19).

If this is the situation, it exists because "bodily pleasures are sought for their own sake, by reason of their intensity, by people who are incapable of enjoying other pleasures" (1154b2). "Because people know only these pleasures, they think there are no others" (1154a1). In addition, these pleasures provide relief for passionate natures,

> since, on the one hand, due to their temperament, their bodies are constantly in torment, and on the other they are always the prey of intense desire; pleasure, however, drives out pain: the pleasure which is opposed to the particular pain, but even any pleasure whatsoever, provided it be intense enough (1154b12–14).

The pleasures accompanying the best activities are of a different kind. Aristotle inquiries after "the best activity of the best disposed subject in relation to the highest objects of that activity. This is the activity that will be the most complete and the most pleasurable" (1174b16–20). He argues that this activity can only be "an activity of the soul in accordance with virtue and, if there is more than one virtue, in accordance with the best and most complete. And we add: in a complete life, for a single swallow does not make a spring, nor does a single fine day, nor does a single day or a short period of time make a human being happy and blessed" (1098a16–20).

Virtuous actions, then, are pleasurable in themselves to those who practice them. "Their life, therefore, has no need of a pleasure that would be added on like a supplementary adornment; on the contrary, the pleasure is inherent in it. Here is a further proof: No person is good who does not find joy in doing good actions" (1099a15–17).

For this reason, pleasure is the best criterion of virtue: "We must see as symptomatic of our moral dispositions the pleasure or pain that follows upon our actions. Does a person find joy in abstaining from bodily pleasures? That person is temperate. Does the abstinence make him cross? He is not temperate" (1104b4–7). For "one cannot feel the pleasure of a just person if one is not just, nor the pleasure of a musician if one is not a musician" (1173b28–30).

This is why the virtuous person supplies the rule and measure for judging in matters of virtue and the good:

In each branch of moral activity the virtuous person judges correctly; in each, things appear to him as what they really are. For each habitual state has its own objects which are beautiful and pleasurable to the virtuous person, and the trait that best distinguishes the virtuous person from every other is undoubtedly his ability to see what is true in each branch of activity, since he is himself as it were the norm and measure (1113a29-32).

In such an ethics a pleasure is morally good if the action which it accompanies is morally good (1175b26).

It is even desirable to feel pleasure in acting properly, for it is in the pleasure that the activity finds its completion. This is true of every activity, even sensation, which attains completeness when the sensing faculty is in a proper and intense relation to the best of the objects proportioned to it. To every activity pleasure adds "a kind of end which is superadded to the activity as a crown, just as beauty is added to the strength of maturity" (1174b31-33).

In this way, pleasure augments the activity: "Those who find joy in doing geometry become excellent geometers; they are the ones who penetrate most deeply into the various aspects of this science, and the same holds for lovers of music, architecture or any other art" (1175a30-36). The same is true of the intellectual life: "The pleasure we find in contemplating and learning make us contemplate and learn all the more" (1153a22). In short, "the pleasures connected with activities intensify these activities, that is, make them better and more lasting" (1175b13).

On the other hand, the activity and its connected pleasure cease to be complete when they are impeded (1175b13). The hindrance may come from the pleasures associated with other activities:

> The pleasure of listening to the oboe prevents the activity of philosophical discussion. The same kind of thing happens in all other cases in which a person is active in two areas at the same time: the more pleasurable of the two activities excludes the other, and the more pleasurable it is the more it will have this effect until finally the person ceases to exercise the other activity altogether (1175b1-9).

Much more will pain exclude the activity with which it is connected. "The person who finds no joy in writing or calculating does not write or calculate" (1178b15).

If an activity is to be accompanied by pleasure, it must be in our power to do it[53] and we must exercise it "in a completely voluntary way" (1110b11). We must desire the activity: "What a person does against his will is painful, but what he does because he wants to is a source of pleasure" (1111a32). There must, therefore, be desire if there is to be pleasure, because "it is what a person loves that gives him pleasure" (1099a7). We must love virtue if we are to be virtuous.

If the virtuous person is the norm and measure in moral matters, the reason is that it is in such a person that we find the love in question, since "as a person's character is, so will the end appear to him" (1114a31). We might regard this motto as befitting to Aristotle: "Tell me what your pleasures are, and I will tell what kind of person you are." For Aristotle observes that "pleasure and pain are the rule by which we measure our actions, some of us more, some less. For this reason, pleasure and pain must be the object of our inquiry [as moralists]. For to rejoice and be saddened at the proper time or at the wrong time is of no little importance for our actions" (1105a4–5).

This is why "we must on every occasion be on guard against the pleasant and pleasure, because we are not incorruptible judges in this area" (1109b7). "We must take note of that to which we are inclined. . . . We can tell what these objects are by the pleasure or pain we feel" (1109b1).

Understandably, then, Aristotle rejects the views of those who regard all pleasure as evil[54] and those who "take less enjoyment than they should." As for "the person who takes pleasure in nothing and is indifferent to everything, he is far from human" (1119a5–10).[55]

Moral education is an education in pleasures and pains. For example, the temperate person has not extinguished all desire, but "he desires only what the right rule prescribes" (1119a14).[56] He avoids certain pleasures, but this is because "he has pleasures of his own" (1153a35). He reaches this state gradually, because virtues are acquired and they grow through being exercised (1103a23): "It is by avoiding pleasures of the body that a person becomes temperate, but when he has become temperate he can more easily avoid them" (1104a33).

Clearly, then, Aristotle bases his ethics on happiness and pleasure: in his view these are "a kind of end" of the moral life; they supply its dynamism and criterion. In basing his ethics on pleasure, he at the same time assigns a value to desire and love.

His moral rule is that of the virtuous person and is based on love of the good and the beautiful. The desire in question is a "desire based on deliberation" (1113a9) which chooses the good of virtue not for the sake of the pleasure that accompanies it, but for its own sake, because it is "noble": "There are many things we would value even if they brought us no pleasure, as, for example, seeing, remembering, possessing virtues; as a matter of fact these things do inevitably bring pleasure in their train, but that is irrelevant: we would choose them even if they were not a source of pleasure" (1174a2–7).[57]

There is no question therefore of an unqualified "hedonism"; the good and virtue are chosen for their own sake and not for the sake of the pleasure which they "necessarily" entail.

Aristotle's moral rule is that of the golden mean, which virtue recognizes and chooses (1107a4):

> For example, in fear, confidence, appetite, anger, pity and, in general, desire or pain, there can be either too much or not enough; in either case one falls short of perfection. On the contrary, to feel these passions at the right moment, for a suitable motive, in regard to the right person, in view of an end for which one should strive, and in the manner that is proper—there you have both the mean and excellence, and this is precisely the mark of virtue (1106b18–22).

The virtuous person attains to this golden mean and this excellence to the extent that he fulfills the three conditions expected of him: "First, he must do them [virtuous actions] with full knowledge. Second, he must do them deliberately for their own sake. Third, in his action he must remain firm and unshakable" (1105a31).

Knowledge and deliberatin are the work of reason. As R. A. Gauthier very properly observes, "the intention is right when reason has so intermingled with desire that the latter is directed toward the object which reason prescribes. This interpenetration of reason with desire is virtue and gives the reason why virtue rectifies the intention."[58]

In this ethics, then, there is no reference at a fundamental level to law, authority, or duty. This is all the more surprising since Aristotle locates his study of pleasure and pain in the field of political philosophy:

> It is the province of the political philosopher to study pleasure and pain.
>
> For he is the architect who determines the end in the light of which we call one thing bad and another good, without qualification.
>
> In addition, an investigation of pleasure and pain is a necessary task of political science. For this science has the virtues and vices of character for its object, and we have already shown that virtue and vice deal with pleasures and pains; virtue has happiness for its object, and the great majority of people say that happiness is inseparable from pleasure. It is because of this connection that the Greek word for "happy" (man), scil. *makarios*, is derived from the verb meaning "to rejoice" (*chairein*) (1152b1–4).[59]

This ethics speaks not of the will (a notion utterly basic to moralities based on duty), but of wish or desire.[60]

The world in which we find ourselves here is thus very different from the world of moralities based on duty. It is true, of course, that Aristotelian ethics is the ethics of an elite, an ethics for "free men" who have enough leisure[61] to devote themselves to philosophy and contemplation. Slaves, peasants, artisans, merchants, children, and even women seem to be excluded from this ethics.[62] Most people need "good laws" and rules that are forced upon them, even if initially they find these rules painful, "because most people obey force rather than a good reason and heed punishments rather than the ideal of the moral life" (1180a4). At the same time, however, in Aristotle's mind these constraints are meant to develop the capacity for "deliberate desires" that cause people to choose with freedom and full knowledge the ideal of a moral beauty and a happy life of virtue that are loved for their own sakes.

The ethics of Aristotle was practically unknown to the early Middle Ages and made its way into Christianity only in the thirteenth centurty via the Arabs. Everyone knows of the extent to which Albert the Great and Thomas Aquinas were disciples of Aristotle, especially in the area of moral thought. But the crisis of the fourteenth and fifteenth centuries doubtless made him suspect and unacceptable[63] as well as irrelevant, despite various attempts to bring him back during the Renaissance.[64]

The morality of happiness, which was such a profound mark of the Greek outlook, entered the more or less hellenized Roman world of the early centuries of our era. "Happiness is there, within the grasp of all: made possible by the *felicitas temporum*, concretized in the delights of the Roman way of life, and conditioned by the vision of life that a triumphant culture brought with it. The theme of happiness recurs constantly."[65] But is this the "happiness of virtue"? We shall soon see that the Greco-Roman world was marked by other more rigid and formalistic tendencies.

The Christian Tradition

St. Augustine
The penetrating power of St. Augustine's thought, the relevance and attractiveness of his words and writings, left a profound mark on the Western world long before Jansenism. And yet the morality he preaches is based on the search for happiness.[66]

But how could it have been otherwise for a man, even one of Augustine's genius, living in the Greco-Roman world in which people generally saw in the quest of happiness (*eudaimonia*) the meaning and goal (*telos*) of human life?

According to Augustine's own admission, Neo-Platonism seemed to him the best[67] of all contemporary philosophies; it was the one that "saved" him from Manicheism. But he also admired the strength of soul of the Stoics[68] and rejected with scorn the "gross hedonism" of Epicurus—but an Epicurus whose thinking had been distorted by the Stoics and especially by Cicero.[69] He seems to have had

hardly any knowledge of Aristotle, although he does give a somewhat Peripatetic definition of the soul.[70] Plotinus, however, is the
philosopher to whom he refers most frequently.[71]

Augustine's eclectic philosophy was given a new organization by
his faith: in his view, the happiness sought by the Greeks can only be
found in the God of revelation. But this conviction does not keep
him from taking the approach that had been classic in the Greek tradition and observing that all human beings seek happiness and the
"happy life." "It is a fact that all human beings want to be happy and
that they desire this alone with a very great love."[72] He writes to
Proba: "In your prayer ask for the happy life. All human beings, the
wicked as well as the good, desire such a life."[73] But "though all seek
it, very few find it."[74] Even as a bishop, Augustine will continue to
present Christian life in terms of happiness.[75]

But he does not stop at this commonly accepted idea; rather, he
experiences it himself, and presents it to others, as transfigured by
his Christian faith. According to him this "happy life" is a gift of
God and specifically of the revealed God,[76] and the happiness which
this God promises is not something but Someone.[77] "That person is
blessed who possesses God."[78] Holte observes quite accurately that

> blessedness is not a state of an ego that is closed in on itself; which is
> not to say that happiness cannot be something conscious. But it is an
> ontic reality and as such, independent of the human subject for the
> same reason that the good, the beautiful, and so on, are independent.
> Every effort to attain to goodness, beauty, beatitude is therefore di-
> rected to a reality located *outside* the subject.[79]

Moreover the very quest and journey toward beatitude are themselves gifts of God: "That which makes you happy is not the virtue
in your soul; it is rather the One who has given you the gift of virtue,
the One who has inspired you with the will and given you the
power."[80] If individuals go astray and fail in their quest for happiness, the reason is that they no longer know who they are; they do
not possess themselves. Therefore St. Augustine has God say in a
lapidary formula: "I will restore you to yourself when I give you to
myself."[81]

Augustine is too much influenced by biblical anthropology and
the incarnation of the Son of God to let himself follow Plotinus,
much less the Manicheans, in their contempt for the body. He does
not reduce the human person to a soul; this is especially so toward
the end of his life. Later on, in his *Retractations*, he will recognize
that, contrary to what he had written in his *De vita beata*, the body
does have its place in human beatitude and the soul can be happy
only when the body is fully subject to it (a state that also represents
the perfection of the body[82]).

When they [the movements of the animal part] are dominated and rendered subject, they become entirely domesticated and live in harmony with us. They are not alien to the movements of our souls. They even draw nourishment in us from rational knowledge, superior moral action, and eternal life, just as we in turn draw nourishment from plants, fruit trees, and green vegetables. Here, for human beings, is the happy and peaceful life: when all movements in the person are in harmony with reason and truth; these movements are then called holy, chaste and good joys and loves.[83]

The morality Augustine teaches is thus not a disincarnate morality; it takes account of the person in its totality: the body and the virtues of the sensible and sensuous world are not neglected,[84] nor are the good or bad "pleasures of the body."[85] The good pleasures are seen as "helps" in our desire and quest of beatitude: "The things we enjoy make us happy. By those we make use of we are helped in our movement toward beatitude."[86]

He does not hesitate to talk of the soul's pleasures in a typically Augustinian passage that must be cited in its entirety:

When you hear the words, "No one comes to me unless the Father draws him," do not think of yourself as drawn against your will, for the soul is drawn by love. Let us not fear the reproaches of those who attend only to the literal meaning of words that are utterly remote from things divine and who accuse us of misusing a word consecrated by the holy gospels. "How," they ask, "can I believe freely if I am drawn?"

I answer, "It is not by your will alone that you are drawn; you are drawn by pleasure." But how is a person drawn by pleasure? "Find your delight in the Lord, and he will fulfill the desires of your heart" (Ps 36[37]:4). Anyone who tastes the sweetness of this heavenly bread experiences true interior joys. If the poet could write: "Each person is drawn by his pleasure" (trahit sua quemque voluptas: Virgil, Eclogues)—note that he says by his pleasure and not by necessity, by delight and not by force—then with how much greater justice should we not say that we are drawn to Jesus Christ. Are the senses of the body to have their pleasures, but the soul is not to have hers? . . . Give me a heart that loves and it will know what I am talking about. Give me a heart that desires, a heart that is hungry, a heart that thinks of itself as an exile in this life, that is thirsty for heaven, that longs for the fountain in the eternal homeland! Give me a heart filled with these sentiments, and it will understand what I am saying.[87]

"Give me a heart that loves": this, for Augustine, is the essential thing. To love nothing is to be dead. "What is it they tell you? To love nothing? Never! Motionless and dead, repulsive and wretched: that is what you would be if you loved nothing. Love, but be careful about what it is that is to be loved."[88]

Love acts like the law of gravity: *Pondus meum, amor meus.* Here is how Augustine understands these few words:

> Under the action of its weight every body tends toward the place proper to it. But a weight does not necessarily travel downward; rather it travels to the place proper to it. Fire rises, a stone descends. . . . My weight is my love *(pondus meum, amor meus)*. Wherever I am carried it is my love that carries me. We are set on fire by your gift, Lord, and carried on high. We burn, we advance.[89]

This love and the delight that accompanies it introduce order into human life. "Order," as Augustine understands it, is not something static but the "harmonious" relation of the human dynamisms or appetites among themselves. It is a proper placing of all of these dynamisms, but with the whole moving in a vitally felt direction. This is why he proposes a "short and accurate definition of virtue: the order of love."[90]

Pleasure has the same function: it, too, is the "weight of the soul" and "establishes order in the soul."[91] The person who lives a just and holy life experiences "properly ordered pleasure."[92]

Human beings attain to this dynamic order by regulating their love and their pleasure in the light of supreme happiness and of God. "Virtues that do not have beatitude as their goal are not true virtues."[93] It is this "ordered love" or, to use another term, virtue that causes "what is inferior to be governed by what is superior" and that enables the person to "keep the deadly passions under restraint and within the measure decreed by nature."[94]

On this point, Augustine is evidently not a Stoic in any sense, especially since he assigns a high value to desire: "It is through desire that we draw nourishment from God,"[95] "the soul grows through desire of that which it seeks."[96]

> Enjoyment is the goal of all desire, for each person strives in his cares and concerns to reach the enjoyment he is seeking.
> He who examines our heart sees our desires, and he who examines the reins sees the goal of our desires, that is, the pleasures we seek. When, therefore, he sees that our desires are not to the lusts of the flesh nor the concupiscence of the eyes nor the flattery of the world (1 Jn 2:17)—all of them, things that pass like shadows—but that on the contrary, our desires reach up toward the everlasting goal which no change can affect, then the God who examines the reins and the heart guides the just man.[97]

The importance thus given to the ordering dynamism of desire, love, and pleasure is regulated and assigned its place, in Augustine, in accordance with the Stoic distinction of useful goods and goods which Cicero calls *honesta* ("right"), that is, which are loved for themselves and not because of their usefulness or the pleasure one expects from them. The good loved by virtue is of this second kind: a good loved for its beauty. Augustine makes frequent use of the distinction between goods that are to be used (uti) and goods that are to be enjoyed (frui), the latter being those of virtue and the "blessed life."[98]

On the other hand, "all our sins are due to the fact that we want to enjoy that which we should only use."[99] Frui, or the "love of enjoyment," is honestum because it loves God for his own sake: "If, then, you love without self-interest, if you truly love, then take for your sole reward the object of your love."[100] To love in this way is love with charity and not with a servile love.[101]

Does all this mean that Augustinian morality acknowledges no obligation? No, it does acknowledge a single but absolutely basic obligation: that of loving God. Love, he believes, longs to submit to God who is both the source and the object of beatitude: "God's grace inspires us with love of him and makes us submissiveto his will."[102] The only divine authority that Augustine seems to recognize is that of scripture and the Church.[103] He does of course speak of the divine law, and in fact he defines sin by relation to this law: "Sin is an action, word, or desire that contravenes the eternal law. The eternal law is divine reason or the will of God who commands us to maintain the natural order and forbids us to violate it."[104] But we should immediately note on the one hand that "the fullness and goal of the law and the scriptures is love,"[105] and on the other that, as Holte observes,

> if sin against the law of God is synonymous with an attack on the natural order, that is, the order of created values, then we must go on to say in what the preservation of this order or an attack on it consists, insofar as the position of the human creature is concerned. This question can quite naturally be formulated thus: "We must ask ourselves what this natural order is as it exists *in human beings.*" The natural order is not a code of morals that imposes its demands on human beings *from outside.* Insofar as human beings are creatures, they are *themselves* part of the ladder of values found in creation. For them to obey God means to respect the order which he has established within his human creatures.[106]

The moral law is promulgated by God, but this law is not arbitrary, nor is it external to the human person; it is, rather, the very law that God has established in human beings. Before being an infraction, sin is a love that subordinates creator to creature; it is a disordered love.[107] To be forced to obey the law is an evil,[108] with the evil consisting in failing to love God and his law properly: "Only one who does not love the law is compelled to obey it."[109]

Augustine does, of course, base his teaching on divine authority, that of the scriptures and the commandments. But, as Ragnar Holte points out,

> divine authority uses *praeceptio* as a means of teaching (*docere*). Here we see the new value assigned to *auctoritas*: when a categorical order (*jubere*) is reformulated as a precept (*praeceptio*) and an exhortation (*admonitio*), it is no longer understood as simply a commandment, but is taken at the same time as an evangelical call.[110]

The same author tells us of another idea of Augustine that deserves our attention: "Nonetheless, this entire external order—incarnation and external teaching—is a purely provisional stage, introduced because of the fall. It is a means God uses for attaining this sole end: the restoration of the original order in which the interior wellspring gave water directly to man."[111]

For Augustine, then, *the* moral obligation is to love the good and the beautiful that are imprinted in human nature, to love this order in its source that is within the human person, to love happiness, to love with the love of charity. When one obeys a commandment because one fears punishment, one does not respect the commandment:

> If this commandment is respected out of fear of punishment and not out of love for the good, then it is respected in a slavish way and not freely, which is to say that it is not respected at all. For no fruit is good unless its root is charity. But when one possesses the faith that works through love, one begins to take pleasure, in the interior self, in the law of God.[112]

The morality which Augustine teaches is evidently completely different from the legalistic morality of duty that was rampant in the Christian world ten centuries after his death. This shift is all the more unexpected and even paradoxical since Augustine's influence was considerable throughout the Middle Ages and in the Renaissance, even among the Jansenists. As far as morality was concerned, many Augustinians betrayed or misunderstood Augustine.

It is also easy to understand why a certain number of modern disciples of Kant accuse Augustine of being a "corrupter of Christian morality" to the extent that he is a "hedonist."[113]

But I can readily turn the accusation back on them: this unqualified rejection of all "hedonism" by Kant and his successors—and, as we shall soon see, by his predecessors as well—"corrupted" Christian morality.

I see no value in presenting the moral thought of St. Thomas Aquinas at this point, since I shall be referring to it throughout the book. In any case, his thought in this area is sufficiently well known.[114] It will be enough here to remind the reader that St. Thomas, like Augustine, is faithful to the gospel and Christian tradition, and that in addition, he uses Greek thought, especially that of Aristotle, in a very free manner to organize the data of the gospel and tradition. It is symptomatic of his entire approach that the very first questions he asks in the part of his *Summa theologiae* dealing with morality are concerned with happiness and the finality it exercises (I–II, qq. 1–5). The decalogue has only a very minor place in the entire discussion (I–II, q. 100).

How was it possible for "Christendom," after thirteen centuries of tradition, to be so changed in its outlook and ways as to reduce morality to obedience to the "commandments of God and the Church" and to barricade itself in the very legalism so forcefully condemned by Jesus Christ himself?

This is the question I shall now try to answer.

Chapter 2

The Smothering of the Spirit by the Letter

With a constancy close to that of a biological law, history shows that no religion and no civilization escapes the sclerosis induced by age. The spirit that gave life in the beginning is gradually smothered under proliferating laws. Institutions, though certainly necessary, also carry the seeds of death in them. "The written code kills, but the Spirit gives life" (2 Cor 3:6).

This is a fate which even Christendom could not escape.

I interpret this inevitable smothering of the spirit by the letter as one effect of the fear or, better, the anxiety that lurks in all human beings and drives them to seek some relief in the (illusory) security afforded by authority and the laws it promulgates.

We can derive some light on this subject from the "mythical" but richly instructive story of "original sin" as interpreted in contemporary exegesis (and not as read by the moralists of duty and law).

The "Original Sin"

The story Genesis tells of the first "sin" may seem to base morality on obedience to God. The whole story begins with a prohibition: "You may freely eat of every tree in the garden; but of the tree of the knowledge of good and evil[1] you shall not eat, for in the day that you eat of it you shall die" (Gen 2:16–17).

If I interpret this mythical account correctly, it means that God reserves for himself the knowledge (or decision) of what is good for human beings and what is bad for them. They may eat from all the other trees, including the "tree of life" (symbol of immortality), but

they are forbidden under pain of death to decide for themselves regarding good and evil. As long as this prohibition is understood and
observed, Adam and Eve live happily as the familiar friends of God
who walks in the garden and talks with them (Gen 3:8).

But the tempter appears on the scene. What follows calls for careful and discerning exegesis. I shall rely on that given by Dominique
Barthélemy,[2] which seems to me to be very much to the point.

The serpent who does the tempting acts after the manner of an ag-
itator. He tries to alter the idea or image that Adam and Eve have of
God by turning him from a loving father into a tyrant who is jealous
of his authority.

The "tempter" begins his work of perversion by exaggerating
God's prohibition: "Did God say, 'You shall not eat of any tree of
the garden'?"[3] This is not what God had said, and Eve immediately
corrects the serpent: "We may eat of the fruit of the trees of the garden; but God said, 'You shall not eat of the fruit of the tree which
is in the midst of the garden, neither shall you touch it, lest you
die" (3:1–3).

As you can see, Eve is already unsettled. The divine prohibition is
beginning to bother her, for in repeating what God had said she in-
troduces some revealing alterations. She avoids giving the tree its
name: the tree of the knowledge of good and evil, and designates it
insteady by its location in the middle of the garden. Because it has
been forbidden, the tree of the knowledge of good and evil takes a
central place in her mind. The prohibition is beginning to exercise
its power of irresistible attraction; she now has eyes only for this
tree, over there in the center, and she avoids giving it its name.

In addition, she exaggerates for herself the seriousness of the prohibition. God had forbidden the eating of the fruit of this tree; Eve
adds that even the touching of it is forbidden. The tree now becomes
taboo.

The reason for this is that the desire to eat from the tree has been
roused: ". . . the woman saw that the tree was good for food, and
that it was a delight to the eyes, and that the tree was to be desired to
make one wise" (v. 6). The prohibition kindles the fire of desire; the
compulsion of vertigo and obsession is being felt.

At this point God turns into an authority lacking in love and interested above all in reserving for himself one of the privileges of divinity: not the privilege of immortality (the tree of life is not forbidden), but in fact the only one that is prohibited, that of the
knowledge of good and evil.

The temptation, therefore, is of the moral order, but its purpose is
the distortion of the image of God. In Eve's eyes, God is no longer a
kind Father with whom she is meant to live, one who does not try to
instill fear. He becomes a jealous dictator: "You will not die. For
God knows that when you eat of it your eyes will be opened, and

you will be like God, knowing good and evil" (vv. 4–5). God has deceived them because he wants this privilege for himself. Such a jealous father is no longer to be trusted. It will be a good act to throw off this arbitrary yoke.

The effect is immediate: hardly have Eve and Adam eaten of the forbidden fruit than God appears before them as a pitiless judge and punisher of the attempt to usurp his rights. They feel compelled to hide; they are afraid.

The story of the "original sin" continues: "Then the eyes of both were opened" (v. 7). And what do they see? The good and evil of which they can judge for themselves? No: "They knew that they were naked" (v. 7). Though they had been naked before their rebellion, they "were not ashamed" (2:25). Now, however, their nakedness is intolerable to them: "They sewed fig leaves together and made themselves aprons" (v. 7). They take refuge behind an adornment; they hide from one another's gaze. They are forced to make a display in order to hide what they have become or, more accurately, to hide that which they have lost, that of which they have been "stripped," the "lack" which they must conceal from the other, from themselves, and from God. "That is what we call self-adornment, to give oneself airs in the eyes of others and then in one's own eyes." Thus Barthélemy, who explains, as follows, the need for adornment which is the first effect of the original sin:

> Man is a being who tries to adorn much more than to dress himself. He tries to appear as someone of importance, to cut a good figure, to have the air of . . . an angel; woman does this also. But strictly speaking, all this is an effort to give the impression of *being*. Man is a being who tries to have the air of being, at least to be somebody in the eyes of others, even if he does not wholly succeed in convincing himself that he is somebody. He finds it soothing at least to consider that he may *seem* attractive or estimable to other people. It helps him to think that he might even really *be* so, and that it would be exaggeratedly pessimistic to think otherwise.

Barthélemy continues: "If one has sinned without anybody seeing, there is only half a sin. If one sins and others see it, it becomes dramatic."[4]

Ever since this "original sin," human beings have felt themselves looked at, that is, judged. The gaze of others is a torment to them. They are afraid of it and yet they cannot do without it. Adornment is a way of showing themselves, while at the same time concealing themselves.

But God's gaze penetrates the adornment and the hiding-place: "They heard the sound of the Lord God walking in the garden in the cool of the day, and the man and his wife hid themselves from the

presence of the Lord God among the trees of the garden. But the
Lord God called to the man, and said to him, 'Where are you?' And
he said, 'I heard the sound of thee in the garden, and I was afraid, because I was naked, and I hid myself' " (3:8–10).

"I was afraid." And in fact, God exacts a terrible punishment (vv.
14–19), the worst part of which is exclusion and banishment from
"paradise," or the loss of happiness.

Since that time, the image human beings have had of God distorts
both God and themselves. An abyss now separates the two. Human
beings are afraid of the judge who is constantly spying on them in
order to condemn them and condemn them even to death; they find
the gaze of God intolerable.

Job's cry of anguish is the cry of a human race condemned to look
upon God as a judge who is both elusive and pitiless:

> Am I the sea, or a sea monster,
>   that thou settest a guard over me?
> When I say, "My bed will comfort me,
>   my couch will ease my complaint,"
> then thou dost scare me with dreams
>   and terrify me with visions,
> so that I would choose strangling
>   and death rather than my bones.
> I loathe my life; I would not live for ever.
>   Let me alone, for my days are a breath.
> What is man that thou dost make so much of him,
>   and that thou dost set thy mind upon him,
> dost visit him every morning,
>   and test him every moment?
> How long wilt thou not look away from me,
>   nor let me alone till I swallow my spittle?

If I sin, what do I do to thee, thou watcher of men? (Job 7:12–20)

Human beings are not only condemned to death; the divine judge
also "spies" on them. This distortion of the image of God is both the
source and the result of the original sin. Dominique Barthélemy
sums up his exegesis of Genesis as follows:

> And perhaps the drama of the first sin lies not so much in the fact of
> man's trying to become God in God's place—man knew perfectly well
> that he could never achieve this, that stumbling against the impossible
> he would be hurled back—but that at the root of this idea there is mis-
> understanding of what the father is, followed by the determination to
> delude himself as to the truth, to imagine the father as a jealous tyrant
> and so justify himself in his desperate rebellion. It is this caricature of
> God's image which is the hardest thing to root out of man.[5]

The crime of Cain has the same effect. God curses him, and "Cain said to the Lord, 'My punishment is greater than I can bear, Behold, thou hast driven me this day away from the ground; and from thy face I shall be hidden; and I shall be a fugitive and a wanderer on the earth, and whoever finds me will slay me'" (Gen 4:13–14).

After the original sin, as after the first subsequent sin (Cain's), the basic problem is to escape from the face of God, for this face has now become threatening and intolerable.[6] In all the Old Testament narratives there is danger of death in seeing the face of God, in seeing his glory, and even in pronouncing his name.

A return to a true image of God is impossible as long as man believes that such a return

> must involve a humiliating deal in which remorse and personal disa-
> vowal of the past would be required of him in order to appease the of-
> fended authority of God. Man has become incapable of imagining this
> return as the rediscovery of a misjudged heart, which in fact is what it
> is. And so from God's point of view, man's return will consist chiefly
> in his becoming tractable once more.[7]

From Abraham to Moses, God will patiently undertake this process of rendering human beings tractable again. Moses, accompanied by Aaron and seventy "elders," is given the privilege of "seeing the God of Israel" on Sinai and of eating and drinking in his presence (Ex 24:9–11). The idolatry of the Israelites (the golden calf) forces Yahweh to show himself once again as an awesome judge.

In its moral and cultic observances, Israel will find a false security and a new way of distorting the image of the true God. This will be the most basic and the most often repeated of the charges leveled by the prophets. God expects Israel to "understand and know me, that I am the Lord who practices steadfast love" (Jer 9:23). Only on this condition will God put his Law in the depths of their being and write it on their hearts (Jer 31:33). "I will betroth you to me for ever; I will betroth you to me in righteousness and in justice, in steadfast love, and in mercy. I will betroth you to me in faithfulness; and you shall know the Lord" (Hos 2:19–20).

Unfortunately, only too often the contrary occurs: Israelites obey the Law like an idol; they use it to maintain a caricature of God and to harden themselves in their false view of him. They cultivate legalism to the nth degree, because they stand, and want to stand, before God as a judge. As Yahweh will say through Isaiah, "this people draw near with their mouth and honor me with their lips, while their hearts are far from me, and their fear of me is a commandment of men learned by rote" (Is 29:13). "I desire steadfast love and not sacrifice" (Hos 6:6).

The Israelites will have to wait for Jesus Christ in order to recover the true picture of God.

Illusory Reassurances

Despite the covenant of Yahweh with his chosen people, despite the repeated admonitions of the prophets, the Israelites, except for a small "remnant," were unable to unshackle themselves from fear of their God.

They looked to the legalistic observance of the Law as a way of alleviating their anxiety and their sense of guilt, both of which were intensified by the destruction of the temple (sixth century B.C.), for they interpreted this as a punishment for their infidelities to the covenant. They hoped that "the broken convenant would be restored thanks to Israel's observance of the Law."[8]

The Torah, which was a revelation of God's love for his people, a body of teaching, and the terms of the convenant, increasingly became in practice a "law" regarding justice. It was overloaded with "commandments of men learned by rote" (Is 29:13), despite the fact that Moses had ordered the Israelites not to add or subtract anything from the Law (Deut 4:2).

This explains Christ's indictment of the lawyers and Pharisees when he blames them for "making void the word of God through your tradition which you hand on" (Mk 7:13), and because they "hold fast to the tradition of men" (Mk 7:8) and "transgress the commandment of God for the sake of your tradition" (Mt 15:3).[9]

When observed in this manner, the Law has ceased to be anything but an unhappy and empty effort to suppress anxiety by bringing about one's own justification. "It becomes an instrument for human beings in their attempt to bring about their own justification."[10] They hope that in this way they will no longer feel guilty and no longer have to admit that "we have all become like one who is unclean, and all our righteous deeds are like a polluted garment" (Is 64:6) and that we do not at all understand what we are and what we do as people condemned to death (cf. Rom 7:15–24).

Rather than acknowledge their wretched state and find their security in the Father's mercy, people seek a deceptive peace through an observance of the Law which they choose to regard as saving. One need only be "in good standing" with the Law in order to have the consolation of a "good conscience" and satisfaction with oneself, for then one can flatter oneself that one is righteous (Lk 18:9). In this way, people hope to hide from themselves the "lack" of which the gospel speaks in connection with the call of the rich man. He was a faithful observer of the Law, but Christ tells him, "you lack one thing" (Mk 10:21; Lk 18:22), or, in Matthew's version, he himself acknowledges that he lacks something and that the Law is not enough for him (19:20).

What he lacks is a liberating detachment from his wealth, from himself, from the satisfaction that his correct observance of the Law brings him. What he lacks is the ability to act like a poor man in making use of his wealth and of the security he finds in it. Leaving everything in order to follow the Messiah means a "fall" into insecurity.[11] For nothing makes one more insecure than being able to count on nothing but a call from God, after the pattern of Abraham, the father of believers, who "by faith . . . obeyed when he was called to go out to a place which he was to receive as an inheritance; and he went out, not knowing where he was to go" (Heb 11:8).[12]

Nothing is a greater source of insecurity than the following of the Spirit: "The wind blows where it wills, and you hear the sound of it, but you do not know whence it comes or whither it goes; so it is with every one who is born of the Spirit" (Jn 3:8).

It is easy to see why the Pharisees and the lawyers could not tolerate the teaching of Christ. They felt threatened—and with good reason—with the loss of the illusory camouflage that concealed their inherited anxiety before God and even more before themselves. They claim they have been "insulted" (Lk 11:45 NAB) and "offended" (Mt 15:12), and they are "filled with fury (Lk 6:11). They begin "a furious attack on him" (Lk 11:52 JB). Together with the Herodians (a group that sides with the Romans), the Pharisees "held counsel . . . against him, how to destroy him" (Mk 3:6). "Why do you seek to kill me?" Christ asks them (Jn 7:19). They will succeed in the attempt, for they find utterly unbearable even the thought of losing their false security which, as I shall point out later on,[13] is a form of idolatry and all the more deadly because it is subtly hidden by the best intentions in the world. Such is the nature of this "leaven of the Pharisees" (Lk 12:1): hypocrisy and blindness with regard to oneself and God.

It is a simple fact that the disciples of Christ have not been able to escape the universal temptation of looking for a degree of security through a legalistic practice even of the very gospel itself. The beginnings of monastic life provide us with an example of the temptation at work. The four "Rules" attributed to Saint Pachomius, and whose chronology and authors have now been established,[14] show, from the first to the fourth, a dismaying proliferation of "precepts" which regulate the life of the monks down to the smallest detail. The end result is a "worship of the Rule": monastic law "saves its practitioners."[15]

In fact, legalism in morality has had a tenacious life, and the "original sin" is perpetuated in us. We are aware, ever since Freud, that human desire is structured by the "law of the father"; by a prohibition (as in the Garden of Eden), namely, the prohibition of incest;

and by the desire for the (symbolic) death of the father who issues the prohibition. Law is the father's word to the child; it brings him into confrontation with the other and thus begins the process of self-identification. Human beings cannot escape this "morality that functions in the super-ego."[16]

This is all the truer since the collective aspect of Christian morality has exerted a considerable influence throughout the course of history. A society cannot exist without norms,[17] without customs and laws, without a "collective super-ego."[18] For several centuries now, we have been overly forgetful of the fact that the moral life is lived in society. The result of this social dimension is that morality inevitably becomes "closed" (I am using Bergson's terminology and drawing on his analysis[19]), whereas the morality of the gospel is essentially "open" and "mystical," even though it is lived in a structured community.

"Christendom," in which political society and ecclesial society were merged, contributed greatly to the "closing" of evangelical morality. It was in this historical context of the mystery of the Church that the dialectic of grace and law was

> developed and illuminated . . . according to which the conceptual and preceptive elements, transubstantiated by grace, become conditionings, "dispositions," according to the unusual expression of Saint Thomas, of the life of the Spirit. There is no longer the question of receiving grace in order to become capable of facing up to the demands of the commandments (such a notion presided over the construction of the Counter-Reformation catechisms) but to live in dependence on the interior movement of the Spirit. In the long run the ethical ideal resides in the fact that man is a law unto himself and not in the fact that he obeys God's command coming from without. Such is the root of Christian liberty which is certainly not the absence of every norm but implies the free choice of a line of conduct conformable to the inner call of grace. Man fixes for himself his own law before God: *Ipsi sibi sunt lex.*[20]

If it be true that the pagans "who have not the law do by nature what the law requires" and "are a law unto themselves" (Rom 2: 14–15), this is allthe more true of the new law which is written in the hearts of those who are inspired by the Holy Spirit.[21]

Yes, it is true—but in fact the history of Christianity forces us to acknowledge that the Spirit has more or less been smothered by the letter, by the law.

The Confusion of the Religious and the Political

In all civilizations, from the most primitive to the most highly developed, the cohesion of a people is created and maintained by an "esprit du corps," an ideology, a myth regarding origins, and so on, in which the religious and political dimensions of life are brought into unity. This means that mores, morality, are also made part of this unity. "Religion, morality, and a social sense—the chief elements in the higher side of man—were originally one and the same thing."[22]

Freud thinks that in the course of Israelite history, this original confusion was deepened, as moraliy gained the upper hand over religion: "Even the exhortation to believe in God seems to recede in comparison with the seriousness of these ethical demands. Instinctual renunciation thus appears to play a prominent part in religion, though it had not been preset in it from the beginning."[23]

There is no need here to appeal to the general observations of ethnologists. We need only remind ourselves that this confusion of the religious and the political reigned unchallenged among the Semitic peoples of the Old Testament period, to say nothing of Egypt. The "kings" were both military and religious leaders, incarnations of the god of the tribe, "high priests," mediators between the god and the people.

Israel was unable to avoid adopting this outlook which was universal among its neighbors and enemies. After the death of Joshua, the tribes were governed by "judges" whom Yahweh raised up (Judg 2:16). But when faced with the Philistine peril, the "elders of Israel" demanded that Samuel "appoint for us a king to govern us like all the nations" (1 Sam 8:5). Samuel was reluctant and consulted the Lord about what he should do. Yahweh's answer deserve to be meditated on:

> And the Lord said to Samuel, "Hearken to the voice of the people in all that they say to you; for they have not rejected you, but they have rejected me from being king over them. According to all the deeds which they have done to me, from the day I brought them up out of Egypt even to this day, forsaking me and serving other gods, so they are also doing to you. Now then, hearken to their voice; only you shall solemnly warn them, and show them the ways of the king who shall rule over them" (1 Sam 8:7-9).

Thus, Yahweh seems resolved to yield to this definitely too demanding need of human beings and to allow the confusion of the political and the religious. Samuel, who is both judge and prophet, will therefore anoint Saul as God's appointee and set him on a throne (1 Sam 10:2-25).

Henceforward, the kings of Israel will be the "anointed" of the Lord; they will be military and political as well as religious leaders, especially from David and Solomon on.

It is not surprising therefore that the Messiah whom Israel awaited should be thought of as a new David, the liberator of Israel from the Romans. This expectation was widespread not only among the Zealots but even among Jesus' disciples and the apostles themselves. The awaited Messiah was to be both a political and a religious figure. A few moments before the ascension, the final question asked of the Messiah by his apostles shows their misunderstanding quite clearly: "Lord, will you at this time restore the kingdom to Israel?" (Acts 1:6). And yet this was a role that Christ had consistently refused, from the temptation in the wilderness (Mt 4:8–10), down to his refusal to make use of the sword when he was arrested (Lk 22: 52). He had hidden himself to keep the crowds from making him their king (Jn 6:15). This rejection of any military and political role ran counter to the views and expectations current among both Jews and Romans. " 'Render therefore to Caesar the things that are Caesar's, and to God the things that are God's.' When they heard it, they marveled; and they left him and went away" (Mt 22:21–22).

This confusion of the religious and the political was widespread among all peoples, especially the Greeks and the Romans. Among them the priests were civic officials.[24] The Roman emperors were sovereign pontiffs and were treated as gods.

Such a need for a powerful, quasi-divine human figure is found in every age and every civilization. Freud explains the function of such a figure when he writes: "We know that the great majority of people have a strong need for authority which they can admire, to which they can submit, and which threatens and sometimes even ill-treats them. We have learned from the psychology of the individual whence comes this need of the masses. It is the longing for the father that lives in each of us from his childhood days."[25]

When the Jews and Romans were baptized and became disciples of Christ, they refused to "sacrifice" to the emperor, but how could they have freed themselves completely from this confusion of the political and the religious that had become such a profound and universal element in human mores?

Did they not receive the following instruction from St. Paul himself? "Let every person be subject to the governing authorities. For there is no authority except from God, and those that exist have been appointed by God. Therefore he who resists the authorities resists what God has appointed" (Rom 13:1–2).

As a result, there would be a good-neighborly relations between the Church and the Empire and eventually an interpenetration of the two when the emperor had been converted to the Christian faith and was called "the image of God," just as the bishop was "the image of Christ." Then the two hierarchical apparatuses (the political and the ecclesiastical), the material sword and the spiritual sword, would help each other in defining morality and seeing to its enforcement; they would thus . . . fill it with a content that was inseparably human and divine both in its judgments and in its sanctions.[26]

This commingling of the political with the religious and therefore the moral appears as early as the second century in the Christian Apologists. It would take solid root in "Christendom" from the time of Constantine and Theodosius and would be restructured with Charlemagne and the "Holy Roman Empire of the Germans," though not without the struggles between the two "swords" that were inevitable given such a confusion of powers.[27] It would then continue on when at the end of the Middle Ages, nationalism and absolute monarchy appeared on the scene in France, England, and then in Spain. The kings of France got the appointment of the bishops they wanted; the British Parliament in the time of the Reformation voted in and published the Book of Common Prayer; and so on. The political conflicts entangled with the Protestant Reformation and the Catholic Counter-Reformation found a juridical and political solution in the principle *Cujus regio, ejus religio* ("In a [prince's] country, the [prince's] religion"); and so on.

In this conception of things, obedience to political authority was bound up with religion. It was therefore quite natural for Louis XIV to say in his *Memoirs*: "He who gave kings to men wills that the latter should respect them as His lieutenants; He reserves to himself alone the right to examine their conduct. There is no principle more solidly established by Christianity than this humble submission of subjects to those who are set over them."[28]

So fully was this doctrine accepted by the subjects of the realm that in 1647, Rotrou could put similar statement in the mouth of a character (Creon) in his play *Wenceslas*: "Faced with the plans of a king as with those of heaven, faithful subjects should close their eyes and, submitting their minds to the power of the crown, should believe the laws, whatever they are, to be good."[29]

Deplorable though such sentiments may seem to us today, they were part and parcel of the mores of the time and greatly contributed to the smothering of the spirit by the letter, that is, to legalism in morality.

In addition, Stoic ethics, which was so widely accepted in the Greco-Roman world of the early centuries, introduced its notions of natural and universal law into Christianity and thus fostered the confusion of morality with law.

In the ethical model of Christian morality, there was a quiet slipping from natural law over to *positive law*, the latter ponderously armed with the scales and the sword. At the same time, the image of God as a monarch was emphasized but also altered: Behind the features with

their worldly cast, of the Master of heaven and earth there took shape
the *politicized* fact of the theocratic sovereign.[30]

Was it possible that the Roman genius, more juridical and political
than philosophical, should not have given morality its coloring by
permeating it with the methods of the law and ultimately causing
"Christian" morality to be based on a catalogue of laws that were
precisely worded and that obliged under pain of sanctions provided
in advance and applied by a "judge"?

That is precisely what happened throughout the course of the history of Christendom.

Chapter 3

Historical Development of the Moralities of Duty

The Early Centuries

In an effort to understand how the "Christian" morality of recent centuries could have read the gospel through legalist glasses and more or less smothered the spirit of the gospel under the letter, I have referred to the inevitable search for a security that is found in the law and to the fusing of the moral and the political.

I would now like to point out some of the historical stages in this unfortunate transformation of the gospel in Western Christendom.

It was not easy for Jewish Christians to free themselves in a radical way from the rigid, legalistic mindset of their ancient Pharisaic or Essene traditions. Gentile Christians, for their part, whether their outlook was Stoic or Plotinian, gnostic or Mazdean, were only too inclined to scorn and even condemn the world of the passions and feelings, of the body and sexuality. This accounts for the exceptionally high value placed on *enkrateia* or sexual continence, even in marriage.

Beginning in the second century, the practice of public penance, with its excommunications and gradual restorations to the community, acquired a dramatic character.

In this system, ethics came to be overburdened with an objectivized and diversified content and an approach that was legalistic and penal, if not arbitrary and comminatory. This content and approach took a consistent shape in the catalogue of sins and sanctions that was used for ecclesiastical penance. This dramatic and legalistic alteration of the ethical model immediately affected the image people had of God. The severity of the Judge now obscured the goodness of the Creator; the "human" face of the Father of mankind was covered with the impassive mask of the magistrate.[1]

Some Fathers of the Church were infected by this outlook, especially Tertullian, and in particular, the Tertullian who became a Montanist and was excommunicated. Authoritarian by temperament and a lawyer by training,

> Tertullian was in search of a Code, and here he found one which at once supplied him with a moral rule conformable to his secret desires, and an authority able to impose it by referring it to a divine source. How could he refuse to make it his own? It was the mind of the ardent lawyer that was first conquered and fixed his choice when it came to having to decide between Montanism and the Church.[2]

Pierre de Labriolle very accurately sums up Tertullian's conception of morality: "The God whom he cherishes is the inflexible and jealous Judge who has established *timor* as the solid base of man's salvation, who scatters temptations in this world in order to prove His faithful ones, and who holds His vengeance ever ready."[3]

But in these early centuries, Tertullian's was a marginal and even heretical position. The primitive catechesis was based on the Sermon on the Mount, the Our Father, and the Creed,[4] and not on the Decalogue.

St. Justin wrote that "in our view Christ has been given as the eternal and final law and as a sure covenant, after whom there are no more laws or precepts or commandments."[5] St. Irenaeus goes so far as to leave the Decalogue to the unconverted Jews and the Stoics, as being a collection of "natural precepts" which all human beings, Christian or not, are bound to observe.[6]

St. Augustine voices the common view when he writes: "For the Law that had been given through Moses was turned into grace and truth through Jesus Christ, when the spirit was joined to the letter in order that the justice of the Law might begin to be fulfilled. When this justice was not fulfilled, it turned men into guilty persons by reason of its transgression."[7]

Later on, during the Middle Ages, when the barbarians were baptized (but hardly evangelized), catalogues of sins and suitable penances would be drawn up. These are the books known as the "penitentiaries."[8] It is also a fact that beginning in the thirteenth century, a certain amount of pastoral attention was focused on the Decalogue, thus preparing the way for the Catechism of the Council of Trent.[9]

Nonetheless, the theologians of the Middle Ages, down to and including the thirteenth century, based morality on love (charity), the quest of happiness, virtue, and "right reason."[11]

Ethically, these twelfth-century collections represent a spiritually oriented version of self-realization. Instead of emphasizing moral obligation by law, they advise the improvement of moral character by the cultivation of the theological (faith, hope, charity) and the cardinal (prudence, temperance, fortitude, justice) virtues.[12]

The same was to be true of the great thirteenth-century theologians, and especially St. Thomas Aquinas. I shall be demonstrating this throughout the present book.

But a great change came during the fourteenth century. A shift of outlook occurred that found expression on the moral plane in the predominance of the law, the Decalogue, submission to political and religious authority, and fear of the implacable judgment of God. The new mentality spread throughout the entire Western World.

How are we to "explain" this spread which played such an important part in forming the outlook of the West for the next seven centuries?

The Endemic Contagion of Stoicism

Perhaps even more than Platonism, Stoicism and its morality were present and played an active role in shaping the mind of the Greco-Roman world and therefore that of the Christians of the early centuries.

This influence has continued, in wave after wave, down through the history of Western Christendom. In order that we may have a clearer grasp of the heritage, explicit and implicit, which Stoicism has left us, I think it worthwhile to recall the major direction taken by Stoic morality. By "Stoic morality" here I mean that of the later disciples of Zeno—men like Marcus Aurelius, Cicero, Seneca, Plutarch, and others—who exerted a very wide-ranging influence on Christianity.

Stoic morality represents a transposition into human actions of a teaching about the world, a comprehensive explanation of the order found in the cosmos, a pantheism which holds that man participates in divine reason, in that divine Logos which is both order and fate or necessity.

The Stoic endeavors to shed light on the laws of the cosmos by studying the divine will and the way in which the world is governed. The wise man finds his happiness in living in conformity and enlightened harmony with nature: "Keep a straight course and follow your own nature and the World-Nature (and the way of these two is one)."[13] Or, as Zeno himself had said, we should "follow the free course of life,"[14] even if this free course leads us into a painful situation and ultimately into death.

The Stoic must persuade himself that whatever befalls him, good or bad, is part of the world order that has been willed by providence. The greatness of man consists in consenting to what befalls him,[15] for providence is good.[16] Man, a member of the immense universe, is privileged to realize this fact and to be able to love himself[17] as part of the universal community and of human society[18] in the bosom of which every human being is a brother or relative to everyone else.[19]

However painful and inescapable the concrete working of the laws of nature may seem to him, the Stoic must submit to it. He is able to do so thanks to the guardian spirit (*daimōn*) which comes to him from God, is a participation in the divine Logos, and serves him as an "interior guide." It is this guide that gives him an understanding of the laws of nature.

A Stoic does not, of course, claim to have a complete understanding of all the laws, although he does all he can to gain this understanding: "As for truth, it is so veiled in obscurity that many reputable philosophers assert the impossibility of reaching any certain knowledge."[20] But whether or not he understands them, the Stoic submits to the laws of the universal Logos. It is by this path that a human being can share in the impassibility of the gods.

A person is capable of attaining this goal to the extent that her *daimōn* enables her to accept the laws with good will and respect. This is within each person's power. Nothing else depends on her, including her body and the breath of life,[21] for her body is an ephemeral thing, a mere "shell which envelops us,"[22] a "corpse"[23] made of "clay and corruption.[24]

This interior guide must therefore be able to act freely and autonomously, not tramelled by the passions, sufferings, and pleasures of the body. Among the "aberrations" Marcus Aurelius wishes to avoid he lists the temptation to self-reproach. When this occurs, the person must say: "This would prove the divine element in me to have been discomfited and forced to its knees by the ignoble and perishable flesh with its gross conceptions."[25] Zeno had said that the passions are "a movement of the irrational soul and contrary to nature."[26]

In order to attain to impassibility (*apatheia*), the interior Logos has only to withdraw from the agitated world of the passions: "Do the ills of the body afflict you? Reflect that the mind has but to detach itself and apprehend its own powers, to be no longer involved with the movements of the breath, whether they be smooth or rough."[27]

In order to detach itself from the passions, the intellect undertakes an analysis of things external to it: "Always remember to go straight for the parts themselves, and by dissecting these achieve your disenchantment. And now, transfer this method to life as a whole."[28] After all, things in themselves are neither good nor bad, it is your opinion and judgment that makes them so. If something external causes you affliction, it is not the external thing itself, but rather, your own judgment on it that produces the disturbance in you. However, it is within your power to rid yourself of this judgment, since the source of your affliction is a disposition of mind that prevents you from correcting your way of seeing things.[29]

The point is not so much to control the passions as to scorn them, detach oneself from them, and get rid of them. They seem to bring pleasure or pain, but this is only a matter of opinion, and your opinion depends on yourself: "Everything is but what your opinion makes it; and that opinion lies with yourself."[30]

The *apatheia* thus attained is the source of the tranquillity and happiness that go with virtue[31] and the interior freedom of the divine Logos, i.e., reason: "How peaceful and at the same time flexible in his actions, how joyful and yet collected is the man who follows reason in all things."[32] In the final analyses, says Marcus Aurelius in an untranslatable play on words, happiness (*eudaimonia*) is a good guiding spirit (*daimōn agathos*).

Thanks to this spirit which enables him to practice *apatheia* in submission to the laws of reason and the cosmos, the Stoic participates in the life of the gods, in the life of "the primordial City and Commonwealth."[33] "Live with the gods. To live with the gods is to show them at all times a soul contented with their awards, and wholly fulfilling the will of that inward divinity, that particle of himself, which Zeus has given to every man for ruler and guide—the mind and the reason."[34]

Herein is to be found the Stoic's happiness which no adversity can take from him, for if misfortune comes, his rule is "not, 'This is a misfortune,' but 'To bear this worthily is good fortune.' "[35] "Zeno proclaims, and the entire Stoic sect unceasingly preaches, that human life has no other goal than moral nobility (*honestas*)."[36]

We must observe, however, that this Stoic *apatheia* is not pure passivity, but is a source of action in the world, in the community that is the universe, and in human societies. "Make up your mind that nothing is of any import save to do what your own nature directs, and to bear what the world's Nature sends you."[37] "Every exercise of our proper natural instincts ought to be esteemed a form of pleasure; and the opportunities for this are everywhere present."[38]

This morality of action is inspired by a faith in the goodness of universal Nature. It aims at imitating the gods by intellectual activity, *apatheia*, and detachment from human beings. The Stoic has contempt for human glory and the good opinion of other human beings and is concerned only to have the good opinion of the gods: "That is the right spirit for a man to have within him; he should never be seen by the gods in the act of harboring a grudge or making a grievance of his sufferings."[39] "Injustice is a sin," as are all the other vices.[40]

Everything can be summed up in this statement of Marcus Aurelius: "I do reverence, I stand firmly, and I put my trust in the directing Power."[41] Stoic wisdom, as Festugière has clearly shown,[42] was a reaction to the political and cultural upheavals of the centuries preceding its development (in 301 B.C.). Stoicism and Epicureanism are "daughters of despair."

Stoicism had something to offer to men of action and to those in government: it gave them "a rule that was based on an order"[43] and brought meaning to their activity by linking this with the beneficent action of the Logos. Stoicism also won an important place in the world of philosophy and religion.

Now, Christianity spread throughout the Greco-Roman world during a period of religious and moral searching that was very eclectic and syncretistic in character. Stoicism had penetrated everywhere thanks to many "preachers" of it who addressed the populace in the public squares; in fact, scholars have even spoken of a "popular" Stoicism that was only relatively orthodox by comparison with the Stoicism of the philosophers.[44]

We know from the Acts of the Apostles (17:18) that St. Paul engaged in debates with Stoics and Epicureans at Athens.

It is therefore not surprising that "the religious and especially the moral atmosphre we find in the writings of the Fathers should reflect rather faithfully the popular Stoicism in the midst of which this generation of Christians was living."[45] This deep influence anteceded the upsurge of Platonism which began around 250. We find Stoic themes in Athenagorus, Clement of Alexandria, Justin, Tertullian, Irenaeus, and the Montanists: universal law, natural law, *apatheia*, attacks on the Cynics and Epicureans, and the condemnation of conjugal pleasure as unacceptable except in the service of procreation.[46]

Through the Fathers of the Church, therefore, and through the reading of Cicero, Seneca, Marcus Aurelius, and Plutarch, Stoicism exerted a very weighty influence on the entire medieval period and even more on the Renaissance period[47] from the reform of Calvin (whose first piece of writing was a translation of Cicero) down to Justus Lipsius (1547–1606) and Pufendorf (1632–1694). There were, of course, occasional resistances inspired by common sense, as in the case of La Fontaine who rejects the views of an "undiscerning" Stoic: "He would cut from the soul desires and passions, good or bad, and even the most innocent wishes. I for my part object to such people; they remove from our hearts the main wellsprings of action; they bid us cease to live before we have died."[48]

Even though Stoicism makes little use of the word "duty," the idea is there, and Stoicism has left its mark on the Western morality of duty. Stoicism played an important part in making acceptable to the Western mind a contempt for the body, a rejection of the passions and affectivity, an exaltation of reason and will, a rule of action that is based on order, the nobility of manly impassivity in submission to the changeless universal laws of nature, and so on.

Chapter 4

The Crisis of the Fourteenth and Fifteenth Centuries

The Advance Signs

At one time, people were either scandalously ignorant of the Middle Ages or had an utterly distorted idea of them. Now we are beginning to see this period and its long history as it really was, and not as it was imagined to be by Renaissance historians and French Romantics of the nineteenth century.[1]

The collapse of the Western Roman Empire and the acculturation of the Germanic hordes ushered in centuries of hardship and chaos. After the eleventh century, however, the Middle Ages saw a remarkable flowering as technical advances in agriculture and industry multiplied: widespread use of the rigid shoulder harness for horses, triennial rotation of crops, the model farms of the Cistercians, watermills and windmills, the pulley-wheel, oarless sailing ships, and so on, and the emancipation of the last slaves.[2]

At the same time, by a relationship of mutual cause and effect, there was a demographic explosion that was facilitated by a period of peace and security. The population of Europe, which is estimated to have been 42 million in the year 1000, rose to 73 million by 1300.[3]

In the sphere of culture this was a period of intense intellectual life. The long reign of monastic culture[4] led to the various, more or less innovative movements associated with St. Anselm (1033–1109), Abelard (1079–1142), St. Bernard (1090–1153), and the Victorines, and, later on, those centered around St. Albert the Great (1193–1280), St. Thomas Aquinas (1225–1274), St. Bonaventure (1221–1274), and others. Via the Arabs of Spain, European thinkers

discovered, to the accompaniment of heated "disputations," the
writings of the Greek philosophers and especially Aristotle. Roman
law was rediscovered, and so on.

But a counterthrust came in 1277 when Stephen Tempier, bishop
of Paris, issued a condemnation of 219 propositions, among them
certain Aristotelean positions that had been more or less baptized by
St. Albert the Great, Siger of Brabant, and St. Thomas Aquinas. The
consequences of this condemnation were to be serious for the future
of theological and philosophical thought.

From the end of the thirteenth century on there was a spreading
infatuation with Roman law, which had been recently "discovered."
This law would provide a juridical framework and a centralized political system (cf. the "legists" of Philip the Fair), as well as a regulation of trade, the need of which was urgently felt by the "merchants" or "bourgeois" who were in the ascendancy at this time.
The wealthiest members of this class sent their sons to study law in
the new universities at Bologna, Montpellier, and other centers.

The development of cities now emancipated from the control of
the feudal lords and administered by an assembly of citizens who
elected their own magistrates meant a revolution in mores and mentalities. The cultivation of trade brought with it a new system of
values:

> At a time when others lived from the soil they tilled or defended, the
> townsman chose to live by trade, without producing anything himself.
> As a result, he was preoccupied with profit in an age when people gen-
> erally were content to satisfy their needs and nothing more. However
> much they may have tried to adapt, the bourgeoisie stood in contrast
> with the rest of society because their way of life, their concerns, and
> the simple fact that trade exists for profit gave this class a special out-
> look of its own.[5]

At this time the gap began to widen between the mentality of the
merchants and that proper to the older, "good and faithful" economic system that was still taught by the theologians (St. Thomas
among them) and called for by the papal Decretals (Gregory IX). In
this older system it was the common good, and not profit, that was
to regulate prices and therefore, trade.[6]

Land itself, which to countryfolk was identified with the soil one
tilled for a livelihood, became for the middle class "property to be
exploited for money."[7]

Buying for the sake of later profit (the definition of trade) was forbidden. It was a form of usury, just as lending at interest was. St. Leo
the Great had written that "interest on money brings death to the
soul."[8] The result was a serious conflict between the Church and the
middle class and between the urban (and even the rural) populace

and the merchants or bankers: "People saw money-changers, almost all of them from beyond the Alps (they were called 'Lombards') making enormous fortunes that were all the more scandalous in an age when life was pretty much the same for everyone, and uniformly simple."[9]

With their money, the middle class obtained power—not only in the cities, but in the countryside where they bought up lands formerly belonging to feudal lords. They purchased offices in the service of the king (some became "citizens of the king"), gained entry into the nobility, and played an active part in political, military, and even religious life. "The merchant had become a landowner. He took the name associated with the property and entered the nobility through purchase, marriage or prescription; his son then obtained some office or other, or military rank, or an ecclesiastical benefice; by the third generation at the latest access was gained to the council of the king."[10]

While the great middle class families were competing in their ambitions, a proletariat was coming into existence in the cities. This proletariat was harshly exploited; the result would be many a riot and uprising.

This, then, was the situation at the end of the thirteenth century and the beginning of the fourteenth. It was now that the latent crisis burst into the open and led to profound and far-reaching change and even to a cultural transformation.

The Crisis

During the first half of the fourteenth century, a series of disasters struck Europe. First there was a famine, the result of climatic disturbances (rain and cold) from 1314 to 1317. Above all, there was the "Black Death" which decimated the population from 1348 to 1350. "It is generally agreed among historians that there was in Europe an overall demographic loss of 33 percent to 40 percent (higher in the cities than in the countryside, as one might expect)."[11]

Deserted villages, fields lying fallow for lack of manpower, ensuing famines throughout the country. There was panic: according to the chroniclers of the time, fear of the plague was so intense that people fled, leaving their kinfolk to die alone and be buried in haste by people who were hired at great cost from among the peasantry and who subsequently died of the plague themselves. Those who overcame this universal fear and attended to the dying out of "Christian generosity," were most likely to succumb to this terrible affliction. The losses sustained were not just numerical; they were losses of human and Christian values.

"Life expectancy in England fell from thirty-four years at the beginning of the 14th century to seventeen in 1348; it reached thirty-
four again only in 1420."[12] The loss of life was immense:

> It began with the great plague of 1348–1350. In a short time, 14,000
> died at Basel, 50,000 in Paris, 60,000 in Florence, 100,000 at Venice.
> In Germany, the Friars Minor alone lost 30,000 religious to the epi-
> demic. In order to evaluate these figures properly we must bear in
> mind that the population of the cities was far, far less than today. The
> death-knell could be heard ringing uninterruptedly, and funeral pro-
> cessions were to be seen passing through the city in a never-ending
> line. The communal graves were not big enough to take the mass of
> corpses. Contemporaries estimated that it was easier to count the sur-
> vivors than the dead. These vast slaughters had a profound effect on
> men and women and changed the way they looked at the world. In the
> ensuing period, the populace continued to be shattered over and over
> again by the plague which came and went like an intermittent fever.
> From 1325 to 1400 there were 32 years of plague; from 1400 to 1500
> there were 41.[13]

"In about 1320–1330 the population of France (modern borders)
probably came to over 17 million. Around 1440 it had decreased by
at least 10 million."[14]

In addition to the plague, war raged, and a mercenary war at that,
carried on by "great companies" that held for ransom, pillaged, and
killed without restraint. The Holy Roman Empire of the German
Nation was now a thing of the past; France was caught up in the
chaos of the Hundred Years' War (1337–1453), and in the impassioned struggles involving the Houses of Orleans, Burgundy, and
England. The lack of any strong and unchallenged political authority
aggravated the general anxiety, as people began to strive for what
would eventually become national unity.

This political anarchy was accompanied by a very profound transformation of social, economic, and cultural life. The feudal world
was collapsing and bringing confusion and anxiety to contemporaries who were as yet unable to see the foundations being laid for a
new world that would later be known as the Renaissance. The period
was a passage through a void as far as the "being in the world" of
several successive generations was concerned.

There was chaos in the Church as well: from 1377 to 1414 there
were two popes claiming authority at the same time (and even a
third in 1409), and the critical situation led to the Council of Con-
stance (1414–1417). The dioceses, religious orders, and political
powers were divided by obedience to one or other of the popes. Even
the saints of this age who were later canonized were divided in their
decision as to allegiance. The moral and financial wretchedness of
the clergy was great: "The priests have nothing to eat and go collect-

ing alms from house to house with promises of saying Masses for the deceased."[15] "We see a Church that never before reached the low state it is in today."[16] The "Great Schism" of the Eastern and Western Churches was completed in 1378. The robe of Christ was torn, and popular belief had it that ever since this sacrilegious rending, it was impossible for anyone to enter Paradise.[17]

Islam was on the offensive again. The fall of Saint-Jean d'Acre, the last fortress of Christendom, occurred in 1291. Soon the Turks were invading the Byzantine Empire, the Balkans, Hungary, and Poland. The Christian defeat at Nicopolis came in 1396.

"All goes badly": the "end of the world" is at hand. This is the widespread feeling that is well expressed in a poem of Eustache Deschamps: "Now the world is cowardly, decayed and weak. Old, covetous, confused of speech: I see only female and male fools. . . . The end approaches, in sooth. . . . All goes badly."[18]

The widespread and much prolonged anxiety caused reactions that are to some extent analogous with those of an individual suffering from an obsessional neurosis. It is possible in these circumstances to speak of a collective neurosis.[19]

The mood of the populace alternated between a tragic sense of guilt and outbursts of hedonism:

> So violent and motley was life, that it bore the mixed smell of blood and of roses. The men of that time always oscillate between the fear of hell and the most naïve joy, between cruelty and tenderness, between harsh asceticism and insane attachment to the delights of this world, between hatred and goodness, always running to extremes.[20]

Not without reason, the chief object that became the irresistible focus of anxiety was death, "hideous and threatening."[21] It was impossible to avoid seeing it every day. In the course of a single century France lost 7 million inhabitants out of a total of 17 million. I must emphasize the effects of this slaughter,[22] if only so that we may understand the atmosphere in which the "new" morality developed which dates from this period.

The collective anxiety intensified the sense of life's precariousness. Here is a lament of Jean Meschinot, three-quarters of a century after Deschamps: "O miserable and very sad life! . . . We suffer from warfare, death and famine; cold and heat, night and day, sap our strength; fleas, scabmites and so much other vermin make war upon us. In short, have mercy, Lord, upon our wicked persons, whose life is very short."[23]

The anxious fear of death found expression in dramatically exaggerated ways that were authentic symptoms of neurosis. For example, one popular belief was that after his resurrection, Lazarus lived in continual horror of the death he had experienced.[24] This same period saw the appearance and spread of the images of the "wheel of fortune," the works on "the art of dying well," and those dealing with "contempt for the world." In the cemetary of the Innocents at Paris, "hysterical" crowds gathered to celebrate burials in which the horrible was the order of the day.[25]

Woodcuts for popular use illustrated the most terrifying aspects of hell and death. Painters did the same; recall, for example, Grünewald's famous Crucifixion at Colmar in which the body of Christ displays signs of premature putrefaction.

The execution of condemned robbers and witches became fascinating spectacles that drew mobs of people. Huizinga remarks:

> What strikes us in this judicial cruelty and in the joy the people felt at it, is rather brutality than perversity. Torture and executions are enjoyed by the spectators like an entertainment at a fair. The citizens of Mons bought a brigand, at far too high a price, for the pleasure of seeing him quartered, "at which the people rejoiced more than if a new holy body had risen from the dead."[26]

The authorities went so far as to refuse to allow the condemned to confess their sins, in order to make it more certain that they would not escape the terrible pains of hell.

Death and hell so fascinated people with their horror that preachers made these the habitual subject of their sermons. Processions of penitents became extraordinarily popular, and even more so the processions of flagellants who preceded and accompanied the great itinerant preachers such as St. Vincent Ferrer (1350–1419). During these celebrations, "popular devotion" allowed itself the free expression of every violent emotion. Everyone wept warm tears. "Each time that he [Vincent Ferrer] consecrated the host he shed so many tears that everyone present began to weep and a wailing arose that was like a funeral lament. So sweet were these tears to him that only reluctantly did he dry them."[27]

People would ask God for "the daily baptism of tears,"[28] as they meditated on all the details of Christ's passion and on death and the threat of hell. The dramatic stanzas of the *Dies irae*, or at least the final sixteen, date from this period, as do the multiplication of Masses for the dead, "founded" Masses, and so on, all of them being celebrated with a complete panoply of lamentations.

In order to escape this unbearable anxiety as far as possible, some sought compensation in the exercise of imagination (stories of chivalry, heroic narratives) or in mysticism[29] or even in the practice of magic (geomancy, necromancy, astrology) which Bishop Tempier had already condemned in 1277. Witchcraft and the occult sciences attracted a passionate interest,[30] as did alchemy, to which people turned especially in order to make gold (a sign of the times!).

"Jacques Coeur founded a chapel and sacristy in the cathedral of Bourges, but his reputation was already that of a man who made use of black magic, while in his circle, diabolical practices were attested, as far as such attestation was possible."[31]

Another symptom of neurosis was the spread of ritualism: at the courts of princes and kings there was an etiquette regulated down to the last detail, including the color and style of dress;[32] the same was true of secular and religious ceremonies.

This formalism took on a magical character in everything dealing with religion. We need think only of the practice of indulgences, which was based on the doctrine of the "treasury of the Church" and received its official form right at this time, in 1343, in the Bull *Unigenitus* of Clement VI. The same tendency to magical formalism was found in sacramental practice and in the cult of the saints: people carried "amulets" of Sts. Roch, Christopher, or Sebastian as a protection against "foul death" and hell.[33]

All of these practices fitted in only too well with the collective fear of death and sin[34] that afflicted the entire West at this time. Just as an individual suffering from an obsessional neurosis invents rituals for himself, "little tricks" that provide him with a magical security and a very temporary alleviation of his anxiety, so too did Western society seek to allieviate its collective anxiety through ritualism and moral formalism.

> The entire spirituality of the feudal period was strongly oriented toward eschatological perspectives: the glorious return of the Son of man in the "modern" age. But in the tenth to the thirteenth centuries, we observe that while the scenario has not changed, the meaning is no longer quite the same. The focus now is less on the Second Coming than on the Last Judgment; Christ appears in his glory, but primarily as a Judge who will reward the good and punish the wicked. . . . All this shows the influence being exerted by a juridical mentality and even by a mercantile mentality on the manner in which relations between God and his creatures are conceived.[35]

The connection between anxiety and moral legalism is both psychologically and historically clear.

The world made up of merchants, bankers, and other "bourgeois" saw their business threatened, ruined, and rendered impossible by the general insecurity of society: fluctuation of prices, constant devaluation of money, confusing regional variations in law, the venality of judges, and so on. It was vital to them to obtain some minimal security through "order": a legal order, promulgated and imposed by an effective central authority, an order comparable to that which had been provided by Roman law, the model whose study "was at this period part of the vast movement of ideas that was exciting the whole of Christendom."[36] "It is very peculiar to see the extent to which juridical formulations henceforth made their way into every area of life, and how important the magistrates were to become in France."[37]

Such an "order" could be established only through a concentration of power, which Louis XI was to begin (1423–1483).[38] This is why the growing influence of the bourgeoisie was directed more and more to the reinforcement of the power of the monarchy (the influence of a good part of the nobility was exerted in the opposite direction). The bourgeoisie shared increasingly in the regional exercise of royal power. Some of its members served on the council of the king, whom they aided with their wealth[39] and their understanding of centralized organization. Feeling their power to be slipping away, the great lords protested and entered the lists against those whom they scornfuly called the Marmousets (1388).[40]

The concentration of royal power, which was supported by the legists who had been won over to Roman law, soon led to encroachments of the political power into the religious sphere.

> The juridical sphere was certainly the one in which, despite or even because of the disturbances, the authority of the monarchy advanced most irresistibly, in the sphere of "both laws," that is, canonical and civil. By reason of his anointing, the king had at all times jurisdiction in ecclesiastical matters; on this ground, his people in Parliament claimed the right to "cap" the Church's tribunals and to intervene between the clergy of the realm and the court of Rome. Conferences at Vincennes in 1328 had endeavored, not without difficulty, to settle these conflicts of jurisdiction. The Schism hatched the initial seeds of Gallicanism. In a kind of anticipation of the disputes of the seventeenth and eighteenth centuries, Parliament and the University joined to emancipate the clergy of France from the control of the Curia.[41]

In the Pragmatic Sanction of Bourges (1437), "the monarchy by unilateral action claimed control of the clergy; for practical purposes, the nomination of the principal dignitaries was left to its discretion."[42]

It was the state, more than the Church, that initiated the hunt for witches and heretics. "Crimes of heresy" would be under the jurisdiction of the civil courts and not of the Inquisition.[43]

The king of France was king "by the grace of God." He possessed "not only temporality but divinity," wrote the bishop of Arras in 1380. "He is an ecclesiastical person as well as a lay person" (Jouvenal des Oursins). He is a "most Christian king, king by miracle and anointing, a spiritual and priestly king" (Gerson).[44]

The sacralization of political power and the politicization of the religious sphere were now more closely connected than ever before in the history of Christendom. As a result, the king profited by all the ideas which the legists had pulled together since the now distant days of Philip the Fair, and which in the fifteenth and sixteenth centuries were summarized in a few formulas that gave a theoretical foundation for what a Louis XIV would put into practice: "The king is king and emperor in his realm and can issue laws and edicts at his pleasure," the legist Jean Boutillier had written in his *Summa ruralis* (1400). Whence the formula, "For such is our pleasure," which began to be current in royal acts in the 15th century.[45]

Merchants or bankers, landowners or "citizens of the king," all profited by their power to avoid taxes,[46] leaving these to be paid by the poor whom they exploited. Rebellions broke out which threatened "order" and were therefore harshly put down.[47] But these events troubled the consciences of some, especially since the Church still maintained its condemnation of lending money at interest and other "usurious" practices, as well as of speculations and fraud in buying and selling. Some felt that they were guilty and would go straight to hell.

> While those who used their money for business were violating ecclesiastical prescriptions at every moment, and while there are individual examples of cynicism on the part of habitual usurers, we also find frequent evidence on the part of businessmen of a sincere piety that generates remorse, however belated this remorse may be.[48]

To mitigate their guilt, many, during their lifetime or at their death, left gifts for the poor or for the building of churches and hospices, "gifts which increasingly resembled a kind of insurance policy with regard to eternal salvation."[49]

I felt it necessary to sketch a brief portrait of this widespread and dramatically expressed anxiety which Europeans experienced for more than a century at the end of the Middle Ages. It helps us understand the need they ultimately felt for some bit of security, a security they hoped to obtain from an authority sufficiently strong and unchallenged that it could introduce order into activity and ideas of every kind: religious, moral, economic, social, and political.

The Moral Teaching of William of Occam

This period of anxiety saw the formulation and rapid spread of moralities based on a divine authority that imposes arbitrary laws to which human beings have no choice but to submit on pain of the sternest sanctions in the hereafter.

An outstanding example was the theological and moral system of William of Occam.[50] Occam was a Franciscan of English birth who died in 1349; he developed a moral system which responded only too well to the anxious expectancy that marked the end of the Middle Ages.

Like Stoicism, which came into existence and found a following in a chaotic period in the history of Greece, Occamism reveals its full meaning when we situate it in its historical context. Occam soon came to be called *Venerabilis Inceptor* (the "Esteemed Beginner"), and that is precisely what he was: an innovator who is the ancestor of the Western moral systems that sprang up from the fourteenth century on, those moralities based on law and duty which most unfortunately represent "traditional" Christian morality.

Occam's moral system was connected with the beginnings of nominalism and voluntarism,[51] and seemed at the time to be an innovation which would supply the desired security people needed. The majority of later theologians followed his lead enthusiastically: from Roger Bacon to Gerson and Gabriel Biel, whom the young Luther took for one of his masters. This system of thought left such a strong mark on the outlook of the Western world that we find in Occam positions still being echoed to some extent in Leibniz, Kant, Hegel, and Jean-Paul Sartre.

As a nominalist, Occam maintained that only singular entities existed. A universal is only a word, and a word (Latin: *vox*) "exists neither really nor substantially in the thing which it signifies."[52]

Only singular things exist, each of them unique. Each is closed up in what Lagarde calls its "insularity"; somewhat like Leibniz's monads, it has no relations with other things. Here we have the theoretical basis for the individualism of later centuries.

It is true, of course, says Occam, that human beings live in society, but society is only a sum of beings, nothing more. In society, these human beings occupy certain positions relative to one another, but such positions establish relations and obligations that are purely external to the beings themselves; they are relations of force (perhaps foreshadowing Hegel?).

The relations of human beings with God are likewise conceived as relations of force which remain extrinsic to them and depend exclusively on the omnipotence of God. In Occam's view, God is absolute freedom; this means we cannot define him as having a nature which would set limits to his sovereign freedom. God therefore has no nature. But neither does the human person, since all that exists is singulars. Created as they are in the image and likeness of God, human beings too have freedom.(Occam all but says, with Jean-Paul Sartre, that man must create his own freedom.)

In Occam's view, the human person exercises this freedom in submission to God and his commandments. The latter are arbitrary, since they are not based on any nature, either divine or human. Human beings have no "natural" inclination in their will, nor any desire of the good or of beatitude.[53]

It is God who decides, with sovereign freedom and according to his own good pleasure, what is to be good or evil, what he is to forbid, allow, or require. Thus, once God decides things, man's only function is to obey. God can always decide differently; otherwise he would not be free. He can very well decide, for example, that it is evil and forbidden to love him and that he is to be hated. We, in turn, would then have to obey.

Obligation, and it alone, is thus the basis of morality: a morality of submission to commandments of God for which we are to seek no justification except in the absolute authority and freedom of God. Moral obligation is "completely extrinsic to the human person; it is even irrational and has no connection with a human nature or a natural human desire."[54] Surely, the perspective here is already that of Kant's categorical imperative.

Natural law is simply the expression of the arbitrary will of God who dictates to man's "right reason" what he is to do and not to do. It is no accident that this morality of "God's good pleasure" is contemporary with the politics of "the king's good pleasure."

In summary: according to Occam, human perfection consists in submitting blindly, but also freely, to the law imposed by God. Such a morality was seen as the best possible "tranquillizer." It enabled people to "get right" with God and their consciences and thereby find (illusory) peace. During this lengthy period of political and religious anarchy, it enabled people to rely wholly on divine and ecclesiastical authority which, by determining what was allowed and forbidden (under pain of serious sin), spared them all the risks of personal responsibility, since they now had only to obey.

It was a great consolation for people to know, in a precise and secure way, what they had to do to avoid hell. If they did break the law, they had only to pay their debt and make reparation in a more or less magical way through prescribed practices (ranging from indulgences to confession that focused on "the commandments of God and the Church").

Once this pattern was established, everything was in order, and the anxieties felt by conscience were to a great extent alleviated—not completely alleviated because, despite everything, the sense of guilt was still present and active, thus reinforcing the entire process.

Beginning in this second half of the fourteenth century, mores and theory reinforced one another in the way described and thus led to the transformation of Western morality that has lasted down to our own day.

Chapter 5

The Legacy

Religion as Prop for the Moral, Social and Political Order

Should we regard the effects of the crises of the fourteenth and fifteenth centuries as a sudden transformation or rather as "a process of change which had been under way for a long time and which a brutal shock, a violent upheaval, brought to its completion"?[1] Our knowledge of the laws (if indeed there are any general laws) governing the birth, growth, and decay of civilizations is too imperfect for us to be able to answer such a question. Are we better off following custom and speaking of the Renaissance? If we do, we must understand it not only as a rebirth of Greco-Roman civilization but also, at the same time, as the attainment of that which had been so desperately sought during the "waning" of the Middle Ages, what Michel Mollat would like to compare with a springtime or an adolescence: "The end of the Middle Ages shows the characteristics of adolescence: the confusions, the unrest, the intense need of security, but also the enthusiasm, the tireless search for balance."[2]

As Jacques Soustelle puts it,

Each culture, each civilization, is a contingent set of technical, juridical, and ethical phenomena which the group or groups in question attempt, without ever succeeding completely, to integrate into a structured whole. At each moment of its duration a particular culture shows itself to be a compromise between what has been *received* from tradition and outside influences and what is *produced* by the society in its functioning at the given moment.[3]

The makers of what would later be called the Renaissance showed a distorted perception of what came to them from the most recent tradition. To them, the Middle Ages represented nothing but "obscurantism." The cathedrals were judged to be "barbaric"; medieval philosophy was nothing but base Scholasticism which deserved no attention from subsequent generations. In other words, there had been only an empty gap for a thousand years. The models for Renaissance men were those of the Greco-Roman world; these they copied rather than drew inspiration from for something new.[4]

I am convinced that all the distinctive characteristics of "modern times" came into existence, received their structure, and were spread throughout the West during the crisis of the fourteenth and fifteenth centuries. I am afraid that the historians and thinkers of the sixteenth and seventeenth centuries were not sufficiently aware of this.

This is particularly clear in regard to morality. There is no other way of explaining the extraordinary success of the Occamist moral system from the end of the fourteenth century on. Luther rebelled against this morality, and rightly so, but in his case he had a counter-dependence of his own that was overly conditioned by his personal problems in relation to his father.[5]

Occamism, mingled with the Stoicism that was finding a new lease on life at that time, gave their structure to both Catholic[6] and Protestant moral thinking, which were organized around the Decalogue and, for Catholics, around the "commandments of the Church" as well. Morality and religion were taught in the catechisms, moral treatises, and preparation for confession, and the focus at all times was the law. This legalism was matched by an exaltation of will power (voluntarism), submission to religious and civil authority, and a discussion of subtle problems raised by the uneasy conscience. In addition, morality sought the support of the "essentialism" of the age; this contributed the false security afforded by an immutable and universal order, the order of "natural law" (Stoicism) that shut its eyes to the historical, evolutive, and diversified aspect of human life.

Aristotle had been well aware of this aspect of human life: "In matters having to do with human action and with what is expedient, nothing is strictly fixed and unchanging, any more than in matters of health" (1104a3). Renaissance morality, on the other hand, aimed at providing security. But "the rejection, in the name of the Absolute, of the conditions set by history and its contingency meant abandoning the human measure, the temporal limits set to reason and freedom; it was, by that very fact, an abandonment of morality, due to a failure to accept the conditions required for its production."[7]

This security-producing order held sway in priestly and religious life as well, as it did in "reforms of the clergy" (Synod of Sens, 1485;

Reform Commission of Tours, 1493; Council of Trent, 1545–63) and in the renewal of 1600–1640. But this widespread legalism did not stifle the spirit that worked in the saintly founders or in those who inspired the great spiritual movements at the end of the sixteenth century and the beginning of the seventeenth.

Both the Reformation and the Counter-Reformation, however, which already bore the impress of two centuries of Occamism, the revival of Stoicism, and the cult of Roman law, found in moral legalism one more motive for following and having others follow a moral and religious practice that was based on the fear of hell and damnation, on rigorism, and on submission to a God seen as a Judge.

Jean Delumeau's books have clearly brought out this attitude on the part of the "elite," both Catholic and Protestant, who could not stand the sight of the Christianity of the masses, with its excessive mixture of paganism and superstition.[8] They found "popular" religion intolerable. This accounts for their zeal in regard to the masses, but it was a zeal equivocal in its motives and in its effects (as seen in Jansenism and Protestant puritanism). We see it in Catholics after 1640, when the "devout" and the members of the Compagnie du Saint-Sacrement, (founded in 1630 and comprising primarily princes, nobles, and men of the upper middle class) used their political influence for the purpose of introducing order "in the streets." "In their own minds," these people "identified social and Christian action with the values of their own class."[9]

These devout persons applied to the masses the same moral and religious principles that inspired their own zeal; consequently they did everything they could to "convert" ordinary men and women through fear.

Their efforts led to the foundation in 1656 of the Hôpitaux Généraüx, which were subsidized by the crown and governed by twenty-six directors (twelve of whom were members of the Compagnie du Saint-Sacrement). They proceeded to "confine" all undesirable subjects in the hospitals of the Pitié, the Salpétrière, Bicêtre, and Scipion: beggars, the elderly, the sick, but also prostitutes and the insane—and even Protestants. These hospitals were simultaneously prisons, alms-houses, houses of correction, and asylums for the insane. The poor "internees," thus intermingled, were not likely to find solace in their wretchedness, but at least people who kept good company would no longer have to see them wandering the streets of Paris and causing scandal with their bad habits.

The "morality" thus imposed was regarded as Christian, and no doubt it was in its own way—as conceived by the elite of the day and by the ideology of the aristocracy and middle class.

More than ever, religion and politics were intermingled under the twofold authority of king and pope. For political centralization around the authority of the monarchy had its homologue in the centralization of Church government—a development that would lead in 1870 to the dogma of papal infallibility.

In secular society the combined action of the two political and religious powers became important and traditional. It was exercised in every area, from the appointment of bishops and monastic abbots, to the hunt for witches and other disturbers of public order. The control of the Church by the political power continued under Napoleon[10] and during the Restoration.[11] This state of affairs was supported by public opinion, even that of freethinkers who agreed with Voltaire: "I want my steward, tailor, and valets to believe in God; I imagine that then I'm less likely to be robbed."[12]

Religion and the morality it enforces are the guarantee of social order and submission to the political authorities: this belief would be reinforced during the nineteenth century, after the upheaval of the Revolution of 1789.[13] Nietzsche would find it possible to write: "Naiveté: as if morality could survive when the God who sanctions it is missing! The 'beyond' absolutely necessary if faith in morality is to be maintained."[14]

This moral order (for other people) which religion promoted and sanctioned was in fact more "bourgeois" than Christian. It showed a high regard for wealth and the cult of property [15] and material progress; it kept women in subjection,[16] encouraged political and military actions for commercial ends, had contempt for manual labor,[17] and exploited the proletariat and the indigenous peoples of colonized countries.[18]

The mores and religious morality of modern times are indeed the fruit of a mentality created back then; and, as Philippe Ariès rightly observes, "this includes the secular morality of the nineteenth century."[19] It was a morality developed by merchants, bankers, and aristocratic and middle-class men of government, all of whom were eager for everything that could bring them security: the security of a good conscience that obeyed the law, the security provided by political, social, and economic order. Religion and a legalistic morality that was sanctioned by a divine Judge gave them valuable and much appreciated aid.

Among the moral systems that have successively arisen in the modern age there is one that, by reason of its consistency with the mentality described, the philosophical rigor of its structure, and its considerable influence even in our day, deserves to have its main principles recalled. I am speaking of the ethics of Immanuel Kant.

Kantian Ethics

It was Kant's role to systematize the morality of duty and thus to strengthen its mental and cultural structures in the Western world of the nineteenth and even the twentieth centuries.

His ambition was to construct a metaphysics of morals that would be centered on law. This moral law does not itself require a justification, and the obligation it imposes cannot "be proved *a posteriori* by experience, and yet it is firmly established of itself."[20]

Kant's is thus an *a priori* morality, a demand flowing from the very operation of reason: "Pure reason practical of itself is here directly legislative,"[21] and "a law . . . must carry with it absolute necessity."[22]

Moral obligation, then, is an immediate datum of consciousness, a categorical imperative that is objectively and universally necessary. The reader probably knows Kant's formulation: "I am never to act otherwise than so that I could also will that my maxim should become a universal law."[23]

In short, this morality of duty has its existence "in itself" and imposes itself in an unqualified way on the conscience, the latter being subject to it as to a constraining rule. Kant goes so far as to speak of "an internal, but intellectual, compulsion."[24] The internal compulsion is exercised by reason which recognizes the justice of submission. The moral law begins as exogenous, but in this way becomes endogenous.

Moral law is sacred because the categorical imperative has its origin in God.[25] God is the subject who issues the command.[26] "The concept of God is that of a subject who is external to me and who imposes an obligation on me."[27] Despite this, "God should not be represented as a subject external to me but as the supreme moral principle within me."[28]

As thus conceived, this metaphysical, rational, and a priori morality excludes any seeking of happiness. The moral act compels recognition of itself and for itself, and has no other purpose but itself. Duty has no element of the pleasurable in it.[29] Kant rejects without qualification everything that he regards as moral "eudaimonism." In his view, to practice virtue while being inclined to do so by pleasure or happiness is "the euthanasia (painless death) of all morals."[30] Happiness is self-centered, subjective, individual, and empirical; therefore it cannot be the basis of morality.

> Happiness is the satisfaction of all our desires; *extensive*, in regard to their multiplicity; *intensive*, in regard to their degree; and *protensive*, in regard to their duration. The practical law based on the motive of *happiness* I term a pragmatical law (or prudential rule); but that law, assuming such to exist, which has no other motive than the *worthiness of being happy*, I term a moral or ethical law. The first tells us what we have to do, if we wish to become possessed of happiness; the second dictates how we ought to act, in order to deserve happiness. The first is based upon empirical principles; for it is only by experience that I can learn either what inclinations exist which desire satisfaction, or

what are the natural means of satisfying them. The second takes no account of our desires or the means of satisfying them, and regards only the freedom of a rational being, and the necessary conditions under which alone this freedom can harmonize with the distribution of happiness according to principles. This second law may therefore rest upon mere ideas of pure reason, and may be cognized *a priori*.[31]

The only place happiness has in Kantian morality is in connection with the next life. It is in no way a principle of virtue. It is radically rejected as a formal constituent of moral motivation; it can only be a result of morality, inasmuch as morality renders the person worthy of receiving happiness from the Supreme Good. But the Supreme Good is not of this world; its attainment postulates the immortality of the soul and the existence of the God who will reward virtue with happiness.[32]

For Kant, then, morality has nothing empirical about it: it is an *a priori*, one of the categories of reason, which are indefinable.[33] The categorical imperative has a divine character,[34] and the field of human freedom is that of obedience to this necessary, absolute, universal, and unfathomable imperative.

This morality of duty, like that of the Stoics and Occam, is thus based on obedience to a "sacred" law which is its own justification and is imposed by divine authority. Kant's successors will find ways of locating the source of moral obligation elsewhere than in God: in the state, in history, or in the universal Will (Hegel). In every case, however, the morality remains a morality of the categorical imperative, of duty. So deeply imprinted is this morality in the ideology of the Western (and bourgeois) world, Christian or not, that many are incapable of freeing themselves from it. In their own way, they are "victims of duty."

Thus, some people talk of a "duty of being happy"—which is enough to make you lose your desire for happiness. When Eric Weil tries to reintroduce happiness into morality, he is unable to free himself from Kantianism and looks for a way out by saying:

> It is not because either his own interest, properly understood, or a duty toward others demands it that a person wills to observe the moral law. It is because the person owes it to himself to be reasonable and because he has chosen to seek happiness in and through reason, even if this means renouncing all happiness for his empirical self. Duty to self is specified as the duty of being happy precisely as a reasonable being.[35]

It is this kind of Western morality, born of the crisis of the fourteenth and fifteenth centuries, that is today being questioned and challenged. It is questioned, that is, except where people barricade themselves up in it to avoid the dizzying loss of a moral system that gives security and seems to be "traditional" (it is, but only for the last six centuries) and "Christian" (it is, insofar as it is that of Western "Christendom"), but that is hardly either traditional or Christian by the standard of fidelity to the gospel.

Chapter 6

The Damage Done by "Traditional" Morality

"Christian" Morality Is Barely Christian

The new covenant can be summed up in three words: "You shall love." The comandment of love is "new," but without ceasing to be old (1 Jn 2:7), inasmuch as it was there "from the beginning."[1] "If I . . . have not love, I am nothing" (1 Cor 13:2).

All the moralities of duty and law, on the other hand, can be summed up in the formula, "You shall obey." You are and will be judged and condemned if you do not submit to all the orders of an absolute, "sacred," and ruthless authority who issues laws as it seems good to him and without reference to your desires, capacities, and difficulties.

The fundamental law of the new covenant is incompatible with this morality of obedience, because it is not possible to love out of duty, that is, solely for the reason that authority imposes on me the obligation of loving. All love is spontaneous; it proceeds from the innermost personal depths of the subject. If love has a law, it is an endogenous law, a law of life and its development. Love belongs to the order of free inspiration that is constitutive of the person.

This is why Christ so often emphasizes the priority that must be given to what "proceeds from the heart" (Mt 15:19; etc.), on the vigor of the tree that determines the quality of the fruit (Mt 7:17; 12:33–37; 15:1–20), on the "soundness" of the eye (Mt 6:22), and so on. "You blind Pharisee! first cleanse the inside of the cup . . . that the outside also may be clean" (Mt 23:26).

This single commandment of love is no longer a law imposed from without; to this extent it is not a commandment[2] since its obligation is that of love and not of authority. This commandment does, of course, imply many others which we read in the gospel and St. Paul and which the Church teaches us, but we must see and practice these for what they really are: concrete applications of charity and meant to help its growth. These commandments are true and effective only if their observance is inspired by love: "If you love me, you will keep my commandments" (Jn 14:15). Without this love it is impossible to observe these commandments, even according to the letter. One falls back under "the curse of the law" (Gal 3:13).

This is certainly the morality of the gospel; yet through the ages, it has been deformed and Christians have chosen instead to inflict on themselves the excessive burden of laws and prohibitions which, as Isaiah had already said, started as "the precepts of men" but became in time "the tradition of the elders" (Mt 15:2-9). We find St. Paul already writing to the Colossians:

> Why do you live as if you still belonged to the world? Why do you submit to regulations, "Do not handle, Do not taste, Do not touch" (referring to things which all perish as they are used), according to human precepts and doctrines? These have indeed an appearance of wisdom in promoting rigor of devotion and self-abasement and severity to the body, but they are of no value in checking the indulgence of the flesh (Col 2:20-23).

Why this regression by Christians into legalism and the "leaven of the Pharisees" (Mt 16:6-12), unless because human beings find it difficult to free themselves from the spirit of the world and the "flesh"[3] and because the kingdom of heaven, though now present, is also still to come?

As they wait, human beings are hard pressed by the inescapable effects of original sin and by the distorted image of God as a judge who is jealous of his authority, instills fear, and is inflexible. As a result, the old self of which St. Paul speaks[4] continues to take shelter behind the observance of the law and "human traditions," far from the face of the God of mercy.

To the extent that the "traditional" morality of duty seeks security in the observance of the law, it has been unfaithful to the gospel. It has not cleansed itself of the old leaven (1 Cor 5:7). It has gone back to the righteousness of the lawyers and the Pharisees and "rejected the purpose of God" for us (Lk 7:30), a plan of mercy for all human beings as soon as they are willing to acknowledge the anxiety their wretched state and their poverty cause them.

To the extent indicated, this morality, contrary to the common view, is not Christian. "O foolish Galatians! Who has bewitched you?" (Gal 3:1). What is it that has bewitched Westerners for seven centuries if not the ascendancy of the letter, with its gift of an illusory security, over the spirit which it smothers, an ascendancy fostered by the desperate state of the times?

The "Prevalent" Morality Mutilates

The hardly Christian morality that has reigned in the West for seven centuries seems in our time to be under increasing challenge and to be showing clear signs of decline.

I admit I am glad that this is so, although I am at the same time concerned about the confusion such an upheaval brings with it and about the more or less satisfactory attempts to find a more authentic morality.

By way of ending my discussion of the morality of duty, I shall quickly list the accusations that are to be made against it, not only in the light of the gospel but also in the name of the truth about the human person. For this morality has excessively mutilated the human person and made it the prisoner of the Western neurosis, whether this last be diagnosed as schizophrenia, paranoia, or, as far as mores are concerned, clearly an obsessional neurosis.

A Morality that Promotes Infantilism

The morality of duty reduces to a matter of obedience to law and to the authority that promulgates it. Its imperatives call for passive submission and allow only a very secondary role to human desires, to understanding, and to personal judgment. *Stat pro ratione voluntas* ("will takes the place of reason").

As a result, the Christian people expect the divine authority, as transmitted, applied and sanctioned by the pope, the bishop, and the parish priest, to decide what is permitted and prohibited.

It is true that authority provides security. When a child feels weak or threatened by something frightening, it calms its fear by taking shelter in the authority of his or her parents. In a similar way, the believer whom responsibility makes anxious finds a certain security by falling back on the authority of the pope and the priest (paternal figures) and of the Church (a maternal figure).

This kind of fundamental dependence on authority fits in only too well with the nostalgia for childhood that dwells in every human being. It is an obedience to another that eliminates the need for obeying oneself. "He who cannot command himself should obey."[5] A morality based on submission to authorities can have only two outcomes, both of them "immature": the acceptance of infantilism or rebellion, the latter being only a counterdependence.

A Morality of Subservience to Political Authority

Such a morality of infantile submission offers every kind of political power a well-prepared ground on which to establish readily its own authority over subjects who are morally submissive and content to be so.

Like Freud in his day,[6] Gérard Mendel in his sociopsychoanalytic studies has analyzed the "phenomenon of authority."[7] Authority only accentuates and exploits the fact that, especially as a result of the blackmail practiced by love, people remain afraid of being abandoned or, to state the matter very precisely, they retain a sense of guilt. The fear of being abandoned—which is now anachronistic since it is no longer relevant but relates to the first months of life—leaves an ineradicable, unconscious mark on the person and leads first the child, then the adult to submit by an almost automatic, conditioned reflex to a "grown-up."

This need of infantile submission facilitated the meddling of political authority in the religious sphere throughout Western Christendom: France and England, Spain and Portugal, Russia and the Austro-Hungarian Empire.

In nineteenth/century France, the clergy was regarded as "the sublime preserver of public order," according to Count Molé in 1840,[8] while the Catholic hierarchy was looked upon as exercising the "sacred power: the power of commanding in the name of Jesus Christ."[9]

In a lecture in 1816, Freyssinous assured his listeners that "religion protects morality" and that "morality protects the laws." For this reason "religion is the first foundation of the moral order."[10]

Religion and the morality it sanctions are thus expected to give a sacral quality to the social order established by the ruling class. As late as 1914, the national catechism of France would be teaching children that "from the hour of birth some are marked out for submission, others for command."[11]

The same principle seems to be accepted for the Church itself: In 1906, in his *Vehementer Nos*, Pius X stated that "only the body of pastors possesses the right and authority needed for directing all the members toward the goal of the society. The multitude, for its part, has no duty but to allow itself to be led and, like a docile flock, to follow its shepherds."[12]

It is understandable that people, especially those supposedly marked from birth for submission, should have resisted the Church and that the Church should be frequented almost exclusively by those who are "submissive" and docile: children and women. Bishop Dupanloup of Orléans made the comment in 1865 that "in the villages where I preach the gospel the Church has the women and the old folk, the school has the children, whom it also leads to the Church, and the newspapers and the taverns own the men and the young people."[13] Parents would tell their children: "We forbid you to go to confession; the priests use confession in order to control the consciences of the village."[14]

Such are the confusions and compromises to which a morality of submission to the laws promulgated by authority only too readily leads.

A Class Ideology

The morality of duty developed and was established in connection with the birth of the "bourgeois" world and its acquisition of control over economic, social, and political life. This morality has all the characteristics of a class ideology in the sociological and Marxist sense of this term.

Thus, the morality of duty is an "imaginary representation by individuals of the real conditions of existence"; it is

> an unconscious and conscious concealment of reality; it exercises its power within social structures (family, school, work, government, churches); it is a mental and sociological structure that interprets social relations and both justifies and controls the social groups in power.[15]

It is a morality that preserves the "established order."[16] As Nietzsche described it: "Morality, source of preservation for great collectivities, whose members it disciplines; an instrument."[17]

This conservative attitude found its philosophical justification in the revival of Stoicism and in the Kantian systematization of the idea of "universal law" in morality. But the attitude was, in fact, part of the security-motivated search for a stable and even immutable social consensus. "A morality of universal law is always strictly political in the sense that it becomes a pledge of an order based on stable structures."[18]

An ideology is needed for any kind of social life; mores and moral theories always have been and always will be historically conditioned by some ideology or other. "Traditional" morality is not the only possible morality. It is legitimate and even necessary to develop a morality that will be proper to our own age.

A Sacralized Morality

Moralities centered on submission to authority lend themselves, more than any other kind, to a confusion between the religious and political orders. They take on a "sacral" character that is highly ambiguous and very harmful to them.

Nothing is more stupid (since nothing is as Louis-Philippe-ish and as Monsieur Thiers-ish) than to lump morality and religion together in this way. It might almost be said that everything taken by grace is taken from morality. And everything won by the morality in question, everything recovered by the morality in question, is automatically covered over by the glaze which I have described as impenetrable to grace.[19]

The sacredness of this so-called morality is ambiguous, and the human sciences have revealed its historical and psychological sources. It will be enough here to recall Freud's analysis of it: "What is sacred was originally nothing but the perpetuated will of the primeval father."[20]

When sacralized in this way, "Christian" morality proves to be so firmly built on the principle of submission to the commandments of God and the Church that it seriously minimizes the "primacy of love," which, until the fourteenth century, had traditionally been the life-giving principle of morality.[21] This development explains why it is that within the Church relations are of the kind marked by dependence on authority.[22] But the gospel shows us that another kind of relation is possible.

A Legalistic and Casuistic Morality

The morality of duty suffers from another kind of confusion as well. In it, law and morality are inadequately distinguished both in object and in method. Such a confusion is inevitable in a morality that has its source and basic point of reference in law as promulgated by authority.[23]

In such a perspective moral obligation is exogenous. Law "descends from heaven." Being external to the subject and imposed upon him, this morality is "very uncomely and tiresome," to use Kierkegaard's description.[24]

One symptom of this confusion is to be seen in the fact that, at least until recently, it was the professor of canon law who taught moral theology in the seminaries. I fear that canon law suffered from the confusion, but that moral theology suffered far more.

In this legalistic conception of morality, "mortal" sin was "*formally*" defined as "an act that substantially *violates the order* established by divine law."[25] In the Middle Ages, on the other hand, mortal sin was an action that kills love.[26]

Moral legalism reduces moral obligation to a reference to a duly promulgated law. The result is that in this "canonico-moral" perspective there can be no sin in refusing a "vocation" to the priesthood or religious life, even if such a call is, by hypothesis, absolutely certain. The reason is that a call of this kind involves an individual case, whereas law can only be general and bind all its subjects. No law, no obligation.[27]

Religious life (which by definition aims at fostering the practice of charity and the evangelical counsels) was presented in such a way that the emphasis was placed on its canonical obligations. Instruction on the vows of religion concentrated on their negative side, the aspect of "privation" and "destruction": "The *direct* object of the vow is a self-imposed privation: e.g., one deprives oneself of the possession or free use of temporal goods by the vow of poverty. The object of the virtue is the destruction of *inordinate affections*."[28]

In the older tradition, virtue had been a structured dynamism that in turn structured the person.[29] Here it is presented as destructive; what it destroys is indeed "inordinate affections" (inordinate relative to the law), but can the subject avoid being also destroyed in the process?

A reading of the treatises in moral theology that were used in the seminaries is a dismaying experience. I shall give but one example, taken from Heribert Jone, *Moral Theology*: "If one—either deliberately or by mistake—has eaten two full meals on a fastday, one can no longer observe the fast and, therefore, he may eat to satiety again."[30]

I could draw up a lengthly list of views of this kind which today seem to us deserving of the reproaches Christ addressed to the Pharisees and the teachers of the law.

An A Priori Morality

As we saw in the previous chapter, Kant rejects any and every empirical basis for morality. His is a "formal," categorical, and a prioristic morality. It obliges in an absolute, necessary, and universal manner, in the name of a categorical imperative that is unfathomable and divine.

This morality expressly refuses any information from or confirmation by experience. It rejects all "empiricism" and "subjectivism." Such a rejection, however, is a methodological defect that excludes any study of morality in its historical implementation and as lived by human beings. There is no place in Kantian (and post–Kantian) moral thought for any contribution from the human sciences.

In Aristotle (and St. Thomas Aquinas) we find an entirely different method and an entirely different conception of morality.[31]

For Aristotle the rule and measure of moral goodness is to be located in the action and judgment of the virtuous person.[32] Here is what R.-A. Gauthier has to say about this approach:

With regard to the subject matter of morality, current opinion necessarily includes a degree of valid perception. Such opinion may be analyzed in a superficial way (by the kind of dialectic that would satisfy a
rhetorician), but it is also possible to apply an appropriate critique and
bring to light the truths this opinion contains. This is what ethics
does, and that is why ethics is not reducible to dialectical knowledge,
even though it takes current opinion as its point of departure. Must
we say, then, that ethical knowledge is "scientific" knowledge? On occasion, Aristotle has no scruple about using this description, and it is
he who developed the concept of "practical science" in order to cap-
ture what is specific to ethics.[33]

When Kantian moral thought refused to consider morality to be a
"practical science," it condemned itself to a radical misunderstanding of human actions and of the moral subject. It is "empty of any
existential content."[34]

"A Thief of Energies"

All these unfortunate characteristics of traditional morality explain why it had a mutilating effect on the human person—and on
the Christian—and why it has been possible to describe it as "a thief
of energies." The phrase is from Arthur Rimbaud who, sad to say,
wrote it in accusation of the Christ who had been taught to him at
the time he was preparing for his first communion:

> I was very young, and Christ corrupted my breath.
> He filled me beyond measure with disgust.
> Christ! O Christ, eternal thief of energies.[35]

This morality has been a thief of energies because it has failed to
recognize the human possibilities of freedom and creativity. Those
who were and still are its victims can exercise their freedom in only
three ways: by rejecting it, or by an unconditional submission to
duty, or by engaging in juridical subtleties that allow them to act as
they please without incurring any sanctions.

This last alternative describes the basis on which casuistry became
so widespread for centuries, as it made systematic use of the principle: "This or that must be done (or avoided) under pain of mortal
sin." To use a simile, casuistry's aim was to make its way through
the electrified barbed wire mesh of the commandments of God and
the Church without getting electrocuted.

But the whole procedure excessively reduced the field of human
freedom and even debased its activity. Everyone is familiar with the
impassioned yet sound criticisms Nietzsche made of this kind of
moral thinking:

In summa: what is the price of moral improvement?—Unhinging of reason, reduction of all motives to fear and hope (punishment and reward); dependence upon a priestly guardianship, upon pedantic formalities which claim to express a divine will; the implanting of a "conscience" which sets a false knowing in place of testing and experiment; as if what should be done and left undone had already been determined—a kind of castration of the seeking and forward-striving spirit; *in summa:* the worst mutilation of man that can be imagined presented as the "good man."[36]

An exclusively deductive ethics of principles and laws has no choice but to ignore the subject in his concrete life and "individual mystery": "When a churchman does nothing but raise problems or is enthusiastic only about causes, without ever even beginning to attend to the individual mysteries which these problems call into play, then the deadly process of objectification has been set in motion. . . . Incapable of sacrificing an idea in order to save a human being."[37]

This moral system of the canonists, the casuists, and the armchair professors claims to be "objective," but its objectivity is idle, for it bears no relation to its real subjects.[38]

This failure to take account of subjects with their desires, capacities, and individual difficulties is one of the unfortunate effects of every ideology in the realm of morality. The collective "superego" of the Christianity of recent centuries has not escaped this accusation. Freud observes that the collective superego "troubles itself too little about the happiness of the ego, in that it takes insufficient account of the resistances against obeying them [the commands and prohibitions of the superego]—of the instinctual strength of the id [in the first place], and of the difficulties presented by the real external environment [in the second]."[39]

"Anyone thus compelled to act continually in the sense of precepts which are not the expression of instinctual inclinations, is living, psychologically speaking, beyond his means, and might objectively be designated a hypocrite, whether this difference be clearly known to him or not."[40]

Need I remind the reader that this is precisely the hypocrisy of which Christ accuses the Pharisees (Mt 23:3, 15; etc.)? Such is the inevitable lot of any morality based on law and duty. As Montaigne remarked: "Between ourselves, there are two things that I have always observed to be in singular accord: supercelestial thoughts and subterranean conduct."[41]

There is another point the morality of duty fails to recognize: it seems to be ignorant of the fact that the subject lives in time. Individually and collectively, the subject "becomes."[42] He advances into the future on the basis of his past. Moral life has its stages; it develops to maturity. When it chooses to ignore the laws of this growth,

traditional morality imposes the same universal and absolute "objective" obligations on all its subjects and on each of them alike, re-
gardless of whether the individual be child, adolescent, or adult,
neurotic or non-neurotic, a member of this class or that, this culture
or that. An education based on such a morality makes improper use
of ethical demands and is therefore doomed to failure. Some remarks of Freud seem to me to be especially relevant here:

> That the education of young people at the present day conceals from
> them the part which sexuality will play in their lives is not the only re-
> proach which we are obliged to make against it. Its other sin is that it
> does not prepare them for the aggressiveness of which they are des-
> tined to become the objects. In sending the young out into life with
> such a false psychological orientation, education is behaving as though
> one were to equip people starting on a Polar expedition with summer
> clothing and maps of the Italian Lakes. In this it becomes evident that
> a certain misuse is being made of ethical demands. The strictness of
> those demands would not do so much harm if education were to say:
> "This is how men ought to be, in order to be happy and to make others
> happy, but you have to reckon on their not being like that." Instead of
> this, the young are made to believe that everyone else fulfills these eth-
> ical demands—that is, that everyone else is virtuous. It is on this that
> the demand is based that the young, too, shall become virtuous.[43]

The "morality that functions in the super-ego"[44] is characteristic
of a "guilt-culture" (the West has no monopoly on the guilt-culture
market): "In a guilt-culture, the need for a supernatural assurance,
for an authority transcending man's, appears to be overwhelmingly
strong."[45] This statement holds for the West.

By obliging its subjects to live "beyond their means," the prevalent morality renders them unhappy, neurotic, or rebellious.[46] It
arouses in them an aggressiveness against the prohibiting authority,
and this aggressiveness, more or less repressed, does not allow them
to live the law as mediational. "Once the law ceases to mediate between 'No' and 'Yes,' the prohibition it necessarily lays upon the
person is no longer experienced as a mediation of the presence of the
other; rather, the presence of the other is directly felt as a prohibition, as a challenge to my own existence."[47]

The morality of duty is responsible for many obsessional neuroses.[48] It is significant that the word "scruple," in its modern sense,
first appears in French at the beginning of the fifteenth century, under the pen of Gerson who was a disciple of Occam.

The neurotic sense of guilt tends to blind the moral subject to his
true guilt, as Paul Ricoeur pertinently remarks:

An authentic transgression is a concealed transgression that always requires another person to bring it to light. It is here that the criticism of the archaic, morbid sense of guilt takes on its full meaning: the morbid sense of guilt tends to lay an enormous affective emphasis on an unreal transgression and thus to camouflage the access to the more authentic strata of guilt. Due to his atypical position the prophet penetrates to this level of unvoiced guilt. The more authentic the guilt and the closer it is to the wellsprings of the personality, the more it conceals itself.[49]

To the extent that the superego is sadistic in its relation to the ego, it is pitiless[50] and drives the person to despair, self-hatred, and a failure to exonerate himself:

What a wilderness or, better, what a Kafkaesque castle we find ourselves in when a Christian has lost the sense of forgiveness while retaining the sense of sin! The worst thing that can happen to a human being is to "believe in sin," for in fact there is no Credo except in the forgiveness of sins. Such a state of affairs represents a real inversion of the spiritual world. A culture in which the preaching of sin has replaced the preaching of forgiveness, and in which a cramped juridical sense of social prohibitions is combined with an inflexible practice of competition and profit—such a culture, lacking any sense of generosity, is the seed ground not only for a sense of unreal guilt but also for a failure to achieve self-exoneration. One is tempted to say that this kind of spiritual world, one that Christendom has often brought into being, falls below the level of the tragic; when there is no longer even a chorus to weep over him, man is delivered up to terror that is unalleviated by pity.[51]

The superego not only presents itself as a pitiless judge; it is also the "ideal of the ego." In his situation of littleness, weakness, and imitations of "grown-ups," a child seeks security by projecting into his future, dreams of limitless greatness and power. The "megalomania" of the child is satisfied by an ideal of perfection for himself. This process—a common and fruitful stage in growth to maturity—is narcissistic in nature;[52] it reflects a love of self that draws back in the face of a reality felt to be too frustrative of its desires. The love finds expression in the play of imagination and of the ideal.

This narcissism may persist in the adult as an intellectualism that is unconsciously sustained by "the kind of self-sufficiency and solitary self-assertion which compensates for the essentials of human desire by intellectual control or seduction."[53]

In the realm of morality, such narcissism often finds expression in "perfectionism": the person wills to be, imagines himself to be, perfect: like God. This is one of the subtlest and most unfortunate forms of the delusion that leads to the sour condemnation of others and to a sense of guilt, despair, and self-hatred when the narcissistic illusion is unable to withstand the test of reality.

This kind of narcissistic idealization, whether intellectual or moral, withdraws the subject from object-centered relations and gives rise to insoluble conflicts due to the rejection both of the instincts and of reality. As a result, "narcissism turns morality into a form of autoerotic enjoyment in which even the enjoyment is eliminated."[54] Thus, "what is given value is not the satisfaction nor the frustration (as in the case of masochism), but the privation. . . . As soon as there is need of renouncing some satisfaction, moral narcissism becomes wilful."[55]

We can see now why Western morality based on the categorical imperative should have had the effect of confining people within themselves ("my soul and God") behind a flattering but deceptive façade, and of bringing to a midcourse halt the process of growth and access to a "morality of the ego,"[56] a secondary narcissism that is capable of investment in reality outside the subject.

Far from promoting this kind of successful maturation of the person, traditional morality keeps him or her immature:

> The aim of moral narcissism is to make use of morality in order to achieve emancipation from the vicissitudes affecting ties with objects and thus indirectly to obtain liberation from the servitudes entailed in the relationship to objects. This in turn enables the id and the ego to win the love of a demanding superego and of a tyrannical ego-ideal. But this deluded effort fails. It fails first because the superego is not so easily deceived and second because the demands of the id do not cease to make themselves heard despite the asceticial maneuvering of the ego.[57]

This false asceticism is matched by a false image of God.

> The goal is to be pure and therefore to be alone, to renounce the world and its pleasures as well as its vexations—for we know it is possible to derive pleasure even from vexation. It is within the power of many to corrupt the subject by an inversion of pleasure. It is more difficult and more tempting to rise above both pleasure and pain by making a vow to resist, to be a solitary or even a hermit—all of these being conditions that bring us near to God. After all, does God hunger or thirst? Is he dependent on the love or hatred of men? Men may think that he is, but they do not understand what God really is: the Unnameable One.[58]

The result is a conservative attitude[59] or a pride that is paranoiac or schizophrenic in nature; these seek in the "unreal" world of ideas or utopias a sedative for anxiety.

This, I am afraid, describes the state of mind of many of the authors of treatises on morality that were quite recently being used in seminaries.

We may even follow Theodor Reik in thinking that the finicky and authoritarian preoccupation with the formal aspects of theological propositions and ritual practices, as well as the rigid and inviolable observance of these, are symptomatic of an ambivalence: they are an overcompensation for the anxiety induced by uncertainty and by a latent connivance with the very freedom that is being resisted.[60]

The effect of such overcompensation is to idealize an instinct by "making it pass for something that it is not";[61] this in turn leads to "perversions" (in the psychiatric, not in the moral, sense).

The morality of the superego can also lead to masochism:

Conscience and morality arose through overcoming, desexualizing, the Oedipus-complex; in moral masochism, morality becomes sexualized afresh, the Oedipus-complex is reactivated, a regression from morality back to the Oedipus-complex is under way. This is to the advantage neither of the person concerned nor of morality. An individual may, it is true, preserve the whole or a certain amount of his morality alongside his masochism, but, on the other hand, a good part of his conscience may become swallowed up by his masochism. Further, the masochism in him creates a temptation to "sinful acts" which must then be expiated by the reproaches of the sadistic conscience (as in so many Russian character-types) or by chastisement from the great parental authority of Fate. In order to provoke punishment from this last parent-substitute, the masochist must do something inexpedient, act against his own interests, ruin the prospects which the real world offers him, and possibly destroy his own existence in the world of reality.[62]

Such, among others, are the unhappy and often pathological effects of a legalistic morality that is primarily concerned to avoid sin, hell, and the pitiless judgment of the false god who wears the mask of the superego. They are the bad effects Freud had in mind, I think, when he spoke of a "neurotic civilization."[63]

The morality of duty must also be blamed for ignoring history. Although it is evident even to a nonspecialist that the ways of understanding the gospel and putting it into practice have varied according to periods and places and that mores are both causes and effects of cultures, treatises of Catholic moral theology would have nothing to do with history. Although history has left a decisive mark on the methods of biblical exegesis, the liturgical renewal, and even the understanding of dogmas, the history of morality is still unappreciated by the majority of moralists.

While working in his own distinctive manner on a "real history of morals,"[64] Nietzsche clearly grasped the central issue:

In all "science of morals" so far one thing was *lacking*, strange as it may sound: the problem of morality itself; what was lacking was any suspicion that there was something problematic here. What the philosophers called "a rational foundation for morality" and tried to supply was, seen in the right light, merely a scholarly variation of the common *faith* in the prevalent morality; a new means of *expression* for this faith; and thus just another fact within a particular morality; indeed, in the last analysis a kind of denial that this morality might ever be considered problematic—certainly the very opposite of an examination, analysis, questioning, and vivisection of this very faith.[65]

We are beginning, of course, to see works on the history of morality being published, but you can still count on the fingers of one hand the places where any systematic instruction is being offered in the history of mores and moral laws. When will we have a university-level chair in the history of moral thought and—why not?—a chair in comparative morality?

Another serious deficiency in the morality of duty is its "individualism." This morality fails to recognize the fact that the moral subject lives in a community. In the minds of the ancients, especially Plato and Aristotle,[66] moral philosophy was part of political philosophy, but the morality of duty is hardly interested in anything but the individual and the exercise of power. This is certainly the reason why it has no answers to the questions being raised for it today by the communal, sociocultural, economic, and political aspects of human life.[67]

As a final heading in this lengthy indictment, I shall mention the bogus spiritualism of traditional morality. This morality fails to recognize the basic unity of soul and body. The "dichotomist" conception of the human person and the consequent contempt for the body undoubtedly has ancient roots in tradition (though it is a tradition more Greek and Mazdean than Christian). Undoubtedly, too, that conception was confirmed by the "idealist" philosophies (from Descartes to Kant), though these were themselves reflections of the mentality of the time. The fact remains that the separation of soul and body is part of an anthropology which is not that of the Bible and which contains errors and has unfortunate consequences now being brought to light by the human sciences. Here again, contempt of the body has to be seen as both an effect and a cause of the moral narcissism cultivated by the morality of duty. "The body as outward manifestation and as source of pleasure, seduction, and conquest of others is banished in moral narcissism; hell is not other people (narcissism has gotten rid of them) but the body."[68]

The morality of duty is resolutely blind to the reality of the human person in its body-soul unity, its communal life, its history as individual and as member of a collectivity. It is also blind to itself to the extent that its rationalizations conceal from it its own unconscious motivations.[69] Nietzsche had already called attention to these motivations: "The prudence of the idealist consists in not knowing himself. An idealist: a person who has reasons for not seeing clearly into himself and who is intelligent enough not to bring these reasons out into the clear light of day."[70]

Nietzsche also asks some very pertinent questions regarding Kant:

> Even apart from the value of such claims as "there is a categorical imperative in us," one can still always ask: what does such a claim tell us about the man who makes it? There are moralities which are meant to justify their creator before others. Other moralities are meant to calm him and lead him to be satisfied with himself. With yet others he wants to crucify himself and humiliate himself. With others he wants to wreak revenge, with others conceal himself, with others transfigure himself and place himself way up, at a distance. This morality is used by its creator to forget, that one to have others forget him or something about him. Some moralists want to vent their power and creative whims on humanity; some others, perhaps including Kant, suggest with their morality: "What deserves respect in me is that I can obey— and you *ought* not to be different from me."—In short, moralities are also merely a *sign language of the affects.*[71]

This is doubtless the reason why they are so ineffective. As Marx had already noted: "Moral theology is impotence in action. Every time it attacks a vice it gets the worst of the fight."[72]

We badly need a moral theology that refuses either to ignore any aspect of the human person or to mutilate the person in any way.

PART
II

Chapter 7

A Morality of Pleasure?

The morality of duty has little that is Christian (or, in any event, little that is evangelical) about it, and in addition, ends up mutilating the human person. As a result, for some decades now it has been less and less accepted and put into practice. It has been challenged and disputed, sometimes quite noisily and with the blindness induced by a counterdependence.

Out of this have come a great confusion and impassioned divisions of opinion, with some people retreating to the shelter of "traditional" morality while others, thinking to free themselves from it, have taken the opposite tack. This state of affairs is an unavoidable social phenomenon; it will take time to achieve freedom from a mentality and an ideology that have struck such deep roots in the West over the course of seven centuries.

Of course, the search for a morality that rejects the primacy given to duty and law is nothing new in the West. During the Renaissance, a certain number of Italian philosophers drew their inspiration from Platonism and even from Epicureanism. England saw, first, the "ethical self-centeredness" of Thomas Hobbes (1588–1679), then the "utilitarian ethics" of John Stuart Mill (1806–1853). France in the age of Jean-Jacques Rousseau and Romanticism believed in "nature as good," while the positivists believed in science and progress. I may mention Jean-Marie Guyau and his *Esquisse d'une morale sans obligation ni sanction* [Outline of a Morality without Obligation or Sanction] (1885); the writings of Henri Bergson; the work done in the philosophy of values and then in existentialism; finally, the publications of Charles Odier[1] and A. Hesnard[2] who write as psychoanalysts.

All these approaches have not, however, been enough to liberate the Western world from its legalist framework. I shall offer only a single example: Paul Tillich, whose outlook was so confined by the morality of the categorical imperative and submission to law that he described a conscience which rises above it as "transmoral":

> A conscience may be called "transmoral" if it judges not in obedience to a moral law, but according to its participation in a reality that transcends the sphere of moral commands. A transmoral conscience does not deny the moral realm, but is driven beyond it by the unbearable tensions of the sphere of law.[3]

Even Jacques Maritain, Thomist though he was, spoke of a "supramorality" when discussing a morality that does not make the law its basic foundation.[4]

Among contemporary efforts to find an "endogenous" morality,[5] the most interesting, in my judgment, are those based on freedom.[6] For a truly human and evangelical morality cannot be built except upon freedom, and this is the direction being taken in contemporary theological work.[7]

But what is freedom, and how is the degree of moral responsibility to be gauged in a concrete act? The philosophers and theologians of every age have raised this question; so have the sociologists and psychologists of our age, although these, most of whom are "determinists," deny freedom. At what point does alienation begin?[8] How is it possible to escape a freedom that is "terrifying" because "there is no duty to guide it"?[9]

While fully convinced that the source and norm of morality can be found nowhere except in freedom, I would like to open up another avenue of study (an avenue no less difficult than that of freedom), leading to a morality that has for its object the affective life of the human person and, more particularly, the human search for happiness and pleasure.[10]

To do this is to take a course diametrically opposed to traditional morality—Kantian, Stoic, or Jansenist—for which all pleasure and even all happiness are suspect, forbidden,[11] culpable. They are regarded, as Nietzsche says, as devilish "temptations": "Life as punishment (happiness as temptation); the passions as devilish, confidence in oneself as godless."[12]

Kant drew upon himself the sarcasm of Nietzsche for excluding "eudaimonism" as the foundation of morality:

> Kant's categorical imperative should have been felt as *mortally dangerous!* . . . The theologian instinct alone took it under its protection!
> —An action compelled by the instinct of life has in the joy of performing it the proof it is a *right*: and every nihilist with Christian-dogmatic

bowels understands joy as an *objection*. . . . What destroys more quickly than to work, to think, to feel without inner necessity, without a deep personal choice, without *joy*? as an automaton of "duty"? It is virtually a *recipe* for *decadence*, even for idiocy. . . . Kant became an idiot.[13]

Nietzsche is echoed by Albert Camus: "Why . . . should I deny the joy of living, as long as I know everything is not included in this joy? . . . But today the fool is king, and I call those who fear pleasure fools."[14]

"Traditional" morality sanctified "the formula: the more you enjoy, the more you will be punished—a formula that has been the basis of all the moralities and all the religions."[15] This is an overstatement, and my whole purpose is to prove it. Nonetheless, Nietzsche had some justification for thinking that "Christianity gave Eros poison to drink; he did not die of it but degenerated—into a vice."[16]

I am convinced of the feasibility of a morality that has been taught and lived within Christianity and that gives happiness and pleasure a good and important place. A morality of love (*agapē*) is a morality of joy, for joy is the first effect of love;[17] I mean the joy that Paul tirelessly urged upon his readers[18] and that Christ himself gives to those who believe in him (Jn 15:11), a joy that is shared.[19]

This morality of happiness was the commonly accepted one—not only among the Greeks, but also in Western Christendom—until the fourteenth century.

Aristotle considered the affective life to be the very object of morality: "Human problems, that is, those that involve character and the passions, these are the problems to which we shall be devoting attention."[20] St. Thomas took the same approach. For him, the affective life (which he calls the appetitive power, *vis appetitiva*, or desire) is the "material" object of morality,[21] while the moral virtues, that is, the structured dynamisms that give structure to the way of acting, are the virtues that humanize the appetitive power[22] through the regulatory and finalizing action of the rational and loving intellect. It might be said that the moral person is one whose affective life is "sinewy": strong, skilful, adaptable, and a source of pleasure.

St. Thomas believes that joy is necessary and fruitful, and he explains this point in a number of places, among them his commentary on St. Paul's advice to the Corinthians: *Chairete*, "rejoice," "be happy" (2 Cor 13:11): "This feeling is necessary if you are to be upright and virtuous, because no one is upright and virtuous who does not rejoice in actions that are virtuous and upright. . . . And indeed you must rejoice always, because joy sustains a person in habits of doing good. For no one can long persevere in what is a source of sadness to him."[23]

All human beings want to be happy: this is the desire that moves them; this is the finality that energizes, directs, and structures their lives. Aristotle observes that "not to have one's life organized toward some end is a mark of great folly."[24] This end that sets the person in motion is the satisfaction of what St. Thomas calls our "appetites."

St. Augustine, for his part, says that morality

> has to do with the supreme Good: that to which we relate all our actions; that which we desire for its own sake and not as a means to an end; that whose possession bestows a happiness which fulfills all our desires. This is why we call it the "end," for it is for its sake that we will everything else.[25]

In an age when the scientific community was ridiculing the idea of finality, it took courage for Freud to maintain that the psychic life has a finality and that "it seems that our entire psychical activity is bent upon procuring pleasure and avoiding pain."[26]

There is, then, nothing novel about basing morality on the affective life as finalized by the search for happiness. Such an approach is consistent with what has been observed by psychoanalysts and psychiatrists.[27]

I believe it preferable to speak of pleasure rather than of happiness as the foundation of this morality. This is because the Western tradition distinguishes between happiness and pleasure and even opposes the two.[28] Pleasure is coarse, suspect, culpable; happiness is noble.

In my view, there is no opposition between pleasure and happiness unless one takes the former to be a "totality that brings a completion, but only a limited and univocal completion,"[29] and defines happiness as "fulfillment by the infinite that presents itself to desire."[30] It is true enough that there is danger of looking upon pleasure as a self-sufficient totality, yet I believe that it is the nature of pleasure to lead beyond itself,[31] as is the case with every human affective experience.

The etymology of the Latin word reminds us of this truth about pleasure, for *affectus* (ad-fectus) says first of all "relation to," "connection with," then "mode of being," "disposition," and finally "affection," "tenderness."

I shall come back in a moment to this relational aspect of the affective life and to my refusal to regard it as an "affection" in the pathological sense of the term.

As I see it, the view that happiness and pleasure are necessarily opposed is one of the most striking and regrettable traits of the Western schizophrenic mentality, its Platonic conception of happiness, and its Stoic attitude to pleasure.

Happiness is defined in a way that is excessively "spiritualist" and Kantian and is regarded as reserved for the next life, as a reward. I shall therefore speak here of pleasure, in order to make room for an anthropology that sees soul and body as a unity. I prefer to speak of pleasure precisely in order to make happiness an "incarnational" thing. The choice may shock some readers (as does Freud's choice of the term "libido" when speaking of love). Nonetheless, I think it a timely choice and consistent with human reality which has a biological basis, as Bergson has reminded us: "Let us then give to the word biology the very wide meaning it should have, and will perhaps one day have, and let us say that all morality, be it pressure or aspiration, is in essence biological."[32]

St. Thomas noted that "the animal is begotten before the human."[33] The pleasure of a human being is the pleasure of a human animal. From this St. Thomas concludes that in perfect beatitude the fulfillment of the entire person will involve the joy of the "higher part" overflowing upon the "lower part," but that in this life the opposite is true: "completion of the lower part precedes the fulfillment of the higher part."[34]

I make my own the remarks of Dr. Jean Trémolières, a dietician, who wants us to "be present once again to our subtlest sensations" and to regain "the joy of savoring each bit of contentment."[35] His conclusion: "If the very meaning of life, the real 'savoir-faire,' eludes us, is not the reason that in our affective life we have lost the ability to enjoy the somewhat mysterious values contained in the humble realities of everyday life?"[36]

By "pleasure," I understand the Greek (and especially the Aristotelean) hēdonē, the delectatio of St. Thomas Aquinas,[37] and the human reality that comes under the observation of the human sciences: physiology,[38] sociology, economics,[39] and politics. In short, to study pleasure, as thus understood, is to take as our subject the whole of the affective life in what is most typical of it[40] and most accessible to observation.[41]

In addition, even in Freud the term "pleasure" is no less suitable for expressing the "finer and higher" satisfactions of mental activity than it is for those of the senses; he means, for example, the pleasures of intellect and art.

By "pleasure," then, I understand all the various kinds of satisfaction of human desire, whatever be the "level" of the satisfaction and the way of experiencing it. I thus include all that goes under the names of happiness, joy, enjoyment, jubilation, beatitude, consolation, security, comfort, contentment, well being, alleviation of a pain or an anxiety, and so on.

This way of talking about pleasure seems to me in conformity with ancient and even modern usage, as the Grand Robert dictionary notes under the entry Plaisir. It defines this term as "a basic affective state . . . an agreeable sensation or emotion, connected with the satisfaction of a tendency or need or with the harmonious exercise of vital activities. . . . It is used to describe everything that can give the person an agreeable sensation or emotion, everything (objects or actions) that is the source or occasion of such a sensation or emotion." It is in this sense that I use the word "pleasure," while not rejecting its primitive meaning: "That which it pleases some one to do or order, that which he judges good, that which he wills."

In speaking of pleasure, I am therefore speaking of a privileged experience of human affective life.

Finally, I intend to include in what I am calling "pleasure" the special content to which the Bible is pointing when it uses the word "beatitude" or "blessedness" and the phrase "Blessed he (they) who. . . ."

The Greek New Testament uses the adjective *makarios*, "happy, blessed, fortunate," about fifty times.[42] In classical Greek, the adjective was used first of the gods,[43] then of men who died as heroes.[44]

Happiness thus has an element of the divine in it,[45] for it means that one has received a "good spirit" (*eu-daimon*) from the gods. Aristotle gives a (relative) place in art[46] and in morality to the idea of happiness and unhappiness: "But because the happy man also needs fortune, some people think that good fortune is the same as happiness, which it is not. The proof of nonidentity is the fact that if good fortune becomes excessive it is an impediment and perhaps should then not be called 'good' fortune, since the criterion of 'good' fortune is its connection with happiness."[47]

The virtuous person puts up well with the whims of fortune; even if great misfortunes descend upon him, "his moral beauty shines through, if he endures unshaken many and great misfortunes, not because he is insensible of them but because he is noble and magnanimous."[48]

In the same way, the biblical idea expressed in *makarios* and in *chara* (joy) connotes something of the divine; the blessedness and joy are a gift of God. "Blessed are you, Simon Bar-Jona! For flesh and blood has not revealed this to you, but my Father who is in heaven" (Mt 16:17).

The proclamation of salvation is a "promise of happiness" to both Jews and pagans (cf. Rom 4:4–5). It is "good news of a great joy which will come to all the people" (Lk 2:10). "Blessed are those who are invited to the marriage supper of the Lamb" (Rev 19:9).

That is how we are to understand the meaning of the beatitudes in the Sermon on the Mount. They are gifts of God which enable human beings to enter into true life, present and future, and to live fully their response to the invitation issued by the Father of mercies, in fidelity and conformity to the life of Jesus Christ. In short, "all is well": you are on the right track, you are fortunate, and your happiness is a gift of God. It is a blessing:[49] the kingdom of heaven is at hand.

Conversely, unhappy are they who do not follow this way and do not respond to God's invitation, to the call given them. "Woe to me if I do not preach the gospel!" said St. Paul (1 Cor 9:16).

The joy which Christ's disciples experience is a gift: "These things I have spoken to you, that my joy may be in you, and that your joy may be full" (Jn 15:11).

If there is an evangelical morality, it is a morality based on the divine gift of joy as source and goal of a truly human life.

This is the proposition I must now establish by locating the foundations and explicating the laws of a morality based on pleasure.

Chapter 8

The Search for Pleasure

All Human Beings Seek Pleasure

Every age and every culture attest to the fact that human beings seek happiness.

To the Greeks, this was both self-evident and basic. As Aristotle observed, "the fact that all beings, brutes and men alike, seek pleasure is an indication that pleasure is in some sense the supreme good."[1]

St. Augustine notes: "It is true that all human beings want to be happy, that they desire this with the most intense love, and that it is for the sake of happiness that they desire everything else."[2]

St. Thomas Aquinas echoes this when he says that "a human being cannot not wish to be happy," for "to desire happiness is simply to desire the satisfaction of the will, and everyone wants that."[3]

Montaigne says the same with regard to the (Stoic?) philosophers: "All the opinions in the world agree on this—that pleasure is our goal—though they choose different means to it. . . . Whatever they say, in virtue itself the ultimate goal we aim at is voluptuousness:"[4]

And everyone is familiar with the famous saying of Pascal:

All men seek happiness. There are no exceptions. However different the means they may employ, they all strive towards this goal. The reason why some go to war and some do not is the same desire in both, but interpreted in two different ways. The will never takes the least step except to that end. This is the motive of every act of every man, including those who go and hang themselves.[5]

Even Kant, a firm antihedonist, wrote that "to be happy is necessarily the wish of every finite rational being."[6]

The fact, then, is so universal and obvious that no observer of human mores can fail to see it.[7]

In tackling the theme of his *Civilization and Its Discontents*, Freud asks himself a question and immediately answers it: "We will therefore turn to the less ambitious question of what men themselves show by their behaviour to be the purpose and intention of their lives. What do they demand of life and wish to achieve in it? The answer to this can hardly be in doubt. They strive after happiness; they want to become happy and to remain so."[8]

This human search for happiness is even beginning to be a concern of politicians, and they now aim at a "comfortable society."[9] A recent French poll dealt with "The French and Happiness."[10] All this brings us back to Plato and Aristotle, for whom happiness was the object of political practice.

Sociologists, for their part, note that "modern man thinks of himself as a being who looks for happiness and has a right to it."[11]

If human beings thus seek happiness and pleasure, it is because these are the expression and goal of life: "Philosophers who have speculated on the meaning of life and on the destiny of man have failed to take sufficient notice of an indication which nature itself has given us. Nature warns us by a clear sign that our destination is attained. That sign is joy. . . . Joy always announces that life has succeeded. . . . All great joy has a triumphant note."[12]

Aristotle had already made the same point: "We see now that life and pleasure are inseparable, because without activity there is no pleasure, and pleasure completes activity."[13] Pleasure is not a kind of subsequent addition to life, "as though it were something adventitious; rather life has pleasure as part of itself."[14]

Aristotle also asks:

> But do we value life for the pleasure it brings, or do we value pleasure because of the life it augments? We may leave this question aside for the moment. To have pleasure is to live, and to live is to have pleasure; the two form a unity. To desire life is to desire pleasure, and this is why all living things seek pleasure.[15]

And yet, they scarcely find it.

Disappointments

According to Pascal, "all men seek happiness." But "all men complain. . . . While the present never satisfies us, experience deceives us, and leads us on from one misfortune to another until death comes as the final and eternal climax."[16]

And according to Péguy in his *Clio*: "A man of forty knows that he knows, and he knows that he is not happy." More recently, André Malraux has passed on to us these disillusioned views of General de Gaulle: "On the whole, women think of love and men of military decorations of something similar. For the rest, people think only of happiness—which does not exist."[17]

The search for happiness and pleasure brings disappointment and never ends in full and lasting satisfaction. Such is the testimony of all "wise men." Our affectivity, says Antoine Vergote, "is indivisibly compounded of imagination, deception, and desire for true happiness."[18]

In the language and perspective of a thirteenth-century theologian, St. Thomas writes:

> A certain degree of happiness is possible in this life, but true and perfect happiness is not. This can be shown by two considerations. First, by an appeal to the generally accepted notion of happiness: since happiness means the complete and self-sufficient good, it excludes all evil and fulfills all desires. In the present life, however, all evils cannot be eliminated. Our present life is subject to many evils that cannot be avoided: ignorance on the part of the mind, unregulated affections on the part of the appetite, and many kinds of affliction on the part of the body, as St. Augustine explains in detail in Book XIX of his *City of God*. In like manner, the desire for good cannot be satisfied in the present life. For man naturally desires that the goods he has should be permanent, but they are in fact transitory just as is life itself, which we naturally desire and will should be permanent, for man naturally flees death. It is therefore impossible to have true happiness in the present life.
>
> Second, there is the consideration of the object in which happiness essentially consists, namely, the vision of the divine essence. This vision is not possible for man in his present life, as I have shown in Part I of this work. These considerations show that no one can attain to true and complete happiness in this life.[19]

Freud, for his part, observes that while the pleasure principle determines the goal of life, "yet its programme is at loggerheads with the whole world, with the macrocosm as much as with the microcosm. There is no possibility at all of its being carried through; all the regulations of the universe run counter to it. One feels inclined to say that "the intention that man should be 'happy' is not included in the plan of 'Creation.' "[20] The result is the *Unbehagen*—the malaise or uneasiness, the discontent—that forces human beings "to moderate their claims to happiness."[21] But the disappointment experienced in the search for pleasure is not the doing solely of civilization; Freud ventures the following hypothesis: "Something in the nature of the [sexual] function itself . . . denies us full satisfaction and urges us along other paths."[22]

To Marie Bonaparte, Freud wrote: "The moment a man questions the meaning and value of life, he is sick, since objectively neither has any existence; by asking this question one is merely admitting to a store of unsatisfied libido to which something else must have happened, a kind of fermentation leading to sickness and depression."[23]

Freud is not the first to have noted the fleeting or, as he puts it, the "episodic" nature of pleasure.[24] "It is the fate of sensual love to become extinguished when it is satisfied; for it to be able to last, it must from the beginning be mixed with purely affectionate components—with such, that is, as are inhibited in their aims—or it must itself undergo a transformation of this kind."[25] The development of the ego, as well as the demands both of "reality" and civilization are accompanied by inhibitions, repressions, sublimations, substitute satisfactions, affective investments, and other processes which make possible and give value to familial and social bonds, the pleasures of intellectual research and artistic creation, and so on. Access to such satisfactions, which Freud, using quotation marks, calls "finer and higher,"[26] requires a "taming" of the instincts (libido and aggressivity), a control of their "primary" urges. "There is an undeniable diminution in the potentialities of enjoyment. The feeling of happiness derived from the satisfaction of a wild instinctual impulse untamed by the ego is incomparably more intense than that derived from sating an instinct that has been tamed."[27]

When thus "desexualized," the "sexual impulsions are not capable of complete satisfaction, while sexual impulsions which are uninhibited in their aims suffer an extraordinary reduction through the discharge of energy every time the sexual aim is attained."[28] The inescapable conclusion is that, whether sublimated or not, the instincts are incapable of leading to complete and lasting satisfaction.

With this hypothesis of the "lost object," Freud is able to explain to some extent the experience of a radical failure of satisfaction in the search for pleasure: "Objects . . . have been lost which have formerly afforded real satisfaction,"[29] so that "object-finding is really a re-finding"[30] or, better, to find the object is "to convince oneself that it is still there."[31] Desire is permeated by nostalgia for the primal experience of satisfaction: that which accompanied the relationship of fusion of child with mother. This is why "the original lost object [of an instinctual desire] is often replaced by an endless series of substitute-objects, none of which ever give full satisfaction. This may explain the lack of stability in object-choice, the 'craving for stimulus,' which is so often a feature of the love of adults."[32]

The lost object cannot be found again, nor can the full and complete satisfaction which it offered.

Freud's hypothesis of the lost object enables us to understand to some extent the inevitable disappointment experienced in the search for pleasure. To this explanatory factor he adds the goals and effects of which he calls the "death instinct." Observing the compulsion that is present in the repetition of psychic phenomena and is opposed to the pleasure principle, he explains this fact by "a compulsion inherent in organic life to restore an earlier state of things,"[34] namely, the inorganic state. " 'The goal of all life is death' and, looking backwards . . . 'what was inanimate existed before what is living.' "[35] "The death instincts seem to do their work unobtrusively. The pleasure principle seems actually to serve the death instincts,"[36] since the most they can do is to try to put off the inevitable day.

By reason both of their origin (the lost object) and of their end (death), desire and pleasure are thus destined for radical unsatisfaction. So "displeasing" is this that human beings try to escape it by every possible means (cf. Pascal's "diversion"). To use Jacques Lacan's phrase, they try "to hide from themselves the gaping abyss" of desire.

Once again, the point being made is not a new one. Aristotle remarked long ago that "desire by its nature knows no limits, and most men live only to satisfy it."[37]

In order to escape the profound sense of frustration caused by the nonsatisfaction of the desire for pleasure, human beings seek compensation not only in substitute objects of many kinds, but in the exercise of the imagination, "the dominant faculty in man, master of error and falsehood, all the more deceptive for not being invariably so."[38] Whence the fascination exercised by illusions—which Freud lists in his Civilization and Its Discontents: drugs, religion, nirvana, and so on, without forgetting "value judgments": "Man's judgements of value follow directly his wishes for happiness— . . . accordingly, they are an attempt to support his illusions with arguments."[39] This also explains why "people commonly use false standards of measurement— . . . they seek power, success and wealth for themselves and admire them in others, and . . . underestimate what is of true value in life."[40]

Consequently most people are satisfied with mediocre forms of happiness, and for this Nietzsche despises them:

I walk among this people and I keep my eyes open: they have become smaller, and they are becoming smaller and smaller; but this is due to their doctrine of happiness and virtue. For they are modest in virtue, too—because they want contentment. But only a modest virtue gets along with contentment.[41]

Nietzsche's Zarathustra goes on to say:

Modestly to embrace a small happiness—that they call "resignation" —and modestly they squint the while for another small happiness. At bottom, these simpletons want a single thing most of all: that nobody should hurt them. Thus they try to please and gratify everybody. This, however, is cowardice, even if it be called virtue.[42]

And yet, the radical character of the unsatisfaction experienced in the search for pleasure may not be either denied or ignored. Despite his pessimism, Freud sees the search as a spur to "all that is most precious in human civilization":

> The repressed instinct never ceases to strive for complete satisfaction, which would consist in the repetition of a primary experience of satisfaction. No substitutive or reactive formations and no sublimations will suffice to remove the repressed instinct's persisting tension, and it is the difference in amount between the gratificatory pleasure which is demanded and that which is actually achieved that provides the driving factor which will permit of no halting at any established position but, in the poet's words, *ungebändigt immer vorwärts dringt* ["presses ever forward unsubdued": *Faust* I]. The backward path that leads to complete satisfaction is as a rule obstructed by the resistances which maintain the repressions. So there is no alternative but to advance in the direction in which growth is still free—though with no prospect of bringing the process to a conclusion or of being able to reach the goal.[43]

It is precisely the lack of satisfaction in the pursuit of pleasure that "distinguish[es] our lives from those of our animal ancestors," and stimulates us to the progress in civilization which aims "to protect men against nature and to adjust their mutual relations,"[44] so as to pass from "egoism" to "altruism."[45] By imposing on human beings a renunciation of instinctual satisfaction, civilization bestows on them the special kind of satisfaction we call "security."[46] Concern for security dominates the ego, whereas the id obeys only the pleasure principle.[47]

But this security is constantly threatened and proves inadequate: "In adversity I long for happiness; in happiness I fear adversity."[48]

Must we therefore think that, as Voltaire says in the final chapter of his *Candide*, "man was born to live in the convulsions of anxiety or the lethargy of boredom"?[49] Or as Oscar Wilde puts it in one of his plays, that "in this world there are only two tragedies. One is not getting what one wants, and the other is getting it. The last is much the worst, the last is the real tragedy!"[50]

St. Bernard had already observed that "in his voraciousness man continually desires what he still lacks, but he wearies of it as soon as he obtains it. . . . So many people are prisoners in that labyrinth!"[51]

On the other hand, it can be thought that this restlessness and lack of satisfaction are the source of "salvation" as Kierkegaard understands the latter. "Occasionally you plunge into pleasure, and every instant you are devoting yourself to it you make the discovery in your consciousness that it is vanity. So you are constantly beyond yourself, that is, in despair."[52] But "it is my sincere conviction that it is a man's true salvation to despair."[53]

This despair is an invitation to an elsewhere:

Beyond where cares and boredom hold dominion,
Which charge our fogged existence with their spleen,
Happy is he who with a stalwart pinion
Can seek those fields so shining and serene:

Whose thoughts, like larks, rise on the freshening breeze,
Who fans the morning with his tameless wings,
Skims over life, and understands with ease
The speech of flowers and other voiceless things.[54]

In the light of all this, what are we to think of the search for happiness and pleasure that is, on the one hand, the motive force, energizing power, and goal of human life, and, on the other, a source of radical disillusionment; the search which is for some people salvation and a spur to move "ever forward," while for others it is a source of illusion, whether it brings them into the blindness of unrestrained sensuality or into the "haphazard" resignation of mediocrity?

Nothing is more ambiguous than pleasure.

The Dangerous Ambiguities of Pleasure

To all these ambiguities we must add fear and even anxiety: the dizziness induced by the "lack," the anxiety caused by alienation in substitutive satisfactions that hide the abyss from us. An often vague and unconscious sense of danger accompanies self-abandonment to pleasure. The person is afraid he or she may not be able to control this abandonment. "*Measure* is alien to us; let us own it; our thrill is the thrill of the infinite, the unmeasured. Like a rider on a steed that flies forward, we drop the reins before the infinite, we modern men, like semi-barbarians—and reach *our* bliss only where we are most—in *danger*."[55] But even if pleasure itself is not always experienced in this Dionysiac fashion, the search for it is experienced as at once a thirst for freedom and a thread of alienation.

For pleasure that is sought and experienced for its own sake is an executioner:

Now while the common multitude strips bare,
feels pleasure's cat-o'nine tails on its back,
and fights off anguish at the great bazaar,
give me your hand, my Sorrow. Let's stand back.[56]

The adult is trapped by pleasure to the extent especially that "the lost paradise of childish loves" is a mirage and threatens regression to a childhood that is forever lost. And yet, the child who is always present in the adult wants these archaic satisfactions.

Fixation in affective immaturity or regression to it further compli-
cates the ambiguity of desire. Thus, the frequent ambiguity found in
love and hate "is to be traced in part to those preliminary stages of
love which have not been wholly outgrown."[57]

The education of desire and pleasure is not easily accomplished.
"The erotic instincts are hard to mould; training of them achieves
now too much, now too little."[58]

For Baudelaire, pleasure is the locus of conflict between God and
Satan:

> In every man, and at all times, there are two simultaneous yearnings—
> the one towards God, the other towards Satan.
>   The invocation of God, or spirituality, is a desire to ascend a step;
> the invocation of Satan, or animality, is a delight in descending. To
> this latter one should relate one's enamourments with women, one's
> intimate conversations with animals—dogs, cats, etc.[59]

And yet psychoanalysts see it as a sign of "psychic health" that
the person has a capacity for happiness, a capacity for experiencing
pleasure when the objective conditions for such an experience are
present.[60]

Part of every neurosis or psychosis is "an attempt at flight from
the satisfaction of an instinct."[61] One symptom of a neurosis is the
inability to experience pleasure under conditions in which people
normally do experience it: "There is no doubt that all neurotic unpleasure is of that kind—pleasure that cannot be felt as such."[62] "In
reality, perverts are more likely to be poor devils who have to pay
most bitterly for the satisfaction they manage to procure with such
difficulty."[63] The flight into nervous illness is a flight from a pleasure that brings only "substitutive satisfactions,"[64] or else it is a
transformation of unpleasure into pleasure: "The masochist . . . enjoys the act of torturing when this is being applied to himself."[65]

Although the term "neurosis" is not applicable here, Freud acknowledged in himself certain obstacles to pleasures of an esthetic
kind: "Some rationalistic, or perhaps analytic, turn of mind in me
rebels against being moved by a thing without knowing why I am
thus affected and what it is that affects me."[66] He also reminds us
that it is sometimes difficult to accept a piece of good news (because
of an unconscious sense of guilt or feeling of inferiority?) or a success (this being interdicted by an unconscious desire to slay the Father?): "It is one of those cases of 'too good to be true' that we come
across often. It is an example of the scepticism that arises so often
when we are surprised by a piece of good news, when we have won a
prize, for instance, or drawn a winner."[67]

Freud analyzes still another obstacle: the transiency of even our
highest pleasures. He tells that when walking one day in the hills

with a young poet, the latter "admired the beauty of the scene around us but felt no joy in it. He was disturbed by the thought that all this beauty was fated to extinction. . . . All that he would otherwise have loved and admired seemed to him to be shorn of its worth by the transcience which was its doom."[68]

There is in truth no pleasure that is not ambiguous, not even that of the self-satisfaction which we call a "good conscience." Freud has brought to light the unconscious wellsprings of this "good conscience": "The Ego feels uplifted; it is proud of the renunciation [of an instinct] as of a valuable achievement."[69] " 'Natural' ethics, as it is called, has nothing to offer here except the narcissistic satisfaction of being able to think oneself better than others."[70] But the gospel already warns us against the illusions and dangers of the good conscience possessed by the Pharisees.

It is understandable that for all the reasons we have been reviewing the moralities which make happiness, the goal should receive bad reviews:

> All these moralities that address themselves to the individual, for the sake of his "happiness," as one says—what are they but counsels for behavior in relation to the degree of *dangerousness* in which the individual lives with himself, recipes against his passions, his good and bad inclinations insofar as they have the will to power and want to play the master; little and great prudences and artifices that exude the nook odor of old nostrums and of the wisdom of old women.[71]

Since the search for happiness may be considered, not without reason, as the source of all sins, many Christians (more or less influenced by Stoicism, Manicheeism, and later Jansenism) have believed that the happiness promised by God cannot be had on this earth, and that if we are to obtain it we must reject all "earthly" pleasure. Their attitude makes it possible for Freud to say: "Religions have been able to effect absolute renunciation of pleasure in this life by means of the promise of compensation in a future life. They have not, however, achieved a conquest of the pleasure-principle in this way."[72] His statement may be a misinterpretation of the true nature of religion, but is it false in fact?

In any case, pleasure rouses fear. In order to escape from this fear and to avoid all the ambiguities and compromises associated with pleasure, many spiritual families seek to distance themselves as far as possible from pleasure (and pain). "I would prefer," Antisthenes said, "to be a madman than to experience pleasure. Pleasure is not worth the effort of extending one's hand for it."[73]

This is the attitude of most of the Greek philosophers, from Democritus down to Epicurus himself; it is even truer of the Stoics. In all of these philosophies, the ideal set before the wise person is *atar-*

axia or *apatheia*. In order to attain this impassibility, this indifference, this insensibility to suffering and pleasure, "we must kill desire."[74] Only on this necessary condition will the wise person reach a repose of soul like that of the gods and become sinless. This same ideal, further strengthened by gnostic,[75] Mazdean, and Manichean influences, left a profound mark on Christianity, both initially and subsequently.[76] Other philosophers such as Kant locate happiness in the next world and, in their conception of morality, reject any and every kind of hedonism; as they see it, something so subjective, empirical, changing, ambiguous, and dangerous can have no place in an "a priori" and "universal" system of morality.

Thus—to offer an example—a philosopher like Raymond Polin, a believer in values like freedom and action, refuses to regard happiness as an end: happiness "is not a moral value" but a "technical value"; it "has lost its meaning."[77] "A free man and a man of action are not happy and have no concern to be so. This does not mean that they renounce happiness; they are simply not interested in it. . . . A free man is not happy. Insofar as he is a moral being, he has no need of being happy and no longer even dreams of becoming happy."[78]

Many people, like the philosopher Alain, think that "as soon as a man looks for happiness, it is certain that he will not find it. . . . Happiness is a reward that comes to those who have not looked for it."[79] The same attitude can be found in some psychoanalysts, for example, Denis Vasse, who writes: "The pleasure principle cannot be regarded as equivalent to the idea of pleasure as an end. This principle is not endowed with an intentionality that would direct human action and behavior along the lines of a hedonistic morality which aims at obtaining pleasure."[80]

Some sociologists take the same view, believing that "we must neither pursue pleasure systematically nor flee it in an obsessional way. Pleasure comes along subsequently, as it were, and without being sought; it is something superadded."[81]

We find the same outlook in the ancient wisdom of India: "Work alone is your proper business, never the fruits [it may produce]: let not your motive be the fruit of works nor your attachment to [mere] worklessness."[82]

How can we explain such a denial of a fact that is so evident and universal, namely, that human beings seek happiness as an end? Is not the Kantian refusal of all hedonism in morality itself a symptom of "a pathology of cultural communities"?[83]

For my part, I think that pleasure is both in fact and by right an object of intentional striving. It functions as an end to be attained. This is a fact verifiable by scientific and empirical observation. It is also an end by right to the extent (and this extent is in my opinion the object of morality) that pleasure as an end is ordered to something other than the pleasure itself, namely, to the reality or object with which it is connected.

It is one thing not to desire "egoistic" happiness,[84] but quite another to seek happiness in the fullness of what it is (and aspires to be), that is, in its power to lead us to the reality of the Other and others. "An affect is an epiphany of the other to the subject."[85]

Any and every rejection of pleasure, from apatheia to nirvana, and every devaluation of happiness seem to me unacceptable. I regard them as false. The human fabric, both in the material that makes it up and in its empty spaces, is woven of the search for happiness and pleasure. To experience and desire these is to be alive. We must not reject them or alienate ourselves from them.

The whole problem of morality is to experience pleasure in the right way.

Whatever its ambiguities and dangers, pleasure, or rather the way of experiencing it, is the very object of the art of living and therefore of morality.

Chapter 9

The Authentic Experience of Pleasure

There Are Pleasures and Pleasures

As I explained above, I understand by "pleasure" every human experience felt to be pleasurable or the source of happiness. This definition covers the entire field of affectivity, from the most "animal" to the most "spiritual."

I may note in passing that ever since the rise of the "voluntarist" systems (which are linked to the moral legalism of the fourteenth and fifteenth centuries) we have no word in French (or in any other European language except Spanish) for the affectivity of the intellect, that is, for all those affects that are invested in objects perceived by the intellect and in the laws proper to the functioning of the intellect. Before voluntarism captured the European mentality, this understanding of the heart was called "the will." Initially "will" was not a synonym for firmness and a more or less tight-jawed energy; "to will" meant to love with the mind.

In losing this ancient meaning of the word, we reduced the field of affectivity to sensation, emotion, and passion, while at the same time limiting the scope of the intellect to the cold gaze of "reason." Yet despite this development, it is impossible to overlook the fact that there is no authentic experience of friendship, tenderness, and love in which the intellect does not play a role. This role is all the more necessary because, as Freud constantly insists, the dominance of the reality principle over the pleasure principle is the work of the intellect and the ego and because "we recognize the essential precondition of neuroses in this lagging of ego development behind libidinal development."[1]

I therefore follow Aristotle in regarding pleasure as connected with every kind of human activity.

It follows from this that we must distinguish as many kinds of pleasure as there are kinds of activity. "The activities of thought differ specifically from those of the senses, and within each of these two areas, activities differ specifically among themselves. Therefore, the pleasures which complete these activities also differ specifically among themselves."[2]

Psychoanalysts also observe specific differences among pleasures. "To each satisfaction there corresponds a specific action."[3] The quantitative factor is not the only one that comes into play here. Several times in his writings, Freud ventures the idea that there is a qualitative difference among pleasures:

> Pleasure and "pain" cannot, therefore, be referred to a quantitative increase or decrease of something which we call stimulus-tension, although they clearly have a great deal to do with this factor. It seems as though they do not depend on this quantitative factor, but on some peculiarity in it which we can only describe as qualitative. We should be much further on with psychology if we knew what this qualitative peculiarity was. Perhaps it is something rhythmic, the periodical duration of the changes, the risings and fallings of the volume of stimuli; we do not know.[4]

Freud and his disciples have devoted little attention to this qualitative aspect of pleasure,[5] even though the effect of analytic therapy is described by saying that "the supremacy of the quantitative factor is brought to an end"[6] and even though Freud speaks[7] of the pleasure principle, which prizes above all else the quality of pleasure, as causing a development "into a purified pleasure-ego."[8]

Such a development can be seen in the case of the "higher" cultural activities, which are made possible by the sublimation of the instincts:

> One gains the most if one can sufficiently heighten the yield of pleasure from the sources of psychical and intellectual work. When that is so, fate can do little against one. A satisfaction of this kind, such as an artist's joy in creating, in giving his phantasies body, or a scientist's in solving problems or discovering truths, has a special quality which we shall certainly one day be able to characterize in metapsychological terms. At present we can only say figuratively that such satisfactions seem "finer and higher."[9]

The day does not seem yet to have come when psychoanalysts are able to specify the qualities of the pleasures of the mind. But at least psychoanalysis does not deny their existence, although it does assert their "sexual" origin: "It can be said that intellectual work in its turn is nourished by sublimated sexual impulses."[10] No one should be shocked by this statement; in fact, it is not even anything very new. Long ago, Aristotle was of the opinion that the superiority of the human being over the brute animal is due to the development of the sense of touch and that "as far as the human species is concerned it is due to this sense organ, and to nothing else, that some men are well endowed, for human beings whose flesh is hard are ill-endowed in regard to intelligence, while those whose flesh is soft are well-endowed."[11] This rather strange sounding statement is not unfounded, as St. Thomas shows in his commentary on the passage. Since the sense of touch is the basis of all sense life,[12] it is the object of the virtue of temperance.[13]

It is not only intellectual pleasures but those of friendship as well[14] that are nourished by the sublimated sexual instincts.

The human person knows no pleasure proper to a "pure spirit," since such a person is not a spirit but an animated body. It is for this reason that I understand "pleasure" to include all possible satisfactions of needs, desires, and exigencies, without excluding any aspect of the specifically human complexity of these. The human person is neither angel nor beast. The same must be said of his or her pleasures, whatever be the quantitative and qualitative modalities of these.

Is Pleasure to Be Absolutized?

"Pleasure," says Aristotle, "is a kind of indivisible whole; at whatever point in its duration you may examine it, you will never find a pleasure which will be essentially more complete if it lasts longer."[15] This peculiarity of pleasure probably accounts for the illusory temptation to absolutize it and find in it a momentary taste of eternity.

"Joy wants itself, wants eternity, wants recurrence, wants everything eternally the same."[16]

The Greeks, from Plato to Aristotle, had already formulated in their own way this search for eternity that goes on not only in sexual reproduction (which ensures the perpetuity of the species), but in pleasure as such. According to Aristotle, the desire of God is at the source of all the "movements" of the universe and human beings,[17] while according to Plato, a lover is possessed by a god.[18]

Our contemporaries look upon pleasure as an alienation and a madness.[19] It is an attempt to transcend the limits of the human condition, and to this extent it is experienced as something "religious." The "sacred" is connected with "sex," as the history of religions shows.

It is this fact that justifies Georges Bataille's claim in his book on eroticism that "eroticism is primarily a religious matter and the present work is nearer to 'theology' than to scientific or religious history."[20]

What meaning is to be attributed to this "divine" aspect of pleasure? Is it a matter of the confused search for the original lost object and of the unitive character of the archaic pleasures? Is it a matter of religious feeling along the lines of the "something oceanic," which was so dear to Romain Rolland and of which Freud said he had no experience?[21]

Or perhaps it is a search that goes on at the level of the Freudian "id." In one of the notes found on Freud's worktable after his death, this remark occurs: "Mysticism is the obscure self-perception of the realm outside the ego, of the id."[22] The id knows nothing of time and space[23] or of contradiction, conflict, and anxiety.[24] It obeys "the inexorable pleasure principle."[25] At the level of the id the search for pleasure is an end in itself, and to this extent it can be "religious."

To this we may add the illusory flight from death that characterizes pleasure. "The pleasure principle is the process that causes the desire of perpetual presence to the world, the self, and the other to take root in a body doomed to death."[26] Is not sexual pleasure called a "little death" and does it not, like death, set the person outside of time?

In pleasure, and above all in sexual pleasure, there is an effort to escape the fascination exerted by death and by what Georges Bataille calls the "discontinuity of being."[27] He writes that, in the various forms of eroticism (physical, emotional, and sacral), the "essence [of passion] is to substitute for their persistent discontinuity a miraculous continuity between two beings."[28] He thinks that for this reason, erotic pleasure has a sacral character, and all the more so since to it is added the pleasure of transgressing interdicts and taboos. "But the most constant character of the impulse I have called transgression is to make order out of what is essentially chaos. By introducing transcendence into an organised world, transgression becomes a principle of an organised disorder."[29]

Since taboos, "that make human beings" of us, belong in Bataille's view to the order of the sacred,[30] their transgression is likewise of the religious and sacral order. Transgression means profanation. Bataille supports this statement by citing Baudelaire: "The unique and supreme pleasure of love lies in the certainty of doing *evil*. And men and women know from birth that all pleasure is to be found in evil."[31] Eroticism is accompanied by the pleasure of profanation and pollution. This view is true insofar as, like Bataille, one remains the captive (free though one may claim to be) of a morality which is based on prohibitions and to which one has attributed a sacral character.[32] As early as the Book of Genesis we are warned about the attraction exercised by forbidden fruit.[33]

Pleasure, then—and this is even truer of imagined than of real pleasure—exercises a fascination, that is, an attraction mixed with anxiety: "We cannot avoid dying nor can we avoid bursting through our barriers, and they are one and the same. But as we break through the barriers, as we die, we strive to escape from the terror of death and the terror that belongs even to the continuity glimpsed beyond those boundaries."[34]

> As we are about to take the final step, we are beside ourselves with desire, impotent, in the clutch of a force that demands our disintegration. But the object of our urgent desire is there in front of us and it binds us to the very life that our desire will not be contained by. How sweet it is to remain in the grip of the desire, to burst out without going the whole way, without taking the final step! How sweet it is to gaze long upon the object of our desire, to live on in our desire, instead of dying by going the whole way, by yielding to the excessive violence of desire! We know that possession of the object we are afire for is out of the question. It is one thing or another: either desire will consume us entirely, or its object will cease to fire us with longing. We can possess it on one condition only, that gradually the desire it arouses will fade. Better for desire to die than for us to die, though! We can make do with an illusion. If we possess its object, we shall seem to achieve our desire without dying. Not only do we renounce death, but also we let our desire, really the desire to die, lay hold of its object and we keep it while we live on.[35]

Pleasure issues a challenge to the human person.[36] The wrong, but most spontaneous, answer is to approach it as an end in itself. It is wrong because, as Kierkegaard says, to make pleasure an absolute is to miss the very point of it;[37] it is to become prisoner of what Baudelaire calls a "misunderstanding":

> In love, as in almost all human affairs, sympathy is the result of a misunderstanding. This misunderstanding is the physical pleasure. The man cries out: "My angel!" The woman coos: "Mamma, mamma!" And the two imbeciles are convinced that they are thinking in harmony. The unbridgeable gulf which prevents communication remains unbridged.[38]

In the psychological sphere, to live for pleasure is to remain at, or regress to, the stage of the primary narcissism[39] in which the id, which functions in accordance with the pleasure principle, is in control. St. Thomas, following Aristotle, pointed out long ago that animals and children seek pleasure for its own sake.[40] The person seeking pleasure as an end in itself remains at this primitive stage; he loves only himself, and with an egocentric love: "In the end one loves one's desire and not what is desired."[41]

It seems to me certain that pleasure beckons us to what is beyond itself. In this fact is to be found its truth—and therefore its morality as well.

The Use of Pleasure

Pleasure must be experienced in such a way as to give access to its "beyond." The despisers of pleasure, however, are captives of an alienating narcissism, just as much, though differently, as the sensualists. The beyond of pleasure is accessible only to those who "use it as though they used it not" (1 Cor 7:31).

Pleasure is indeed dangerous inasmuch as the person risks alienating himself in it, but the solution is not to deprive oneself of it completely. Such a solution is both impossible and dangerous in its own way.

A little clear thinking will bring the conviction that pleasure cannot give the complete satisfaction that we attribute to it. Let us take it and desire it for what it actually is: limited, of course, yet necessary and estimable. "The program of becoming happy, which the pleasure principle imposes on us, cannot be fulfilled; yet we must not—indeed, we cannot—give up our efforts to bring it nearer to fulfillment by some means or other."[42]

This advice is simply good sense; it is also the teaching of the Bible, especially in the Book of Qoheleth. In the view of this wise man, the pleasures of human life are simply "vanity" (literally "wind"; cf. Eccles 2:1, and *passim*), for "he who loves money will not be satisfied with money" (5:10). This is true of all possessions, even human wisdom (1:16–18; 4:15). Qoheleth concludes that the only happiness for man is to enjoy his work (3:22), to "eat and drink and find enjoyment in his toil" (2:24); this kind of happiness is "God's gift" (3:13).

According to St. Paul, "God . . . richly furnishes us with everything to enjoy" (1 Tim 6:21).

In these views, there is no trace of the Stoic, Jansenist, or Kantian rejection of pleasure. In the Christian tradition, St. Augustine regarded *apatheia* as "stupidity worse than all the vices"[43] and, in addition, a subtle form of vanity. "Others, with a vanity that is as monstrous as it is unusual, become enamored of their own impassibility to the point of not letting themselves be touched or excited or moved or swayed by the least affection, but instead of thus reaching true tranquillity, they cease to be human. For what is rigid is not necessarily straight, nor is insensibility to be identified with health."[44]

But "the citizens of the holy city, the men and women who live in harmony with God during the pilgrimage of earthly life, experience fear and desire, and feel sad and joyous; and since their love is an upright love, so too these affections are upright in them."[45]

Following Aristotle,[46] St. Thomas thinks that to will insensibility is to fall into a vice opposed to temperance: such an attitude "is not human."[47]

The desire of insensibility is not human. Neither is it Christian. It is to be noted that in listing the vices of the "wicked," St. Paul includes "heartlessness,"[48] and that he constantly urges Christians to rejoice.[49] He means to rejoice in earthly goods, provided they use them as though they used them not, but even more to rejoice in the "fruit" of love and the Holy Spirit, which is joy.[50] It is the joy of Jesus Christ himself that is given to us (Jn 15:11; 16:24; 17:13); the fullness of this joy is as yet only an object of hope, but we already experience something of it in this life inasmuch as the Holy Spirit dwells in our hearts and is part of our life as "pilgrims": "The rule of charity, my brothers and sisters, and its strength, flowers, fruits, beauty, charm, nourishment, drink, food, and embraces, never knows surfeit. If it gives such joy while we are still pilgrims, how great will our joy not be when we reach our homeland!"[51]

The disciple of Jesus Christ does experience joys—the joys, already present, of "earthly" life.

To sum up: in regard to pleasures of whatever kind, human beings must avoid two errors:

The first is to indulge in pleasure for pleasure's sake, to look to pleasure as a "reason for living" and an "end in itself" that are fully satisfying. A giddying indulgence in an unlimited multiplication of pleasures only alienates and blinds. It is a snare.[52] To act in this way is to resemble the bull that charges the red flag without seeing the toreador. It is to lock oneself up in the immediate and in appearances, instead of moving toward the "beyond" to which pleasure itself invites one.

> The love of pleasure binds us to the present. A care for our salvation links us to the future.
> He who binds himself to pleasure—that is, to the present—seems to me like a man rolling down a slope, trying to cling to bushes, and uprooting them and carrying them with him in his fall.[53]

The second error is committed by those who, in order to avoid the snares of pleasure and escape the anxiety which awaits at the goal of desire, reject the entire affective life because they consider it to be a harmful and deadly "affection." They try to mutilate themselves, but the effort cannot succeed.

The next point I would like to establish is that when pleasure is experienced in accordance with its true nature, it becomes a rich invitation to something that lies beyond it. People speak, do they not, of the "transports" of pleasure? That is in fact how pleasure functions. This is an observable fact; it is also what the Good News of the gospel teaches us and makes possible for us.

Beyond Pleasure

Psychoanalytic Perspectives

Desire, and the pleasure which satisfies it, have an "object," "that in or through which it [an instinct] can achieve its aim."[54]

This object may be the subject himself: then we speak of self-love, of narcissism. Or it may also be a reality external to the subject. In this second case, Freud speaks of an investment in an object: the libido leaves the subject in order to invest itself in or lay hold of external objects, a condition that attains its highest development in the passion of love.[55] Narcissistic libido, on the other hand, reaches its greatest intensity in childhood, in dreams, and in somatic and psychic illnesses. This is especially the case "when a definite, very forcible process compels the withdrawal of the libido from its objects. The libido that has then become narcissistic can no longer find its way back to its objects, and this obstruction in the way of the free movement of the libido certainly does prove pathogenic."[56]

Thus it is the easy movement of the libido that permits a successful object investment, though this does not mean the elimination of all narcissistic investment, since there remains the kind of narcissism inherent in the instinct for self-preservation that is common to all living things.[57] Nor may we forget the necessary element of narcissism in object choice.[58]

This investment in external objects is the measure of human maturity[59] and of the maturity of the libido, which develops in such a way that "all the sexual strivings proceed in the direction of one person in whom they wish to attain their aim,"[60] or, in other words, they seek "the attainment of the sexual aim in a strange sexual object."[61]

This development requires an overcoming of the pleasure principle by giving predominance to the reality principle.

As Freudian metapsychology developed, it was enriched by something "beyond the pleasure principle." This something was named by Freud the "reality principle," a complex principle that essentially "represents the influence of the external world." It is the task of the ego to discover this world as something that resists the blind and anarchic impulses of the id but that can, on the other hand, supply it with satisfying objects. "Reality" here means everything that exists outside the subject (nature, society, other human beings), but also the subject himself and his internal conflicts: the compulsion to repetition, the "lack" that is the fate of desire, death, destiny, the "goddess *Anankē*" or Necessity.[62]

The sensorial and intellectual functioning of the ego enables it to "test reality" and thus to avoid confusing reality with the ego's representations of it. A development takes place in the subject that leads to the loss of predominance of the pleasure principle in favor of the reality principle, a development from the pleasure ego to the reality ego. This growth in the ego makes possible a temporary post-ponement of the discharge of tension and a temporary tolerance of the tension associated with pain.[63]

In Freud's view, this development is an advance "by which the mature human being is distinguished from the child," [64] and it ter-minates "in the individual's state of maturity where, having re-nounced the pleasure principle and having adapted himself to real-ity, he seeks his objects in the outer world."[65]

In the final analysis, this very renunciation of the pleasure princi-ple is also a safeguarding of it: the reality ego tends to such pleasure as is possible, for it is the function of the reality ego to take into ac-count the concrete character of each situation:

> Just as the pleasure-ego can do nothing but *wish*, work towards gain-ing pleasure and avoiding "pain," so the reality-ego need do nothing but strive for what is *useful* and guard itself against damage. Actually, the substitution of the reality-principle for the pleasure principle de-notes no dethronement of the pleasure-principle, but only a safeguard-ing of it. A momentary pleasure, uncertain in its results, is given up, but only in order to gain in the new way an assured pleasure coming later.[66]

The reality ego is not characterized by passive resignation; it is able to act upon reality and modify it so that reality may allow the satisfaction of a desire. In the choice of this alternative, Freud sees "the whole art of living":

> One can act upon the external world so as to change it and expressly create in it the conditions that will make satisfaction possible. This kind of activity then becomes the supreme fulfillment of the ego. The spirit of decisiveness that allows one to choose the right time for con-trolling the passions and yielding to reality or, on the other hand, sid-ing with the passions and resisting the external world—this spirit of decisiveness sums up the whole art of living.[67]

Freud does not supply us with an analysis of this art of living nor of the processes which lead to the predominance of the reality prin-ciple.[68] We may at least conclude that the reality ego is a factor in and symptom of psychic health[69] and of maturity. Freud's efforts are directed toward "education to reality"[70] and "a love of truth."[71]

Thus, the search for pleasure, which is a blind and narcissistic search on the part of the id, is susceptible to progress; it becomes a search for pleasure that is really possible, a search for that which is useful, as judged by the ego in function of the always complex and "resistant" reality that it perceives. It is an intelligent search in which pleasure is relativized, in both senses of the word "relativize": pleasure is no longer an (illusory) absolute, and it is related to something other than itself, to a "beyond" which is constituted by reality. This "beyond," in the view of Jacques Lacan and his disciples, is the other, who enters the life of the child by reason of the "break" (faille) which he is forced to acknowledge in the object of his desire:

> It is by discovering, in the weaning process, that the milk is not the mother, that the child becomes detached from the mother and is able to live without her. In the same process the need of milk reveals to the child his desire for the mother. There is a break or split in the object which he had regarded as single, namely milk-mother. This object is not entirely reducible to the need he has of it. The split in the object corresponds to the division which separates need and desire within him. The milk which he can deplete and assimilate at given times and places corresponds to a certain knowledge he has of the *other*, of others. The mother, who continues to exist outside of these specific times and places, belongs to another order: that of a radical difference which can exist apart from need, the order of the Other. It is in this articulation of the other with the Other, of this other which is and is not the Other, that this little human being develops its structure as a *subject* who connects desire for the Other with need of the other. The two do not coincide, and it is from this original break or split, the locus of which is his *body*, that his historical time and the power in his words will emerge. The authentic relationship with the neighbor detaches him from those he loves, to the point of allowing them to exist for themselves at an existential distance.[72]

This "authentic relationship with the neighbor" is the fruit of a radical relativization of pleasure by comparison with a beyond that cannot be grasped[73] but is nonetheless constitutive of the human subject. The subject can then pass from consumption of the other to communion with the other.[74]

This beyond, which cannot be grasped and yet is constitutive of the ego, is already present to a little child in its use of what Winnicott calls the "transitional object." He means by this term "the intermediate area of experience between the thumb and the teddy-bear, between the oral erotism and the true object-relationship."[75]

I may extrapolate this idea of Winnicott and ask whether every relation to a real object may not be called, though in a different way, a "transitional phenomenon." After all, Winnicott observes that "the real thing is the thing which is not there," that "the only positive thing is the negative," and that "all I have is what I do not have."[76] In presenting the main lines of Winnicott's work J.-B. Pontalis speaks of a "blank" which is not the simple blank in which there is no discourse: that which has been erased, that which has been removed by a censor, or the latent within the manifest. There is also a blank of presence-absence that bears witness to what has not been experienced, and thus functions as a call to recognize the non-experienced for the first time and to enter at last into a relation with it in order that this which could not have failed to be overloaded with meaning may come to life. Existence must begin with nonexistence.[77]

It is true, as Paul Ricoeur says, that a "transcending intention" dwells in the passions, but I do not think that this is due solely to "the infinite attraction of happiness."[78] If this were so, we would not have moved beyond the primary narcissism. It seems to me that this transcending intention also includes an openness to extrasubjective reality, to what is "lacking," to "an infinite that I have loved in vain."[79]

To reject this opening to which pleasure urges the subject is to make the self the prisoner of pleasure and condemn the self to the disappointing search for a limitless multiplicity of pleasures; "Between the finitude of pleasure, which encloses a well-delimited act and seals it with its repose, and the infinitude of happiness, the θυμός [thumos] slips in a note of indefiniteness and, along with it, the threat that clings to an endless pursuit."[80]

Such a course represents a misuse of pleasure—which is something finite, a well-delimited and sealed act, but one that carries with it an "invitation to the journey" outside of the self. To understand and experience pleasure in this way is to recognize its true reality and not to denature it, as too many moralists have for centuries spent too much time in doing. "They try to make pleasure moral by denaturing it, i.e., by changing its nature, and they refuse to allow that it can be a good and an end. Their attitude is evidently due to the fact that pleasure can admittedly be turned into an absolute."[81]

To say that pleasure leads to something beyond—beyond both itself and the subject who feels the pleasure—is to acknowledge its true nature. This is possible only for the person who faces up to the anxiety "leading who knows where?" which Baudelaire experienced to such a tragic degree:

Pascal's abyss went with him, yawned in the air—
Everything's an abyss! Desires, acts, dreams,
Words! I have felt the wind of terror stream
Many a time across my standing hair. . . .

Sleep itself is an enormous lair
Full of vague horrors, leading who knows where?
All windows open on infinity.

My spirit, haunted now by vertigo,
Yearns for extinction, insensibility.[82]

To turn pleasure into a self-contained whole that has no "way
out" is to use it as a tranquillizer against anxiety; it is to distort its
nature by deluding oneself that it is self-sufficient and leads only
back to constantly renewed desire.

It is difficult to strip the mask from this delusive and treacherous
approach to pleasure; yet such a stripping is essential if we are to attain the truth of human life and thus, of morality.

"Psychoanalytic work" can help to this desired goal. How far does
it take us? Maurice Bellet asks, and gives this answer:

> Doubtless to the point of recognizing our illusions: we had thought
> that *we could*—could trust our own morality, ideas, and religion, our
> own "free choices" and loves, the world we experienced and the world
> we had made for ourselves—a spurious and perfidious balance. We
> had also thought that *we could not*—that this or that was forbidden,
> that we must not go and look, that we must not experience this or
> that, that we must not follow this comprehensive power of desire (if
> we did, everything would go wrong). Here is a double illusion that is
> carefully concealed, because if it is brought to light we will have to be-
> gin to experience this reality that is at once very much feared and very
> much desired.
>
> It is easy to understand why it should be feared. It represents my
> limit, the end of my desires, and my death. It represents the lack, that
> is, the other, the forever other; the difference inscribed within me that
> forever prohibits my becoming one with myself and tells me that I had
> a birth and will have a death. To awaken to the reality of myself is to
> destroy myself—in relation to my former images of myself. True
> enough, I had already destroyed myself amid these mirages; and my
> knowing this without knowing it (that is, the knowledge was despair-
> ingly repressed) meant anxiety and suffering which were self-con-
> tained, whereas now anxieties and sufferings can be those proper to
> life itself.[83]

Sufferings, anxieties, and pleasures that are no longer locked up
within themselves, but are those of life itself, can be openings. The
psychoanalytic experience enables us to grasp more fully a truth
known before Freud.

Moral Perspectives

In a quite different cultural context, and using a quite different
vocabulary and type of approach, St. Thomas Aquinas, a theologian,
has a view of pleasure which seems to me to move essentially in the
same direction as Freud's.

St. Thomas owes a good deal to Aristotle who considers activity and pleasure as forming an "inseparable" pair.[84]

According to St. Thomas, desire (he is speaking of appetite generally) is centrifugal: it tends toward reality as it exists outside the loving subject; whereas knowledge is centripetal: it draws its object to itself through the image it forms of it.[85]

Desire tends to a reality which the person judges to be a good for him; pleasure supervenes when this good is attained through effective action. The experience is a complex one in which three components can be distinguished, though not separated: the reality (good and desired), the act which enables the subject to lay hold of it, and the pleasure which follows from the attainment. There are relations and subordinations between the three. The reality is the term of the desire and the basic finalizing factor; the act (which connects the subject with the reality) is constitutive; finally, the resulting pleasure crowns the whole.

This complex unity is the object of desire; it finalizes desire. The miser, for example, desires and sets as his goal the money and its possession and the pleasure he finds in possessing it.[86] But in St. Thomas' view, there is also a finality at work within the complex: pleasure is related to the act, and the act in turn is related to the desired reality. This means that in the order of finality, pleasure is desired for its own sake and is aimed at simultaneously with the desired good. But in the order of specificity (formal cause) pleasure is relative to the good which is the object of the pleasure.[87] Pleasure is regarded as a "proper accident" (accidens proprium) of the act (just as laughter is a property of the human being). It is "concomitant" with the act, just as heat cannot be had without fire,[88] and yet the heat is not the same as the fire. The pleasure of seeing does not constitute the act of seeing. To desire is to desire something, just as to see is to see something.[89] Desire and its satisfaction lead to an external reality, an object which specifies both the act and the pleasure which the act brings.

This reference of pleasure to something beyond itself takes on a specific character in the human person thanks to the latter's exercise of intelligence. For St. Thomas, who follows the Greek philosophers in this, intellect makes the human person capable of grasping the general or universal idea of "the good":

> Sense perception does not rise to the general idea of "the good," but is limited to particular goods that present themselves to it as pleasurable. This is why the operations of sense appetite in brute animals have for their object pleasure alone. The intellect, on the other hand, grasps the general idea of "good," the possession of which brings enjoyment, and for this reason it makes the good, and not enjoyment as such, its principal object.[90]

This perception and desire of the good open the human person to a beyond that radically relativizes pleasure. Thanks to this, the person is able (and this describes precisely the "virtuous" person) to act out of love for the good in a form that transcends the concrete embodiment in particular goods. He or she can love the good, like beauty, for its own sake. The person enjoys beauty by contemplating it and not by consuming it.

Kalokagathos

We find in St. Thomas the ancient notion of moral good which the Greeks summed up in the term "beautiful and good" (kalokagathos). Modern writers are perplexed when it comes to translating the word kalon because they are afraid of confusing morality with esthetics. Some propose a literal translation (the beautiful), others suggest honor, the noble, that which is worthy of a human being.[91]

St. Thomas and the Scholastics speak of the bonum honestum, the "honorable good" (the term honestum probably came to them from William of Moerbeke, the translator into Latin of the Neoplatonist Proclus Diadochus). Sertillanges points out the incorrectness of the literal translation "honorable good" and suggests instead "appropriate good" because the good in question is "that which is proper or appropriate to each being as an end or term of development."[92]

Whatever the translation adopted for this morally kalon (beautiful), the concept refers to a human behavior which seems to me of the greatest interest: conduct or activity in which desire and pleasure have for their object a reality that is loved for its own sake. This is exactly the kind of behavior that can be characterized as moral, for in it the good is loved for its own sake.

The Greeks and the Scholastics distinguished three kind of goods: the useful (which is not desired for itself but for the sake of something else), the pleasant or pleasurable (desired for the satisfaction of the desiring subject), and the beautiful (the reality that is loved for its own sake).[93] The morally good (kalon) object calls for (kaleim) or elicits a desire which transcends the attitude of the user, the consumer, and even the enjoyer. It urges the person toward that which is loved "for itself":

> No one would willingly live his life through with no more thoughtfulness than a child shows, even if he were to find his greatest pleasure in the things that please children, nor would he willingly buy his pleasure at the cost of an extremely disgraceful action, even if this action were to entail no pain for him. Conversely, there are many things we would value even if they brought us no pleasure, for example, seeing, remembering, knowing, having virtues; as a matter of fact, these various things do necessarily bring pleasure with them, but that is not to the point: we would choose them even if they brought no pleasure.[94]

It is not the pleasure we expect or experience that makes us choose a morally good act, but rather its "beauty." This does not mean that a morally good act is not pleasureable; on the contrary, the pleasure of it is desired and experienced.

For Aristotle and St. Thomas, a life "according to virtue" is a source of pleasure; it perfects, i.e., completes such a life.[95] This is why the pleasure which good action brings is the best criterion of authentically virtuous activity[96] and the pledge of perseverance in virtue.[97] This "beautiful" way of experiencing the pleasure of virtue in no way excludes sensible and bodily pleasures, provided these are "tempered" and regulated by the intellect. "It is characteristic of the temperate person to desire what is proper and in the proper way,"[98] and therefore to have pleasure. The objects of pleasure and the way of taking it are the two (interconnected) criteria of the morally good (or bad) act. The act and its "concomitant" pleasure are morally good when their object is loved for its own sake, for its goodness and beauty which are open to the universal.

I would like to illustrate these abstract principles with a single example: that of Anne Frank who, while confined to a hiding-place, noted in her diary her attainment of moral maturity, when the good and the beautiful are discovered and loved for their own sake.

She recalls earlier years when she lived for the pleasure of being loved and admired:

Yet I wasn't entirely happy in 1942 in spite of everything; I often felt deserted, but because I was on the go the whole day long, I didn't think about it and enjoyed myself as much as I could. Consciously or unconsciously, I tried to drive away the emptiness I felt with jokes and pranks. Now I think seriously about life and what I have to do. One period of life is over forever. The carefree schooldays are gone, never to return.

I don't even long for them any more; I have outgrown them, I just can't only enjoy myself as my serious side is always there.[99]

The desire to be serious is at the same time a desire for autonomy, for freedom from dependence on others:

The first half of 1943: my fits of crying, the loneliness, how I slowly began to see all my faults and shortcomings, which are so great and which seemed much greater then. During the day I deliberately talked about anything and everything that was farthest from my thoughts, tried to draw Pim [her father] to me; but couldn't. Alone I had to face the difficult task of changing myself, to stop the everlasting reproaches, which were so oppressive and which reduced me to such terrible despondency.

Things improved slightly in the second half of the year; I became a young woman and was treated more like a grownup. I started to think, and write stories, and came to the conclusion that the others no longer had the right to throw me about like an india-rubber ball. I wanted to change in accordance with my own desires. But *one* thing that struck me even more was when I realized that even Daddy would never become my confidant over everything. I didn't want to trust anyone but myself any more.[100]

Finally she reaches moral maturity, a partial reason for this doubtless being that she begins to love a boy friend:

At the beginning of the New Year: the second great change, my dream. . . . And with it I discovered my longing, not for a girl friend, but for a boy friend. I also discovered my inward happiness and my defensive armor of superficiality and gaiety. I due time I quieted down and discovered my boundless desire for all that is beautiful and good.

And in the evening, when I lie in bed and end my prayers with the words, "I thank you, God, for all that is good and dear and beautiful," I am filled with glory.[101]

Another illustration of this love of the morally beautiful good is afforded us by Aristotle in his study of friendship.

Properly speaking, Aristotle is dealing with *philia*, a Greek word that applies to a type of human relations which is much broader than what we think of as "friendship." To Aristotle *philia* means "the concern which any human being awakens in any other" (1155a21). It is *philia* that serves as a bond of unity in states and families (1155a22).

Everything about a person that seems lovable can be the basis of a *philia*, a friendship. Aristotle distinguishes three kinds of lovable things: the useful, the pleasant, and the beautiful, and from this deduces that there can be three kinds of friendship: the useful, the pleasant, and the beautiful(1156a6).

The first two kinds are self-seeking: the "friends" are loved not for themselves but for their usefulness or for the pleasure they afford (1156a8–17). Such friendships are based on "accidental congruences," break up quickly, and do not lead to any intimacy (1156a18–30).[102]

A "noble friendship," on the contrary, is not self-seeking. It is the *philia* of those who resemble one another in virtue, for each desires the good of the other on the same grounds: that the other is "good" (1156b7).

In saying that such friendship is based on virtue, Aristotle means that it is based on love of the morally beautiful (as distinct from the useful and the pleasant). The virtuous person "prefers moral beauty to all other goods (and the more virtuous he is, the greater his passion for the morally beautiful)" (1168a33). This is why the happy person, i.e., the moral person, needs friends. His or her "passion" for moral beauty demands to be shared; it demands a "community of sentiments" (1170b9; cf. 1169b16–22). "Friends have all things in common" (1168b7), and a noble friendship is reciprocal; moreover it tends toward intimacy (1157b6–24).

To love someone is to will the good of that person. The beloved exists for his or her own sake (he or she is morally beautiful) but at the same time for someone else, me or another. "Each of those whose friendship is based on virtue burns with desire to do good to the other" (1162b6), because "friendship consists more in loving than in being loved" (1159a27).

Clearly such a friendship has a realm of experience that is "beyond" pleasure. Nonetheless, like every activity, it is also a source of pleasure: "The activity of a good man is good and pleasing in itself" (1169b30). Moreover the virtuous person is happy to be alive: "Life itself is desirable, especially for those who are good, because to exist is for them a good and a pleasure (by the very fact of being conscious of the good present in them they experience pleasure). But, what a virtuous man feels toward himself, he also feels toward his friend (because the friend is another self)" (1170b3–5).

This love of life does not prevent the virtuous person from being ready to die for his friend (as for his country): "For he will gladly abandon riches, honors, and all the other goods for which men contend and retain for himself only moral beauty. For an intense pleasure, even if only of a moment's duration, is better in his eyes than a mild pleasure, however long it may last" (1169a18–20).

The choice of an "intense pleasure" shows clearly that the virtuous person is motivated by a passion for moral beauty, whatever be the pleasure or utility it may bring. It is loved for its own sake. If a person is to be capable of a love of this quality, he must be virtuous; that is, he must live in accordance with intelligence, since intelligence is the specifying mark of the human being: "We say of someone that he masters or fails to master his passions according as intellect is or is not in control. Is this not as much as to say that the intellect is the man?" (1168b34). This is why children are capable only of "pleasurable" friendships (1156a20–31; 1157a26). On the other hand, conjugal love, however pleasurable and useful it may be, is also capable of developing into a "noble" friendship "when the spouses are virtuous persons, for husband and wife each have their own proper way of being virtuous, and each finds joy in seeing the partner possessing the virtue proper to him or her" (1162a25).

A noble friendship, be it conjugal or of some other kind, renders the friends better persons (1172a9–12); it causes them to grow in justice (1160a7) and live in harmony: "Friends are in harmony, each with himself and with one another, for both are held, as it were, by the same anchor" (1167b4).

Each must be harmony with himself if he is to be in harmony with others,[103] for "the sentiments of friendship which we feel toward others have for their root and model the sentiments we feel toward ourselves" (1166a1).[104]

The virtuous man loves himself. He must be "self-centered" (1169a11), but not after the fashion of

> those who claim for themselves the lion's share of riches, honors and bodily pleasures. These are what the mass of human beings desire; this is what they set their hearts on; in their opinion, these are the greatest of all goods, and this is why there is so much contention over them. Those who set their ambitions on such goods live at the mercy of their lusts and, in general, of their passions, which is to say, the irrational part of their souls. That is the way most human beings are (1168b15–22).

But the right way to love oneself is to love oneself according to "the rational part of the soul," that is, to love the moral good: to love it for oneself, first of all, then "by extension" (1168b5) for others.

This "beyond pleasure," this predominance of the "gratuitous" love of the morally beautiful as the foundation of true friendship, finds felicitous expression in St. Thomas when he writes: "A man's laying down his bodily life for a friend is not due to the fact that he loves his friend more than himself but to the fact that he loves the good of virtue more than bodily good."[105]

I think it symptomatic—and very unfortunate—that for centuries now, moralists have completely ignored this conception of friendship in which so many moral values, dimensions, and criteria are brought together. The whole morality of human relations, the morality of family and politics, could have found radical guidance here; this is something which contemporary studies in a morality based on reciprocity are rediscovering.[106]

Scholars are beginning once again to regret that Freud seems to know only two kinds of good: the useful and the pleasant,[107] and that he did not analyze the quality of the pleasures accompanying the activities of the spirit, the discovery of truth, and artistic creation. He speaks of these as "finer and higher" and adds that "fate can do little against one" when "one can sufficiently heighten the yield of pleasure from the sources of psychical and intellectual work."[108]

Is not Freud speaking here of what the Greeks meant by their *kalokagathos*? Moreover, when Freud does not make similar demands of the pleasures of knowledge and art, why should he require that "religious ideas" should renounce the effort "to preserve anything of the consolation of religion"[109] and that ethics too should renounce "the narcissistic satisfaction of being able to think oneself better than others. . . . So long as virtue is not rewarded here on earth, ethics will, I fancy, preach in vain"?[110] Are "religion" and "ethics" not capable of affording pleasures of the same quality as those of knowledge and art?

An analysis of esthetic pleasure might well be helpful in an analysis of "moral" pleasure. In speaking of "a thing of beauty," Dr. Francis Pasche describes it as "an end without an end": "It is made in order that it may exist, and herein is its value."[111] He goes on to say:

> The quality of a pleasure is the important thing: a pleasure that is provisional, constantly reinitiated, so as never to end in satiety (complete discharge), thus keeping the lover of beauty in suspense and the work still alive, sometimes to the point of immortality; for as often as satiety occurs, it "kills" the object of desire.
>
> But the pleasure must be of a certain quality. What Freud says of humor can be applied to the enjoyment of art: "Without really knowing why we do it, we regard this rather weak pleasure as highly valuable; we feel that it is particularly suited to liberate and exalt us."[112]

My own hope is that moralists, along with psychologists and educators, will rediscover the quality of the pleasures of the moral person: pleasures which by reason of their self-transcendence toward what is beyond themselves, or in other words by their relativization, manifest the true character of their experience of them and of the value set upon them. In Aristotle's opinion, the "complete man" (1165b25) is capable of these pleasures, that is, the man whose passion is that of the *kalokagathos*: a passion for that which is both good and beautiful. Here one and the same word expresses both ideas, just as a single word expresses them in Hebrew and again in New Testament Greek where the word *kalos* is used over 150 times as a synonym of "good."

I believe that the key to the morality I am considering in this book is to be found in this truth: pleasure is a relational experience, and it is such to the extent that moral good is loved for its own sake because it is beautiful.

God Beyond Pleasure?

The search for pleasure and pleasure itself, if these are experienced by a complete human being and in their specifically human truth, urge the person to a "beyond," not only because the total satisfaction of desire is impossible, but even more because "loves posits the other in existence through the desire-for-the-Other of which the other is the locus. The person desires the Other in the need he has of the other. The human person is the place where this relation of the other to the Other is woven."[113]

A metaphysical interpretation can be given of this bringing of the other to the Other, as St. Thomas does in his conception of the relations between part and whole. To the extent that a reality is part of a whole, its very being is relational.

Thus the human person, a "political animal," is part of a community: "We see the part naturally endangering itself for the protection of the whole: the hand, without taking thought, exposes itself to blows in order to protect the body. . . . We find the same inclination in the case of the political virtues: the virtuous citizen accepts the danger of death for the salvation of the entire state."[114]

The individual person is not only part of his people and the entire human community; he is also part of the universe which was created by God and is ordered to him, somewhat as the part is to the whole. "It is evident that the good of the part exists for the good of the whole. From this, it follows that with a natural appetite or love, each particular being loves its own good with a view to the common good of the entire universe: which good is God."[115] "By the very fact that they desire their own completion and the perfections proper to them," all created beings "tend toward God, since the perfection of all things consists in a likeness and participation of each in the divine being."[116]

> It is impossible for the human person to find his beatitude in a created good. For beatitude itself is a complete good that is capable of totally satisfying desire; if there were still something left to desire, beatitude could not be a final end. Now the object of the will, which is the faculty of human desire, is the universal good. It follows that nothing less than the universal good can satisfy the human will, because this universal good is not realized in any creature but only in God; for every creature possesses only a participated good. Thus God alone can fulfill and satisfy man's will.[117]

In this metaphysical and theological perspective, desire and pleasure open the subject to something beyond themselves and beyond the desiring and happy subject.[118]

The human intellect is moved by a desire for an ever greater and better knowledge and for a knowledge of that which it does not already know.[119] Its desire is directed toward the infinite, which, as Aristotle observes, is in itself unknowable.[120] The intellect is indeed capable of moving from effects to cause, but the cause escapes its grasp, since it grasps both effect and cause in a single act of perception in which the cause remains hidden in its effect.[121] Every reality, despite its singularity, has in it something of an infinite "which human reason cannot comprehend."[122] When all is said and done, what human beings are able to know amounts to only a little.[123]

Finally, the human person has a desire to move beyond his way of knowing, which is inevitably anthropomorphic; the reason for this anthropomorphic character, according to Aristotle and St. Thomas, is that what is known is interiorized in the subject, so that a human being knows "in a human fashion," according to his own proper mode of being.[124] In his search for the beyond that beckons to him, he conceives a desire to change his perspective and approach and to find one capable of leading him to the absolute and the unlimited that lies beyond his present grasp.

This never satisfied search for what lies beyond the knowable and desirable tends toward that Other of whom we have an inkling but whom we cannot grasp. This Other is called "God," and God exists beyond any and all the imaginative and conceptual images humans can form of him, and thus beyond the illusions which Freud and many others before him have pointed out. Is it not said of the God of revelation that he "dwells in unapproachable light" (1 Tim 6:16) and that "no one has ever seen" him (Jn 1:18)?

The older theological and mystical[125] tradition had its own meaning for the "lack" and the Other of Lacanian psychoanalysis. Here is St. Augustine's explanation of the lack:

> You do not yet see what you desire; but by desiring, you become capable of seeing, so that when that comes which you are to see, you will be satisfied. Suppose you have something to be filled that is in the shape of a pocket, and suppose that you know how large and extensive that is which you must put in the pocket: you will try to enlarge the pocket or sack or skin or whatever it is. You know how much is available to be put into it and how small the container is, so you try to enlarge it and make it more capacious. So too God, while making you wait, enlarges your desire; by enlarging your desire he enlarges your soul; by enlarging your soul he makes it more capacious. Let us desire, therefore, my brothers and sisters, because we are to be filled![126]

St. Thomas even thinks that this orientation of desire and pleasure toward God was natural to the human person before the "corruption" caused by sin:

> In the state of unwounded nature, man referred love of self to love of God as to its end, and the same was true of his love for all other things. Thus he loved God more than himself and above all else. But in the state of corrupted nature, man has suffered deprivation in the appetite that is his rational will; because his nature is corrupted, he now pursues his private good unless he is healed by the grace of God.[127]

This theological principle accounts in its own way for the pitfalls of pleasure. It is only too easy for the person to turn his pleasure, and himself, into an end and to shut himself up therein. In so doing, he makes himself his God; he worships himself. "God is the ultimate end that fulfills the desires of the whole creation. This is why someone who makes himself his own ultimate end is said to become his own God. The same applies to one who turns the pleasures of the flesh, or honors, or anything else, into an ultimate end. . . . Then God blinds the mind."[128]

Despite the differences among them, the perspectives of the theologian and the psychologist, as well as the experience and thinking of the "wise men" of history, all seem to me to lead to the same conclusion: in the complete, i.e., moral person, pleasure is "ordered,"[129] it is relative to something beyond itself. Its proper function is to provide the person with an experience that urges him or her to search for an absolute "beyond," a beyond which is appropriately called God.

According to St. Thomas, it is natural for a human being, by reason of the very nature of his spirit (*mens*), to seek to know and love God,[130] and this desire cannot be useless and empty (*inane*).[131] But in order for him to be effectively able to fulfill it, he needs a "supernatural" gift.[132]

At this point, morality thus understood leads over into mysticism and cannot be separated from it. As Gaston Bachelard used to say, "man is half-open being."[133]

Chapter 10

The Restoration of Pleasure to the Moral Life

Pleasure Energizes the Moral Life

The search for happiness is the source (St. Thomas says the cause[1]) of the entire affective life; it is also the result and clearest manifestation of this life. It is its purpose: "We give the name 'end' in an unqualified way to that which is always sought for its own sake and never for the sake of something else. But by universal agreement 'end' defined in this way applies above to all happiness."[2]

This motivating function of pleasure can be seen in the virtuous person, who is passionately in love with moral beauty; he or she expects virtue to make him or her happy.[3] The happiness, hoped for and indeed already tasted, which moral beauty gives, motivates action and brings moral completion: "Since pleasure completes an action after the manner of an end, no action can be completely good unless it is accompanied by pleasure in the good, for the goodness of anything depends on its end. Thus the goodness of pleasure is in a sense the cause of the goodness of the action."[4]

Pleasure as thus conceived energizes human and therefore moral life: it makes moral activity complete[5]; it is itself an *energeia*, an action.[6]

If there is any point on which I find myself in complete agreement with Aristotle, it is in thinking that morality is in the order of action and not in the order of speculative knowledge. But action requires a mover. This mover is desire (*to orektikon*), a tension toward a goal.[7]

The goal must of course be known or imagined,[8] and understanding is therefore a necessary constituent of moral action. But what comes into play is the "practical intellect," that is, prudence (*phronēsis*), which looks to an end that is to be achieved. Prudence is activated by desire for the end; it makes it possible to know what the true virtuous end is, but "if virtue is required, it is required not in order to know the end but in order to attain it. . . . In other words, it is required in order that the person may *effectively take as an end* that which prudence says is the end. For this to happen, it is not enough simply to know the end; the end must also be desired, and virtue rectifies the desire."[9]

Knowledge alone does not move us; desire is needed. The motive force of the moral life resides in desire, and specifically in the desire for happiness. Moral progress consists in promoting this desire, and this promotion is the effect of virtue. The virtuous person desires (desires passionately, according to Aristotle) both the morally beautiful and, simultaneously, the happiness to which it leads and which is its end. The virtuous person's desire "has the logos";[10] it is intelligent.

Aristotle distinguishes three kinds of desires: two, he says, "lack the logos," i.e., are nonrational (cupidity and rapture), while one "has the logos" and is rational; this third kind might be called a "reflective wish": "The intellect evidently never produces movement unless there is desire. A reflective wish is a form of desire, and when a person goes into action in accordance with a reasoning process, he goes into action in accordance with a reflective wish."[11]

Nonrational desires and reflective wishes are often in conflct, for (as Freud will later observe in connection with the id) nonrational desires have no sense of time:

> And since desires can be contrary to one another—something that happens when reason and the appetites are in opposition (this occurs only in beings with a sense of time: the intellect orders resistance because of what is to come, while appetite responds only to what is at hand, since present pleasure seems unqualifiedly pleasant and unqualifiedly good when there is no foresight of the future)—it follows that the principle of movement must be specifically one: I mean the desiring faculty as such and, above all, the object of desire.[12]

The virtuous person is moved by a reflective wish for the morally beautiful and for the pleasure specific to it. It is the function of a reflective wish to rectify the nonrational desires (by resisting them, if necessary), in virtue of a demand made by the practical intellect which makes it possible to know and desire something "because it presents itself to us as good, rather than seeming good because we desire it, for the principle in this case is thought."[13]

The reflective wish includes desire of the happiness which virtue brings; it is the mover of the moral life. In the order of intention, says St. Thomas, it is anticipated pleasure that gives rise to desire and love, "for pleasure is the enjoyment of the good, and is in a sense, an end in the same way that the good itself is."[14] As we have already seen, the good (external to the subject) and the pleasure I expect from it or take in it, form a single entity in the order of finality —although the pleasure remains relative to and dependent on the good.

From the viewpoint of the subject, there is no mover in the moral life except his or her search for happiness, that is, for pleasure in the sense in which I have been taking this term here. Moreover, what I am talking about is a moral value: "Virtuous acts are praiseworthy in that they tend [ordinantur] to happiness."[15]

This is a point that has been lost sight of for centuries. But it is also a point that has been solidly established by Freud: "As we see, what decides the purpose of life is simply the program of the pleasure principle. This principle dominates the operation of the mental apparatus from the start,"[16] since the goal of instinct is always its satisfaction[17] and "a satisfaction of instinct spells happiness for us."[18]

In Freud's view, love is defined as the relation of the ego to its sources of pleasure,[19] and the ego "may . . . be defined as the totality of the psi [=psychic]-cathexes at any given moment."[20] This explains why pleasure is a source of energy and a constituent of the ego. R. de Saussure asks:

> How are we to explain the fact that satisfaction itself becomes a source of energy and that pleasure urges us not only to rest but to action? Is it not because pleasure brings us into a new balance, and even at times a new psychic structure, which the ego then invests in a narcissistic manner? The ego then experiences a satisfaction in the exercise of this function.[21]

St. Thomas had already noted that "in all pleasures the appetite adopts an attitude of acceptance of what it has; in sadness, on the contrary, it is in an attitude of flight."[22]

If morality consists in discovering and giving a meaning to human action, then it must make pleasure one object of its study. Pleasure is the energizing source, the goal, and the sign of life.

In restoring pleasure to morality, we are giving it back its moving force. But then we should also study carefully the laws of desire and pleasure in the human person.

I have already shown that one law of "human" pleasure is that it should lead to something other than itself, namely, to reality outside of the subject, and that pleasure, like desire, ends in radical dissatisfaction, in something "infinite." Pleasure has its own laws, its own truth. This will now be the object of my study.

Pleasure Is Natural

Nothing is more interior to a human being than his desire (even while at the same time, his desire is a call and response to the desire of another). His pleasure, which is the satisfaction of desire, has the same quality: it is natural to him.

It is also natural in the same way as desire, if at least desire is conceived as Aristotle conceives it: as an inclination to right action such as is proper to a human being. The pleasure that "accompanies" right action has the same endogenous character. "Man is ordered to happiness by interior principles, since he is ordered to it naturally."[23] Man seeks his happiness by a movement that comes from within himself.

In this respect, the search for happiness is the work of freedom. Referring to Aristotle, who thinks that "he is free who is the cause of himself," St. Thomas writes: "He who acts on his own acts freely. What a man does due to an inclination that is in keeping with his nature, he does on his own."[24]

The "energy" which pleasure is and which accompanies human action, participates in the same freedom as the action does, inasmuch as the person does not passively submit to it but wills it (loves it) and is thus the cause of himself.

But pleasure must also be experienced with a reference to the beyond to which it leads and whence it proceeds. "The beyond of desire is the level at which the subject is established as freedom and at which, paradoxically, he possesses himself prior to desire. . . . This is why it is legitimate to say that the subject constitutes himself as a free being prior to desire."[25]

When experienced in this manner, human pleasure contributes to making the subject autonomous. He frees himself from an alienating dependence on others and on materials goods. His relational life thereby gains in quality and oblativity, while at the same time, he wins a greater independence. Aristotle observes: "We are made independent by that which, when possessed in isolation, makes our life worth living and renders it free of any need. Such I think happiness to be."[26]

It is at this level of pleasure that the subject discloses to himself the meaning of his action. He chooses for himself. Aristotle says that "choice is the origin or moral action," and he continues: "and the origin of choice is desire and planning—the planning which decides on the means for obtaining the end."[27] "Thus choice is either reason that desires or reflective desire, and this complex origin is man."[28]

This choice, which is the man himself in the complex interplay of affectivity and intellect, is the work of virtue: "Virtue is a habitual state which directs choice, and consists in a just mean relative to us; the measure of the mean is the moral norm, that is, the norm a wise man would adopt."[29]

As seen in this perspective, the moral rule is both endogenous (the choice) and exogenous (what a wise person would choose). Freud sees quite clearly that "every man must find out for himself in what particular fashion he can be saved."[30] He also regards choice and the decision on how to act in regard to the passions, as making up the whole "art of living" and "the supreme fulfillment of the ego."[31]

Such is indeed, in my opinion, the source of the moral life. In this respect the moral life is natural.

For, an authentic moral life must be endogenous. It is primarily within a person—in the biological and psychological laws of his or her being and in the laws governing humanization—that he or she discovers the processes of growth toward an autonomous moral life.

The same is true of any living entity. As everyone knows, a living cell is characterized by the presence of macromolecules, which are divided into three groups: proteins, DNA (in the nucleus) which carry genetic information, and RNA (in the cytoplasm) which transfer the genetic information from the nucleus to the cytoplasm where protein synthesis takes place. These molecules are arranged in spirals or helices, and carry the coded program for the cell's growth to a complete organism, in accordance with laws which we are only now learning to decipher.

In this coded program, every living thing finds the laws governing its growth. This does not exclude the favorable or unfavorable action of the "nourishing" environment, on which it depends even before its birth.

> Each of our cells is programmed. The program is inscribed in the cell's code. However, the working out of the program will depend on a dialogue that is carried on with a series of interlocutors. In other words, the working out of the program does not depend exclusively on the determinisms within the cell; it is also influenced by other factors, such as the density and nature of the nutrients in the ego, the topography of the folds in the cell layers from the earliest stages in the development of the embryo, and then on certain contributions from the mother's blood.[32]

This "dialogue" between the endogenous and the exogenous continues throughout biological life and throughout the life of the psyche as well. At this latter level, too, "the succession of the separate phases in the development of the libido probably follows a prescribed course."[33]

Why should the moral life not have its preestablished program, too? Western morality since the fourteenth century has excessively played down the primacy of the endogenous. Morality has been conceived as consisting in obedience to the good pleasure of an authority outside of man (an authority that is both religious and political) that is imposed according to the pattern of the categorical imperative. But such a view imprisons the moral life in the primitive phase of the superego and justifies Freud in thinking that the power to distinguish good and evil is not original, but that in it "there is an extraneous influence of work, and it is this that decides what is to be called good and bad."[34]

In my opinion, the time has come for restoring full primacy to the interior aspects of the moral life, since the laws of its birth and growth are inscribed in the very being of the human subject. Interiority is a law of nature in the human being, as in every living thing, but this is even truer of man since he or she possesses intelligence and the power of "reflective wishing." The gospel only confirms and further exalts this primacy of interiority.

This does not mean we are to downplay the importance of what comes from outside, of that without which interiority could not develop. This is true at the biological level: the digestive system includes in its operation food from outside; the two factors form a sigle, though hierarchized, whole. So too, and even more so, human nature includes "culture."

Obligation

Morality is not simply a science of mores; it carries with it the note of obligation. The thing that has in the course of history led to an overvaluation of the exogenous aspect of morality is undoubtedly the need of grounding moral obligation in a supreme authority, in a sacral "absolute," that is radically external to the moral subject and brings security the easy way. "Liberty, when there is no duty to guide it, [is] terrifying."[35]

In fact, freedom induces fear,[36] and yet it is the dearest of human possessions;[37] people regard it as the source of their nobility and see it as determining the quality of their moral life.

In the Prologue to the part of his *Summa theologiae* that deals with morality, St. Thomas states that he intends to study man insofar as he has been created in the image of God, that is, insofar as he too is "the source of his own actions as one having free will and power over his actions."[38] There is no moral life without freedom. He is free who acts "on his own" and is therefore "cause of himself," because he acts by his own capacity and according to an attraction that is proper to his nature.[39] This is why "he who does something out of love acts on his own, since it is his own inclination that moves him to action."[40]

The person, on the contrary, who acts due to a pressure from outside, is not free. This is the case with a person who submits to laws out of fear of punishment: "He who avoids evil not because it is evil, but because a commandment of the Lord forbids it, is not free."[41] His "reflective wish" and judgment are not free; they do not come from within himself.[42]

The "complete" moral person is not obliged first and foremost from without; rather, he obliges himself. As Jacques Henriot writes, "morality depends on the consent of a self who regards as valid an idea which regulates his own conduct."[43] "It is for the self to judge how it is to impose obligations on itself and whether it should (reason and prudence) act in this way rather than that in reaching its ends."[44]

Obligation here has its origin "in the fact that the self exists"[45] and "exists in an insufficiency and a lack of being"[46] that make it develop an ego-ideal, a plan for its own development. This is one function of the ego whose power of understanding and capacity for submission to the reality principle enable it to recognize in itself and its relational life the endogenous laws governing its existence.

Obligation is admittedly external as well. In this regard, obligation comes from the superego, individual and social. But "it is the ego that obliges itself in the presence of the superego because it makes its own the demands of the superego and recognizes the *preferableness* of the attitudes and behaviors which the superego expects of it. In obliging itself in order to please the obliger, the obliged becomes obliger of itself."[47]

For St. Thomas, moral obligation is basically endogenous.[48] He thinks that the rightness of an action is to be judged according to the suitableness of this action for attaining the end inscribed (*indita*) in the being of the agent. In beings that lack reason, the rightness is measured by the force with which nature carries them on to their specific end: "Every natural inclination to act has its law."[49]

In beings capable of understanding and of reflective wishing, "the proximate rule is human reason, while the supreme rule is the eternal law [inscribed in their being]. Whenever, therefore, the human act moves toward an end that is in accordance with the order willed by human reason and the external law, it is a right act; whenever it deviates from this rightness, it is said to be sinful."[50]

A human act is evil by the very fact that it is not in conformity with the "measure" proper to it by its nature: "A thing is measured by relation to a rule; if it deviates from this rule it is out of measure. The rule for the human will is twofold: one is proximate and homogenous with the will, namely, human reason; the other is the primal rule, namely, the eternal law which is, as it were, the reason of God himself."[51]

In summary, the moral life is the work of existential truth. Man is able on his own to decipher the genetic code of the laws governing his specific growth and of carrying out, with conscience, intellect, and desire, and in an autonomous way, the program of humanization that is inscribed in his own being. This program is his "natural law"; it is homogeneous with him. It is called the eternal law when regarded as the fruit of the creator's mind, but it is manifested to human beings through their specific "inclinations" insofar as these are illumined, criticized, and willed through their intelligence and love. "Right action requires two things: first, that the affectivity be inclined to the good (which is accomplished in us by habits of moral virtues) and second, that reason discover ways suitable for attaining the good of virtue. This discovery Aristotle assigns to prudence."[52]

The precepts of the natural law are based on these inclinations of human affectivity.[53] The human moral law, even when considered as an "eternal law," is endogenous to man and homogenous with him.[54]

St. Thomas does not regard the law enunciated in the Decalogue, which is promulgated by God and therefore exogeneous, to be the source of moral obligation, but looks upon it rather as a body of teaching[55] ("teaching" is precisely what the Hebrew word *Torah* means). It takes on the aspect of obligation from the fact that it was given in view of an end[56] and, specifically, in view of the "ultimate" end of man, namely God.[57] The law in the Decalogue is a "rule" which helps human beings to assess their relations with one another and with God.[58] God's intervention in the Decalogue is undoubtedly external to man, but God acted in this way in order to help man to a better understanding of his own internal law and to a more correct endogenous direction of his desire toward the good.[59]

Here we have what is most specific to the "new law." It is a gift of God and meant to help us through grace,[60] but this gift takes root and lives in the innermost recesses of man's interiority, thus becoming endogenous. The law of the gospel, or new law, as it is called, is more *indita* that any other law of life,[61] for it means that man is "dwelt in" by the Holy Spirit; he is in-spired.

He loves, for in love the entire law and prophets are contained; and it is in this love (of God, himself, and other human beings) that he finds the source of the obligation which binds him.[62]

> The term set to an analysis is the limit that brings the patient up short, and this limit is the point at which the problematic of desire is located. Where analysts see as the goal the capacity for happiness, we shall instead see that which the patient must *promote* (Maud Mannoni). For myself, I think that the essential point is to be found in the word *promote*; at the term of an analysis there is a discovery of what needs to be promoted, of a meaning that transcends the transformation of the capacity for happiness, on the one hand, and the lack of satisfaction, on the other. For who can say that the capacity for happiness does not consist in this constantly recurring feeling, and that the lack of satisfaction, in its full form, is not the simple demand for a meaning which calls for constant implementation?[63]

In addition, it is important to note that the meaning to be given to
the search for pleasure is located in the time proper to the subject. It
is inscribed in a trajectory that goes from past to future:

> The dynamic axis of the person is his unity and his continuity as these
> appear to him and others in the form of a trajectory which has its ori-
> gin in the formation of his first experiences and is directed toward his
> ulterior experiences and ultimate ends. The very finality of the sub-
> ject, and therefore of the person as agent of his own existence, estab-
> lishes his basic structural character. For the guiding thread that binds
> us to our past or to our world is the *existential project*, the very axis of
> our destiny. The ego manifests itself in the direction it takes, that is,
> as the very vector of the being's temporality, the meaning of its life.[64]

It is for this reason, says Madame Amado Lévy-Valensi, that "the
moral person is the person who undergoes changes which cannot be
anticipated and which surprise even him as he emerges from a testing. Nor is he to rest complacently in his surprise, for still other
things await him."[65]

It is indeed here that the meaning of the moral life is to be sought,
for this meaning is independently invented in a process of self-
discovery upon self-discovery. I see this as one of the fundamental
laws of morality, if we mean by morality the meaning and destiny of
human desire and pleasure. "The first moral imperative leads to a
confrontation which allows the subject to emerge from the snares
natural to him. He must innovate, discover his own history over
against others."[66]

"Over against others," for moral meaning comes to the human
person in the form of the truth of his or her relational life. "The discovery of others is inseparable from ethics no less than from desire."[67] Desire and pleasure are forms of openness to the other: "The
act of sucking satisfies the infant's hunger and, at the same time,
through and beyond the object of his need, opens him to another
being. All of human experience is structured by this perception,
through the very act that tries to deny it, of a difference which is
foundational of his own distinctness."[68]

Thus, like desire and pleasure, the moral life advances toward
what some people call "oblativity," or "altruism," or the acknowl-
edgement of the other insofar as he or she is not I. "The person, involved in the experience of a life in which death is at work, learns to
desire beings (of which he, himself, is one) and things for what they
are and no longer for the use he can make of them."[69] The progress
here is toward the "transcending of self" (in its primary narcissism),
"not in order to put on some personal performance but in order to
achieve detachment from self, in all simplicity and without any
complacency, to the benefit of others and the work to be done."[70]

There can be no morality without a rule. The rule can only be based on the laws of desire and pleasure that I have been reviewing, and its aim is to develop these in accordance with their true nature.

> Morality then takes the form of memory. Through responsibility for a destiny that has been accepted and understood, it resists the sterile alternatives of a counterfeit strictness on the part of the superego and a complacent yielding to instinct. We may recall Aragon's saying 'Strictness is true freedom,' which is the law of both art and morality.[71]

We come full circle here to what Aristotle and St. Thomas wrote long ago about the moral rule as based on understanding and the rational search for the truth of man's affective dynamism, and about what "befits" him, when what he is and can become is given, acknowledged, loved, and chosen.

We also come full circle to the primacy of interiority, of which Christ is constantly reminding us.

Compulsions and Frustrations

One of the most valuable contributions of psychoanalysis is to have shown the extent to which compulsion, however external in its origin, is constitutive of desire and therefore of pleasure. Throughout their development, the instincts are structured under the influence of a whole range of compulsions, prohibitions, and frustrations, from the urethral and anal cleanliness imposed on the little child, the prohibition of incest, and everything implied by castration anxiety and the Oedipus complex,[72] on to the demands made by the collective superego.

It is an observable fact that human growth comes by way of frustrations; Freud has shown that these are inevitable but also that they help to give structure. The reality principle, the predominance of which ensures maturity,[73] makes necessary the frustrations caused by all sorts of obstacles, external and internal, to the satisfaction of the instincts of the id. Frustration may be the source of a neurosis, but only if it strikes "at the only form of satisfaction which that person desires, the only form of which he is capable."[74]

Freud goes so far as to say that "the psychical value of sexual satisfaction increases under privation."[75]

Only through testing frustrations can the ego emerge from the id and build itself:

> The immediacy that is part of satisfaction leaves us in direct proximity to the object and even immersed in it. Gradual frustrations (which can take on an Oedipal meaning, though after the fact) and the triangle situation enable us to draw back from the object, and give us a sense of

perspective. . . . In other words, access to the object and the existence of the ego and secondary processes are possible only in the absence of total satisfaction of our desires, a satisfaction that would bring us into union with the mother.[76]

This is a theme that is often developed by Freud's disciples: the suffering and distress caused by frustration are calculated to advance the person in his or her psychological truth.[77]

The frustrations, unconscious repressions, and conscious renunciations that are forced upon the ego by the always unbridgeable gap between the total satisfaction desired and the satisfaction actually experienced are in Freud's view a "driving factor," a goad, "which will permit of no halting at any established position."[78]

In view of this, it is very symptomatic that in the mythical story in Genesis, the first sin is shown to be provoked by a prohibition. Whatever be the viewpoints adopted on the origin of morality, compulsion and frustration always crop up.

"Ethics . . . means restriction of instinctual gratification," Freud remarks.[79] He is referring not only to prohibitions by educators, sociocultural and economic pressures, language, "received opinion," all that comes from human beings, but also to the demands and even threats made by "physical" reality. For our bodies and the cosmos impose inevitable sufferings and frustrations on us. "It is no wonder if, under the pressure of these possiblities of suffering, men are accustomed to moderate their claims to happiness."[80] The reality principle regulates the pleasure principle.

In addition, there is the radical frustration that comes from the expectation of inevitable death. "If you would endure life, be prepared for death."[81] Man is forced to accept this law: life is given to him, and it is marked by a complexity which is constitutive of it and which he did not choose. From this given situation he can emerge with the nobility and freedom proper to him, although he cannot escape his "fate," the goddess *Anankē* to whom Freud gives such prominence and to whom, he tells his friend Pfister, an honest man must submit.[82]

This submission to reality and its laws is the criterion of any scientific procedures. It is also a demand of any authentic morality. In addition, it is one of the best symptoms of psychic health: "Neurosis and psychosis are both of them an expression of the *id* against the outer world, of its 'pain,' unwillingness to adapt itself to necessity."[83]

This constraining general law that weighs on human life also has a structuring function:

In the relation of the human subject to the world, the law shows itself to be the expression of a boundary which distinguishes object from subject (as well as objects and subjects among themselves). We must add, however, that the law possesses this structuring function only in the case of a force or instinct that impels man to make the effort, as Erasmus used to say, to cross the boundary. The law functions in this way, i.e., it structures the human being, only if it is in some way ordered to this crossing of boundaries.[84]

By reason of the constraints it imposes, law is an "interdict" (a "saying between"); it is dialogical.

From the sociologist's standpoint, morality is the expression of the laws which are constitutive of the human community. Man lives in society. He finds therein norms, behavior models, and institutions which regulate the roles of the members and thus facilitate the coexistence of all and their participation in the whole.

These norms weigh heavy; their development meets with tough resistance,[85] is countered by the ambiguities of ideology, and so on.

But the compulsion exercised by these sociological norms should not make us overlook their usefulness. By regulating the relations of human beings with one another, civilization and its ethics "distinguish our lives from those of our animal ancestors."[86] They establish a balance "between this claim of the individual [to freedom] and the cultural claims of the group."[87] This means that "civilization is built up upon a renunciation of instinct,"[88] that is, of libido and aggressivity, anxiety and guilt.[89] Admittedly, one result of this renunciation is "a loss of happiness"[90] for the individual and a lessening in the importance assigned to sexuality as a source of happiness.[91]

The aim of civilization, to make the individual happy, is still there, "but it is pushed into the background."[92] "Civilized man has exchanged a portion of his possibilities of happiness for a portion of security."[93] Inasmuch as this security diminishes threats and sufferings, it is a fom of happiness. But there is something more: "There is, indeed, another and better path: that of becoming a member of the human community, and, with the help of a technique guided by science, going over to the attack against nature and subjecting her to the human will. Then one is working with all for the good of all."[94] Finally, by introducing justice into the relations among human beings, civilization and its ethics aim "at binding the members of the community together in a libidinal way" and endeavor "to strengthen the communal bond by relations of friendship."[95]

The complicated interplay of all the constraints imposed on the civilized person is difficult to evaluate in terms of his or her happiness: it is a source of collective and individual nerouses, but at the same time, it gives access to "finer and higher" joys, those of the mind, art, friendship, and so on.

In short, everything depends on the way in which society imposes its laws and the individual accepts them. "Law is not an in-itself nor does it have its end in itself. It has value to the extent that it is relative, that is, connected with something other than itself: law mediates reciprocity."[96]

It is impossible to see how the struggle against nature, the demands of life in society, and all that Freud means by the reality principle can be accepted and undertaken without constraints and without submission to laws.

Paul Valéry has his Monsieur Teste say: "Anything that constrains me is not me."[97] And in fact, there are constraints which are experienced as external to me. But there are others that can be constitutive of the self, even insofar as they run counter to the primary instincts. Braque often said: "I love the rule that sets emotion straight," and Malraux has remarked that "one day constraint gave birth to art."

This perception is so evident and so widespread that its validity cannot be denied. Nietzsche has given forceful expression to it better than anyone else:

> What is essential and estimable in every morality is that it constitutes a long compulsion: to understand Stoicism or Port-Royal or Puritanism, one should recall the compulsion under which every language so far has achieved strength and freedom—the metrical compulsion of rhyme and rhythm.
>
> How much trouble the poets and orators of all peoples have taken— not excepting a few prose writers today in whose ear there dwells an inexorable conscience— "for the sake of some foolishness, as utilitarian dolts say, feeling smart—"submitting abjectly to capricious laws," as anarchists say, feeling "free," even "free-spirited." But the curious fact is that all there is or has been on earth of freedom, subtlety, boldness, dance, and masterly sureness, whether in thought itself or in government, or in rhetoric and persuasion, in the arts just as in ethics, has developed only owing to the "tyranny of such capricious law"; and in all seriousness, the probability is by no means small that precisely this is "nature" and "natural"—and not that laisser aller.[98]

I gladly make my own what Nietzsche goes on to say about the artist, by adding that the moral man, too, is in his "most natural state," the state of inspiration in which with full freedom he orders, arranges, disposes, and gives form to his human life within the constraints reality imposes on him—his own reality and that of his physical and social environment.

Chapter 11
The Laws of Pleasure

Pleasure as a Moral Rule?

It is a fact that most human beings act for the sake of pleasure and do not look any further for the meaning of life. Those among them who reflect on their behavior justify it by saying that the search for pleasure is indeed the rule of their life. André Gide wrote that "in each action the pleasure I find in it is a sign that I ought to do it,"[1] that "the sincerity of my pleasures, Nathaniel, is the most important of my guides."[2] Subsequently Gide would even discern a moral obligation here:

> It has long seemed to me that joy is rarer, more difficult, lovelier than sadness. And when I had made this discovery, which is doubtless the most important one that can be made in this life, joy became to me not only a natural need (which it was already) but also indeed a moral obligation. It seemed to me that the best, the surest way of spreading happiness about one was to give an image of it oneself, and I resolved to be happy.[3]

The Dutch senator Brongersma tells this story which he attributes to a priest who had been taken by a student "into a hall in which couples of the opposite sexes were dancing, but with them were also dancing couples of the same sex, two boys or two girls":

> He saw there a young man whom he knew quite well and whom he thought of as serious and well intentioned. This young man was dancing with another young man, and his face radiated happiness to such a degree that the priest felt tears spring to his eyes. No doubt about it:

the two young people were madly in love with each other and were making each other happy. And the priest then reflected as a theologian: "God wants his creatures to be happy. For this reason anything that makes them truly happy can never be contrary to God's will. The love which any bystander can clearly see that these two young men have for each other is a good thing; it is a good in the moral sense."[4]

Is the moral rule, then, to be pleasure pure and simple? With Aristotle I would answer with a Yes and a No.

Yes, because we must acknowledge, with Aristotle, that "pleasure and pain are the rule by which we measure even our actions, some of us more so, others less."[5]

No, because, again for Aristotle (I pointed this out earlier) the moral rule and measure are established by the "virtuous man" and by the pleasure such a man experiences in acting rightly. "But the mass of people deceive themselves, and the source of their error seems to be pleasure: it seems to them to be a good even when it is not; it is clear in any case that they pursue pleasure as if it were always a good, and flee pain as if it were always an evil."[6]

If pleasure then is to serve as a moral rule, we must make clear just what is meant by pleasure. In Aristotle's view, it is a question of the pleasures that crown the actions or tasks (to ergon) specific to a human being,[7] namely, the life of knowledge and desire that is proper to the "rational soul." As St. Thomas says very well: "The pleasures of the sense appetite are not the rule of moral good and evil; food, for example, is pleasing to good people and evil people alike. But the will of the good person rejoices in such pleasures insofar as they are in keeping with reason, while the will of the evil person is unconcerned about this."[8]

Using the language of Aristotle, I would say that "the rational soul possesses the rule" and that it imposes its rule on "the part that desires." As a result the latter in a sense participates in the rule of the rational soul "to the extent that it is submissive and obedient to it,"[9] "as one is docile to a father";[10] in so acting it "is in full harmony with the rule."[11]

This full harmony with the rule, a state attained by the temperate and courageous, is neither spontaneous nor easy.

There is also another natural element that is contrary to the rule, struggles against it, and resists it. This is precisely the kind of thing that happens in paralyzed people, though here at the bodily level: their crippled members, which they intended should turn to the right, turn instead to the left. The same thing happens in the soul: the impulses of incontinent persons lead some of them in one direction, others in another. The difference is that in the case of the body, we see what goes astray, but in the case of the soul, we do not see it. But we must think, nonetheless, that in the case of the soul, too, there is something that is contrary to the rule, and resists and opposes it.[12]

Such resistance to the rule is a fact we know only too well. Christian faith sees in it an effect of original sin, but Christian tradition interprets this situation in different ways, depending on whether or not the interpreter is affected by a Stoic or Manichean mentality. According to Augustine, if Adam and Eve had not sinned, sexual union "would have taken place by an act of the will and not been inspired by the desire for pleasure"[13]—pleasure which he regards as a "sickness."[14] He goes so far as to write: "What wise man would not prefer, if it were possible, to beget children without the presence of this desire?"[15]

On the other hand, Augustine's adversary, Julian of Eclanum,[16] and the entire more or less Aristotelean tradition that led to Sts. Albert the Great and Thomas Aquinas,[17] have held the view that prior to original sin, sexual pleasure must have been even more intense:

> Animals are not endowed with reason. If then a human being becomes animal-like in carnal union, it is because he is unable to apply reason to the regulation of the pleasure of carnal union and the heat of desire. But in the state of innocence there would have been nothing in this domain that was not regulated by reason. I do not mean, as some maintain, that the sense pleasure would have been less; as a matter of fact, the sense pleasure would have been all the greater because nature would have been purer and the body more sensitive. But the urge to pleasure would not have turned to this pleasure in such a disorderly way, since it would have been regulated by reason, the function of which is not to lessen sensible pleasure, but to see to it that the sensible appetite does not attach itself to pleasure in an immoderate way (by "immoderate" I mean going beyond the measure of reason). Thus, a sober person derives no less pleasure from food, which he takes in a measured way, than a glutton does; but his urge to pleasure is less focused on this kind of pleasure.[18]

I take particular pleasure in the tradition represented by St. Thomas, for I find more truth in its position that the humanization of our animal body increases with the quality and intensity of its sense life and sense pleasures. "The refinement of the bodily makeup is matched by nobility of soul. . . . It follows that the person with a refined sense of touch has a nobler soul and sharper mind."[19]

This optimistic view does not eliminate the difficulties a human being experiences in mastering his or her "desires." But it does facilitate the task by directing one's efforts to achieving the supremacy of the ego (as Freud would put it): the intelligent, realistic ego that is capable of synthesis, and by relegating to its proper—indispensable but secondary—place the superego with its prohibitions and its cultivation of a sense of guilt.

I think it more in conformity with human reality (and with the faith) to think that the famous recalcitrant "concupiscence" is not a "defect of nature"[20] and that on the contrary, it is natural and good, provided that in a human being it is "humanized" by being brought to participate in the rule of rational intelligence. When it refuses this submission, it becomes disfigured,[21] and this disfiguration can rightly be said to be "against nature."[22]

In this perspective, which I make my own, the object with which morality deals is affectivity. The task of morality is to humanize affectivity, that is, to elevate what is "animal" and infantile in it (domination of the pleasure principle) to the level of rational intelligence, which alone is capable of opening up desire and pleasure to extrasubjective reality, to oblativity, and to the "beyond" that is constituted by their objects.[23]

The moral person is the one who succeeds in making intelligence permeate her affective life. By so doing, she is able to regulate and finalize[24] her desires and pleasures according to the reality principle and the requirements of both her love for truth and her autonomy. "Where id was, there ego shall be."[25] She desires and loves as a human being should. All her powers are "ordered," that is, they are arranged in a "marching order" that is dynamic, gives structure, and leads to the end. Her "lower" affective powers participate of themselves in the manner of loving that is proper to the "higher" affective powers.[26]

The task of morality is to discern the laws which govern human affectivity and are inscribed in it in the form of potentialities; each individual should understand and love these and thus direct his own development. He must use his mind-directed love to exercise over his raw affectivity a control to which St. Thomas gives the name of *imperium*.[27] Contrary to the mind-set which centuries of "voluntarism" have created in the West, this *imperium* is not to be understood as the exercise of a despotic or policelike power. Rather, it is "political" in kind.[28] Its action is to inspire the affections, and takes the form of a call and attraction[29] comparable to the authority of a husband over his wife[30] or of a father over his child, even when this authority takes the form of correction.[31] The higher affectivity "moves" the lower affections,[32] which thereby participate, freely and without struggle or rebellion, in the higher affectivity.[33] The power of love and intelligence that permeates the higher affectivity enables it to humanize and thus render moral the person's entire affectivity.

In summary, the "matter" with which morality deals is the affectivity[34] and therefore pleasures and pains to the extent that these complete the affective act[35] in its (right or wrong) relation to its object. In this perspective the moral virtues are seen as the structured and structure-giving dynamisms of our powers of right love and right action for an end that is desired and that is conformed to the true reality of a human being.[36]

Conversely, sin is a "disorder" and the effect of a distorted or missing finality. "There is disordered love in every sin, and this disordered love results from a disordered desire."[37]

To act with moral rightness is to love rightly; to act wrongly is to love wrongly.

The Pleasures of Right Action

A person who loves rightly is moved by desire for a pleasure which must be declared morally good. The temperate person, for example, does not seek to avoid the pleasures proper to him or her, but seeks them out; on the other hand, he or she does avoid the pleasures of the intemperate person.[38] For the morally bad person finds pleasures in wrong action: he or she is one of those

> who forsake the paths of righteousness
>   to walk in the ways of darkness,
> who rejoice in doing evil
>   and delight in the perverseness of the wicked.[39]

If, then, pleasure can function as a moral rule, this pleasure can only be that of right action, in the sense in which Aristotle understands it. The pleasure is that of the virtuous person; it is the pleasure which crowns and completes the actions proper to a human being.[40]

"A person is not a good person unless he finds his joy in doing beautiful actions,"[41] for "it is impossible for a person to taste the pleasure of the just man if he himself is unjust, just as one who is not a musician cannot taste the pleasure of a musician, and so on."[42] The individual acts in accordance with what he is, and "as the person is, so does the end appear to him."[43]

Whether this end be entirely determined by nature or whether man has had a hand in fashioning it, the tendency to the end (or, as we would say today, the meaning the person gives to his life) is the result of a decision on his part. The virtuous (and vicious) man acts with full deliberation, for he is endowed with the power to act on his own (this is true at least of his actions, if not of his tendency toward his end).[44]

The virtuous man, then, experiences the pleasure of acting freely, that is, with his intellect.[45] The pleasure is basically that of acting in accordance with his desire (of the end) and of reasoning about the means of attaining the end. But "the reasoning must be true and the desire must be right."[46]

We are dealing here with the specifically human pleasure: the pleasure of being human by acting in accordance with the "desiring intellect" or "reflective wish."[47] This, according to Aristotle, is the "right action" the pleasure of which supplies the moral rule and measure. A person must be good in order to experience the pleasure of acting rightly:

> The same things do not seem sweet to the person with a fever as to the man in good health, any more than the same thing will seem hot to a sick person and to a healthy person; and so on. But, by common consent, it is agreed that in every case things are as they seem to the person in the right condition. But if this criterion is correct, as it is unanimously accepted to be, and if the measure of each thing is the virtue of the good man as such, then those pleasures will really be pleasures which seem so to the good man, and those objects truly pleasing in which he finds his joy.
>
> Now it is not surprising that objects which he finds repugnant should appear pleasing to another, for human beings are subject to many kinds of corruption and spoiling. Such objects are not pleasing, however, except to such people and while they are thus disposed. In short, it is clear that the pleasures which it is agreed are sordid should not be called pleasures at all, except for individuals who are corrupt.[48]

If follows from this that the best criterion of authentic virtue is the pleasure which the virtuous person feels. It is possible, as St. Thomas observes,[49] to act in accordance with justice on a single occasion, even though the motive may be fear of punishment or self-interest or something else, or, in other words, without possessing the true virtue of justice. On the other hand, the person who is just will do just actions "readily and with pleasure" and in the way that is most appropriate on each occasion. St. Thomas also formulates this principle, which seems to me to be basic to morality, both theoretically and practically: "A person is judged good or bad above all according to the pleasures of his will, for that person is good and virtuous who takes pleasure in virtuous actions, and he is evil who rejoice in evil deeds."[50] We must even say that insofar as the goodness of this pleasure is desired and serves as an end, it is in a way the cause of the goodness of the action.[51]

The moment has come to ask what these pleasures of right action are. I consider them to be many and complex or even ambiguous.

For purposes of explanation, I shall distinguish between narcissistic pleasures (those of the ego within itself) and relational pleasures (those of the ego in its experience of relations).

The Narcissistic Pleasures of Right Action

The most basic narcissistic pleasure of right action is the pleasure found in the action itself. To act is to live: "Life and pleasure make up a single, inseparable pair."[52] Our powers demand to be exercised and to have their full potentialities actuated, just as the seed tends toward the fruit. The attainment of this goal, if one is aware of it, brings the experience of joy.[53] This is a pleasure which St. Thomas considers to be divinizing, since it brings to fulfillment in us the image and likeness of God. "As the being of God is his action, the supreme likeness of man to God is accomplished in an action. This is why felicity or beatitude, by which man attains to the supreme degree of likeness to God, and which is the end of human life, consists in an action."[54]

But the pleasure of the virtuous person is not the pleasure which accompanies any and every kind of action; it is, rather, the pleasure he experiences in acting in accordance with what is most specific and personal to him and with the greatest possible truthfulness to what he is and wants to become. His pleasure is the "happiness of growth," the "happiness of development," of which Teilhard de Chardin speaks.[55]

This kind of development means a struggle: "the humanization of nature" is the first step in a conquest.[56] A will to power of a Nietzschean kind is at work in it, and this is the source of pleasure for the ego which derives from success in this struggle a confidence in its own powers. "It can be very reassuring to the ego to overcome what is ugly, painful, evil, unharmonious, defective, to make up what is lacking, sew up the wounds, fill in the gaps, and thus achieve control of evil objects and obliteration of castration."[57]

The moral life is not of the speculative order; it consists in action. As Aristotle remarked long ago: "Just as in the Olympic Games it is not the handsomest or strongest who are crowned but those who compete (for it is from this group that the winners come), so too those who act win, and justly so, whatever is fine and good in life."[58]

Right action is victorious action by the loving mind, or intelligent love, and the pleasures of this kind of action "regulate" the pleasures of the passions, with a view not to extinguishing them but to drawing them up into a specifically human and personal harmony.

Whether we speak with Freud of the control or taming of the instincts by the higher powers, or with St. Thomas of a "sovereignty" of intelligent love (which he calls will) over the passions, the point being made is the same: the human being who wishes to be truly human must "temper" or even rein in his or her passional pleasures that are too uncontrolled, in order that these may be experienced in their relational truth.

Even a partial success in this struggle is the source of pleasures which I regard as of the same order as the "finer and higher" pleasures which Freud assigns to the activities of the spirit and to science and art.[59] It was doubtless because Freud did not greatly concern himself with such pleasures that he could make this pessimistic remark: "But so long as virtue is not rewarded here on earth, ethics will, I fancy, preach in vain."[60] But suppose virtue is in fact rewarded with a pleasure of high quality?[61]

The only pleasure Freud seems to attribute to right action is the satisfaction conferred by "the sense of self-esteem," a primary sentiment that develops in the little child. For when a child is forced to recognize his own weakness and imperfection, his self-love and illusory sense of omnipotence are profoundly shaken. The child can then go on loving himself only by projecting an "ideal ego" which is endowed with all perfections (the likewise illusory perfections which he attributes to his parents). Even a partial attainment of this idea is a source of narcissistic satisfaction.[62]

To this Freud adds the satisfactions of the superego:

> When the Ego has made the sacrifice to the Super-ego of renouncing an instinctual satisfaction, it expects to be rewarded by being loved all the more. The consciousness of deserving this love is felt as pride. At a time when the authority was not yet internalized as Super-ego, the relation between the threatened loss of love and the instinctual demand would have been the same. A feeling of security and satisfaction results if out of love to one's parents one achieves an instinctual renunciation. This good feeling could acquire the peculiar narcissistic character of pride only after the authority itself had become part of the Ego.[63]

The result of this is an "increase of self-confidence" and a "progress in spirituality,"[64] such as came to the people of Israel who, "happy in their conviction of possessing truth [and] overcome by the consciousness of being the chosen, came to value highly all intellectual and ethical achievements."[65] This kind of progress in intellectual and ethical life "is accompanied by an extraordinarily high degree of narcissistic enjoyment, owing to its presenting the ego with a fulfillment of the latter's old wish for omnipotence."[66]

From the psychoanalytic standpoint there can be no question of eliminating all narcissism, even primary, from human action.

> The development of the ego consists in a departure from the primary narcissism and results in a vigorous attempt to recover it. This departure is brought about by means of the displacement of libido to an ego-ideal imposed from without, while gratification is derived from the attainment of this ideal.[67]

According to Ferenczi (in his book *Thalassa*), coitus itself makes it possible to satisfy the narcissistic desire to return to the mother's womb and recover the relationship of fusion. Janine Chasseguet-Smirgel comments on this as follows: "The high point of human development thus contains a promise of a return to the maternal womb, that is, to the most archaic phase of the glorious past (of that time when we were our own ideal). But between these two moments the entire psychosexual evolution of the person has taken place."[68]

There is therefore no question of eliminating all narcissistic satisfaction from right action, if for no other reason than that the ideal ego plays a part in maturation.[69]

On the other hand, it is only too true that to settle for the primary narcissism aspect of this pleasure is to fall into the trap of that "good conscience," that moral self-satisfaction which is so accurately brought to light in the parable of the Pharisee and the tax collector (Lk 18:9–14). The Pharisee is there depicted as a lost person, precisely because he derives self-satisfaction from the consoling sight of his own good works and is thereby led to compare himself with other men and to scorn them.[70]

It is possible, nonetheless, to derive from right action pleasures which, however narcissistic, are not narcissistic in the same way in which they were for the Pharisee of the parable, just as it is possible to experience sexual pleasures that transcend the level of the primary narcissism associated with the relation of fusion.

The pleasures of wrong action are revealing in the other direction. This is especially true of the pleasure found in the rebellion of the instincts against the control of the higher powers and especially of the superego, whose aggressiveness gives rise to a counteraggressiveness,[71] that shown in the effort to achieve freedom from the compulsions of the superego and the anxiety caused by guilt.

This accounts for "the irresistibility of perverse instincts, and perhaps the attraction in general of forbidden things."[72]

This is one of the major components of eroticism according to Georges Bataille. The latter makes his own "a universally valid truth" enunciated by Baudelaire: "I say the unique and supreme pleasure of love lies in the certainty of doing *evil*. And men and women know from birth that all pleasure is to be found in evil."[73] And, as a matter of fact, many human beings are fascinated by the pleasure of the "forbidden transgression" and of the subjection of the spirit to the flesh:

> In fact, the individual splits up and his unity is shattered from the first instant of the sexual crisis. Just then the plethoric life of the body comes up against the mind's resistance. Even an apparent harmony is not enough; beyond consent the convulsions of the flesh demand silence and the spirit's absence. The physical urge is curiously foreign to human life, loosed without reference to it so long as it remains silent and keeps away. The being yielding to that urge is human no longer but, like the beasts, a prey of blind forces in action, wallowing in blindness and oblivion.[74]

Such is the most giddying and most specific of the pleasures of wrong action. After remarking that "genitality insofar as it is a definitive reconciliation of the person with himself" is of the order of the ideal and therefore, if thus presented, has an element of illusion in it, Madame Chasseguet-Smirgel writes:

> Conversely, a refusal to allow human tenderness to accomplish the synthesis of the instincts among themselves and of the instincts thus unified with tenderness is even more based on illusion. At issue here would be the very ideas of development and maturation (and therefore difference); there would be an attempt to *abolish the distance* (between desire and satisfaction, between ego and ideal) by denying its very existence.[75]

It is in the nature of things that a human being should take the step "in development from (secondary) narcissism to object-love."[76] This object-love develops thanks to the functioning of the higher powers which regulate behavior according to the reality principle which lies beyond the blind pleasure principle.

This passage from primary ego to secondary ego depends on an understanding of reality as it is (in order then either to submit to it or to change it) and on the investment of libido in objects external to the ego. Only when "the task of the higher strata of the mental apparatus . . . has been accomplished would it be possible for the dominance of the pleasure principle (and of its modification, the reality principle) to proceed unhindered."[77]

I conclude from all this that it is possible for a human being to control his or her primary instincts (up to a certain point) thanks to the action of the pleasure principle (in its mature form, namely, the reality principle). In right action it is possible to move beyond the pleasures of the narcissistic primary ego (ideal ego) and of submission to authority (superego) and experience pleasures that are on the level of the secondary ego. The latter pleasures are those of Eros, which seeks unity in the self and outside the self: 'The aim of [Eros] is to establish ever greater unities and to preserve them thus."[78] These are pleasures proper to the *kalokagathos*.

The Relational Pleasures of Right Action

I consider it of basic importance to have a clear grasp of the extent to which desire and pleasure are structured by and in their relation to the other and by the reality of others. Need I remind the reader that the Latin word *affectus* has relation as part of its primary meaning? This relational structure has to be developed so that in a mature subject it becomes what is now usually called oblativity; the person does not cease to love himself (secondary narcissism), but he also experiences desire and pleasure that have their center outside of himself; his libido is in large part invested outside himself.

In emphasizing the relational character of pleasure I am at one, it seems, with contemporary essays in a "new morality," especially those concerned with a morality of reciprocity.[79]

The morality of reciprocity owes a good deal to the philosophy of existence in which the stress is placed on being-for-others, that is, on the ontological status of the subject in its relation to others[80] and on the irreducible reality of the individual (Kierkegaard). But the inspiration for this morality is not limited to philosophy; it can appeal to observations made by the human sciences and by psychoanalysis in particular. The evangelical morality of charity can only find itself more firmly grounded on such human bases as these.

There is no doubt, of course, that desire and pleasure in their primitive state are very much centered on the emerging ego of the child: Freud observed as early as 1900 that "children are completely egoistic,"[81] as is the primary ego,[82] whereas the secondary ego is altruistic.[83] "The development of the individual seems to be a product of the interaction between two urges, the urge towards happiness, which we usually call 'egoistic,' and the urge towards union with others in the community, which we call 'altruistic.' "[84]

Freud considers "egoistic" and "altruistic" to be "superficial" descriptions. They do nonetheless point to a reality: the fact that "in the development of mankind as a whole, just as in individuals, love alone acts as the civilizing factor in the sense that it brings a change from egoism to altruism."[85]

These metapsychological considerations are based on observation of psychological facts. If from the beginning the pleasure of the individual is correlative with the pleasure of another, then as the ego develops, it can invest its desires and pleasures in one or more "objects" outside of itself. "The capacity for the radiation of libido towards other persons in object-investment must, of course, be ascribed to all normal people."[86] But the actuation of the capacity requires a lengthy developmental process: "At the very beginning, the external world, objects, and that which was hated were one and the same thing."[87]

The developmental process is possible only because libido can undergo "displacements." As a result, libido turns, in particular, into a tenderness thanks to which sexuality acquires a capacity for duration which it does not have by itself: "It is the fate of sensual love to become extinguished when it is satisfied; for it to be able to last, it must from the beginning be mixed with purely affectionate components—with such, that is, as are inhibited in their aims."[88] Freud remarks with good reason that tenderness is the "personal factor of a love relation."[89]

But if tenderness is to play its part, the libidinal tendencies must be partially desexualized and sublimated, so as to allow "a destruction and abrogation of the [Oedipus-] complex."[90] "One who cannot do this falls into a neurosis."[91]

I infer from this that the inability to experience pleasure (sexual or desexualized) in its relational dimension must be regarded as a symptom of a neurosis or a stasis in the maturation process. This seems to be the case with the proponents of "sexual liberation." François Chirpaz has some remarks that are very much to the point:

> By asserting the primacy of satisfaction and of the search for it, the sexual revolution liberates individuals; but it offers them only a fascination with immediate freedom. It does not transform the problem but only turns it around. It reduces sexuality to a matter of pleasure alone. But pleasure is not the whole of meaning. What gives pleasure meaning, what establishes it in its meaning as pleasure, is the encounter to which it invites and calls. A refusal to understand pleasure as an adequate degree of satisfaction is, therefore, not a rejection of pleasure as such but rather an assertion that desire looks beyond satisfaction to a plenitude which only an encounter with another in that other's personal being can ground. The temptation and danger of pleasure is that it may assert itself while forgetting the other.[92]

When pleasure is healthy and has its full meaning, it is a relation to another, to others, in their "otherness" (that by reason of which they are other than, and external to, me) and their "strangeness" (that by reason of which they are different—sex, race, mentality, etc.). It is possible to accept others in this way only to the extent that the ego experiences their otherness and strangeness not as threatening (as a schizophrenic or a paranoiac and a person who is held captive by primary narcissism does), but instead as stimulating and as invitations to explore the unfathomable depths of each human being.

Even if the other be in fact a threat, even if he or she be an "enemy," the gospel requires us to love that person,[93] that is, to cultivate with him or her a relation that lies on the other side of conflict —since persons in conflict do, after all, live an intense relationship that is laden with complex and ambiguous affects.[94] Gospel morality requires that the relation of conflict should not keep us from seeing this enemy as a person: "Bless those who curse you."[95] For "whatever you wish that men would do to you, do so to them; for this is the law and the prophets."[96] We must overcome the (more or less conscious) murderous impulse the other awakens in us; we must not exclude him but allow him to exist as a person:

To allow the other to exist means to judge that he deserves to exist; that, whatever he may be, and however disconcerting or wounding his attitude may be, it is nonetheless better for him to be and live than not to be. In other words, to let him exist means to *begin* by not excluding him and not wishing (unconsciously, of course) that he might not be there but might disappear and even never have been born. . . .

The primary "love" which the other needs is that I should tell him, not in words but by my entire attitude: "I prefer that you should exist." It is clear that any moral judgment on the other which falls short of this elementary affirmation is outside the sphere of the gospel and outside of any authentic "humanness."[97]

In this way human pleasure is given its proper direction: it must be lived as part of a relation to the other as he or she is.

This calls for a firmly established dominance of the reality principle over the pleasure principle. The situation is the same in the relational life of right action as in scientific research, where the first and basic requirement is that the student should observe facts in as objective a way as possible and not confuse reality with hypotheses or theories, however attractive these may be and however filled with promises of glory for their inventor.

If it be true that "every act of knowledge has for precondition an act of libidinal investment,"[98] then it is much more true when there is question of knowing persons as they really are—and not as we might want them to be for the sake of our personal satisfaction, conscious and unconscious.

A firmly established dominance of the reality principle is needed if we are to recognize persons not only for what they are but also for what they are not (as yet?). "The real is not only what is but also all that is lacking to it, all that it must become."[99]

In order to attain this kind of objectivity and oblativity in personal relations and thus experience one of the pleasures most specific to right action, the ego must see to it that the reality principle holds sway over the psyche.

Even at the point of origin of the ego the instincts "required an object."[100] Francis Pasche suggests "anti-narcissism" as a term for designating "the more or less distant external goal and destination of the libido."[101] Once the purely narcissistic stage has been succeeded by the object stage, pleasure and pain signify a relation of the ego to an object.[102] In the beginning, the object of instinct for a child is hallucinatory; a poor distinction is made between internal and external; object relations are of the type in which the body of the child and the body of the mother are fused. This first and original type of relation will never be forgotten and will continue to exert an unconscious influence in the adult. But to the extent that the ego becomes a "reality-ego," its affective investment is made in objects which it recognizes as external to it, even though this very recognition is inevitably mediated by the image or representation it has of the object. The "real" is something in the realm of necessity (anankē): something that is there and resists my desires "but that nonetheless forms the network of meanings in and through which the subject is constituted."[103]

In its relations with objects, the ego cannot avoid experiencing a radical disillusionment, for in these relations it seeks—in vain—to have once again the pleasure, now impossible and forbidden, which it once had in its fusional relation with its first object (the mother's body). The result is the "nostalgia for the lost object," the "lack," the "narcissistic wound," which psychoanalysts observe in their patients.

It is this nostalgia for "the green paradises of childish loves" that spurs the ego to revive its primary narcissism and its centripetal way of relating to objects. But that kind of solution leads to an inhibition or regression of the libido.[104] It means a return to the archaic processes of the libido: fusional relations, oral satisfactions in which the other is devoured, the magical omnipotence of desire, a flight into the imaginary and illusory, an excessive dependence on the object,[105] an inability to endure frustrations, sadistic[106] and masochistic[107] reactions, an "adhesiveness" of the libido,[108] and so on.

Like an army that meets with defenses and counterattacks it cannot overcome, and then retires to positions already won in which it can barricade itself securely, the libido withdraws from objects that cause it intolerable frustrations, and retires within itself. After having overvalued its external object, the libido now overvalues the ego, which is blown out of proportion in the imaginary and illusory world of the ideal ego.[109]

This stasis or regression of the libido is a predisposition for neurosis:

> People fall ill of a neurosis when the possibility of satisfaction for the libido is removed from them—they fall ill in consequence of a "frustration" . . . and their symptoms are actually substitutes for the missing satisfaction. This of course does not mean that every frustration in regard to libidinal satisfaction makes everyone who meets with it neurotic, but merely that in cases of neurosis investigated, the factor of frustration was demonstrable.[110]

Frustrations are inevitable; they can induce illness or, on the contrary, they may help to maturity, depending on the way they are handled (which means: according to the "peculiarities" of the individual) and on the "nature of the frustration":

The frustration is very rarely a comprehensive and absolute one; in order to have a pathogenic effect it would probably have to strike at the only form of satisfaction which that person desires, the only form of which he is capable. In general, there are very many ways by which it is possible to endure lack of libidinal satisfaction without falling ill.[111]

This multiplicity of ways is possible because of the plasticity of the sexual-impulse excitations: "One of them can step in in place of another; if satisfaction of one is denied in reality, satisfaction of another can offer full recompense."[112]

The sublimation of the instincts is the process most frequently adopted; it allows the ego to develop on the basis of the very frustrations themselves. For the ego can gain access to the secondary processes and achieve dominance of the reality principle only if it faces up to the unavoidable fact that at the goal of desires there is "the emptiness of lack"; the lost object (the mother's body) is truly lost.[113]

It is then that the libido can, in a supple and quite varied manner, be distributed between ego and objects. The secondary narcissism is precisely this return to the ego of the libido invested in external objects.[114] Dr. Luquet notes that "when the libido returns to the ego, it retains its objectal character."[115] Love of self is no longer primarily centripetal. The ego, which has not become a "reality ego," is capable of investing part of its libido in external objects precisely as external: the libido activates its centrifugal dimension.[116]

It is to this order that the pleasures of right action belong; that is, they show the characteristics of the secondary narcissism. This kind of narcissism is genuine; the investments of the libido in objects enrich the ego libido in their own way: "If the ego is richly invested, in part through the play of assimilative introjection, then it loves itself as it feels loved; its need of idealized representation is greatly reduced."[117] A certain self-love is necessary and fruitful. This is already true at the level of the primary narcissism, which is "guardian of life";[118] all the more, then, is it true of the satisfactions of the secondary narcissism. Piera Castoriadis-Aulagnier sees in these a pleasure which "identifies" the ego.[119]

Once again, this access to the free operation of the secondary processes is possible only at the (never fully reached) end of frustrations. This is a "bitter experience of life,"[120] but one that makes possible pleasures which, being no longer turned in on themselves, are only the better for this: the pleasures of right action. Only when

the task of the higher strata of the mental apparatus . . . has been accomplished would it be possible for the dominance of the pleasure principle (and of its modification, the reality principle) to proceed unhindered. Till then, the other task of the mental apparatus, the task of mastering or binding excitations, would have precedence—not, indeed, in *opposition* to the pleasure principle, but independently of it and to some extent in disregard of it.[121]

It is a fact that this dominance of the higher levels over the instincts means a reduction in the intensity of pleasures. What is gained in "quality" is lost in quantity of energy.[122] At this level there is question no longer of the effects of repression or other processes of evasion, but of a "rejection based on judgement."[123] As we gradually gain control of our instinctual life, "we are more and more inclined to renounce as unprofitable the formation or retention of such intense wishes as children know" because we see them as empty,[124] or dangerous,[125] or destructive of love,[126] or because the intelligent ego, with its awareness of possibilities, chooses to defer the acquisition of pleasure: "The patient need merely renounce such gratifications as will inevitably be detrimental to him; he need only temporarily abjure, only learn to exchange an immediate source of pleasure for one better assured though longer delayed."[127]

The pleasures of right action are, then, those of the "purified pleasure ego": "Thus the original *reality-ego*, which distinguished outer and inner by means of a sound objective criterion, changes into a purified *pleasure-ego*, which prizes above all else the quality of pleasure."[128]

Freud does not tell us from what this reality ego has been "purified." Perhaps his meaning is that the ego is no longer fascinated by the intensity of the primary narcissistic pleasure and that it appreciates "above all else" the quality of the pleasure which comes to it from its relational life with persons known and loved as they really are. This quality of pleasure would be comparable to the satisfactions which Freud sees in artistic creation and the discovery of truth and which, using an image, he recognizes as being "finer and higher."[129]

Specific though these pleasures of right action are, the "purified reality ego" is not on that account incapable of experiencing primary affects such as pleasures at the unconscious level which become pains at the conscious level. For example, the dynamic manifestation of repressed elements (unconscious pleasure) is experienced as a pain by the conscious ego. "Unpleasure for one system" is "simultaneously satisfaction for the other."[130]

Whatever be the complexities of human pleasures, those that are accessible to the purified reality ego are characterized by an appreciation of their quality and a preference for them on that ground, despite their lesser intensity. In the experience of these relational pleasures, the emphasis is on the other.[131] The ego finds itself enriched therein, even though in safeguarding and developing this quality, sufferings and sacrifices are inevitable. "Happiness is in encounter," says Daniel Lagache. "To be happy means having full experience of

joys but also of failures, griefs, misfortunes."[132] The "love of truth,"
to use an expression of Freud,[133] is a source of relational pleasure,
whatever the pains it may entail:

> Instead [of satisfaction by means of hallucination] the mental appa-
> ratus had to decide to form a conception of the real circumstances in
> the outer world and to exert itself to alter them. A new principle of
> mental functioning was thus introduced; what was conceived of was
> no longer that which was pleasant, but that which was real, even if it
> should prove unpleasant.[134]

There could be no better description of the pleasures of right action.
One final remark, but a very important one if morality is to be
faithful to the reality of the person: the relation experienced in pleasure is two-directional. There is a pleasure to be found in giving
pleasure. My desire is awakened by the desire of the other and responds to it.
The reality involved here is a very primitive one!

> A healthy child and a healthy mother are so well adapted each to the
> other that a single action inevitably brings gratification to both. Some
> good examples one might cite: giving the breast and sucking, caressing
> and being caressed, and so on. For a time, therefore, a healthy child
> feels that there is no conflict of interest—and in fact there is none at
> all—between himself and his environment; that is, he and his environ-
> ment blend together.[135]

The process of maturation, which makes it possible to discover
and acknowledge the other in his external and unique reality, only
enriches the two-directional relational character of desire and pleasure: "Human desire is established . . . under the sign of mediation.
It is a desire to have his desire acknowledged. It has a desire for its
object, the desire of others."[136]
Evangelical morality does justice—and more than justice—to this
relational character of the desire for pleasure.
The gospels teach us that the "favor" or "good pleasure" (eudokia)
of God the Father rests on his Son[137]—who for his part always does
what pleases his Father.[138]
It is the Father's desire and pleasure to proclaim the Good News to
the human beings with whom he is "pleased."[139] It is his good pleasure to "give the kingdom" to those who seek it.[140] It has pleased
him to make us his adopted children[141] and to make known to us his
plan for us[142] or the "mystery" of his will.[143]
The desire of Christ's disciples responds to this desire on God's
part, as they seek to be "fully pleasing to him."[144] Their ambition is
to please him[145] and to please others.[146] In this ambition they find
the inspiration and rule of their behavior: "We do what pleases
him,"[147] while rejecting pleasures alien or contrary to this relation.[148]

This reciprocity in giving pleasure is the central aim of any morality that seeks to be faithful both to the reality of the human person and to the gospel.

Chapter 12

What of the Law?

A morality based on the right use of pleasure has its laws: these are basically endogenous, but there are exogenous ones as well. By its intrinsically relational character, this morality involves a reference to others and the Other. However, it also involves a reference to laws promulgated by political and religious authorities.

The morality of pleasure does not neglect law; it simply puts it in its proper place. It does not make law the first and unquestioned foundation of morality, as seems to have been the case for centuries, if we judge by the "cult" of Roman and Napoleonic law and the almost complete absorption of morality by law.[1]

The place of law is relative in two ways. On the one hand, it is neither the source nor the primary rule of the moral life;[2] on the other, even jurists recognize that written law has its source in the "customs and usages" of a society. Custom is located in the realm of public opinion and brings with it "a conviction, in the minds of those affected, that they are *obliged* to act as they do (*opinio necessitatis*)."[3]

In Aristotle's view, law derives its force from custom.[4] Within the Church it is acknowledged, as St. Augustine thought centuries ago, that "the morals of the people of God are to be taken as laws."[5] What comes first, and is basic, is a way in which people deal with one another, a set of morals, an ethos, an ideology; they find expression and are institutionalized in written law, but they can also cause the application of a given law to become antiquated. Even for jurists, therefore, written law is not an absolute; it is relative in its source, its manner of obligation, and its application.

This is all the more true for the moralist.

According to Aristotle, morality is the "science of the actions that go on in life"[6] and its method must therefore be inductive: it moves from facts to theory.

In his critique of the opinions and theories of his age and his Greek milieu, Aristotle examines those of the "wise men": "In summary, these opinions and theories deserve some credence, but in the final analysis truth in the practical realm is derived from facts and life, for these are the most important thing."[7]

This is why Aristotle bases his morality on a critical observation of views. His point of reference is the moral judgment of the elderly and the wise. "I conclude that we ought to set great store by the statements and views of experienced people, the elderly, and men of wisdom, indemonstrable though these statements and views may be, and ought to treat them as though they were proven truths; for experience has given these persons an 'eye' that enables them to see things correctly."[8]

But, even more than the elderly, it is the "virtuous" who provide the best criterion:

> In each branch of moral activity, the virtuous person judges correctly; in each, things appear to him as what they really are. For each habitual state has its own objects which are beautiful and pleasurable to the virtuous person, and the trait that best distinguishes the virtuous person from every other is undoubtedly his ability to see what is true in each branch of activity, since he is himself as it were the norm and measure.
>
> The majority of people, on the contrary, deceive themselves, and the source of their error is, in all likelihood, pleasure; even when this is not a good, they regard it as one.[9]

In short, the criterion of virtue is defined by the "judicious man": "Virtue, then, is an attitude of the will and consists in a just mean that is relative to us and is defined according to a rational principle and as a judicious man would define it."[10]

When we take as the rule and measure of morality the behavior and judgment of a judicious and virtuous person, we are connecting morality with the morals and opinions of a social milieu, while at the same time being critical of the latter and avoiding both a sheeplike conformism and the counterdependence shown in a rejection we have not been able to overcome.

It is practice, so dear to Marxism, that has been revitalizing this referential aspect of morality[11] which so many centuries of deductive morality had obscured but which St. Thomas did not overlook[12] and Melchior Cano included among his "theological sources."[13]

The thing that holds first place, both in time and as the perduring basis of an experiential morality, is the mores of the human family and group into which each individual is born and within which he or she develops.

Every civilization and every culture give structure to the mentalities[14] and ideologies of its members, as well as to their ways of being present in the world and comporting themselves. As a result, morals are a profound and enduring part of each civilization as a whole and of the more specialized cultures of regions and social groups (esprit de corps, class spirit, spirit of a particular profession, and so on).

A typical example of the social pressure that regulates morality is provided by what we call "fashion." I am thinking here not only of fashions in clothing,[15] but also of fashions in housing and furnishings, work and leisure, holidays, social rituals, funerals, variations in masculine and feminine behavior,[16] and sexual life.[17] There are also fashions in the arts, literature, the sciences, philosophy, theology, and pastoral theory and practice. There are fashions in language, in what is accepted as good manners, and so on.

And who can evade the demands of all these fashions? In fact, do people want to escape them? Are they not only too happy to submit to them in order to "keep up to date"?

The influence of the milieu on morals is also a factor in the ideologies of the various social classes and generations. Those whom we group together as "the young" share a common mentality that finds expression in clothing, vocabulary, the rejection of "bourgeois" society, leftist leanings, the rejection of marriage as an institution, the use of drugs, and so on. Where do such attitudes and mores come from except from their milieu?[18]

At quite a different level, that of the missions, we are becoming aware of the great importance of the cultural milieu in the various "foreign" countries (foreign to the Western world) and of the need for respecting that milieu in the effort to bring into existence in each country a suitable way of receiving and practicing the gospel.[19]

What is true of each milieu is also true of each human being: "To the extent that Jesus becomes for me a vital issue, a being whose identity conditions the meaning of life for me (and he ceases to be simply an indifferent object of study, even exegetical study), I go to him, and interpret him, with all of my experience, all of my moral and political choices, my entire social and cultural situation, and all of my 'a prioris.' "[20]

We are now beginning to take serious account of the important role which the experience of life plays in the regulation of morals.[21] My only purpose in mentioning it here is to shift the emphasis to practice, and thus reduce law and laws to their rightful place. They are not primary, but play only a secondary role in the spread of morals, even when the latter are viewed as having a character of obligation. Bergsom wrote: "It is for closed, simple societies that the moral structure, original and fundamental in man, is made. I grant that the organic tendencies do not stand out clearly in our consciousness. They constitute, nevertheless, the strongest element in obligation."[22]

Social pressure imposes models, "idols," conformisms to which the individual must bend, like it or not, in order to feel accepted and approved by others. We need think only of the "American way of life" or Mao's China or, in Western history, the spirit of chivalry,[23] and later on, the spirit of the "decent man" or the morality of honor or the Jansenist or the Victorian mentality. The eyes of others on us is indeed the essential point of reference, as Baudelaire, who wanted to be a "dandy," observed: "The Dandy should aspire to be sublime, continually. He should live and sleep in front of a mirror."[24]

Even what we call the "milieu" has its laws, which are neither written nor promulgated and yet bind under penalty of death. Every social or professional milieu exerts a pressure and demands a conformity[25] that can reach the point of tyranny: "The tyranny of opinion (and what opinion) is as fatuous in the small towns of France as it is in the United States of America."[26]

The extraordinary development of the mass media further intensifies, for better or for worse, the power of such social pressures and fashions.[27] This is but one more reason for acknowledging their power, both for stabilizing the mores of a people and for altering them—and thus, morality with them.

The moral regulation exercised by the social pressures of public opinion is all the more compelling, and even tyrannical, in that it is not generally felt as such. On the contrary, conformity to it brings pleasure and the security of successful integration into society. The individual regulates his conduct by "what is done" and "what is not done"; he feels himself constantly under the eye and judgment of others. It is in the mirror held up by others that he can attain his own identity, the character he is to play, his role in society.

"The 'exaltation or intensification of emotion' produced in every member of [a group]"[28] becomes a vital necessity for the individual if he is to escape the anxiety roused in him by the threat of exclusion from the society of his fellows. Freud was right in saying that " 'social anxiety' is the essence of what is called conscience."[29]

Woe, indeed, is he who is not "like the others," who is not "normal."[30] He feels—and is—outcast, ridiculed, hated, excommunicated.[31] The collective superego (which is the internalization in the subject of the rules and prohibitions of the familial and social milieu) imposes terrible demands on the ego that wants to avoid blame, loss of self-confidence, and guilt. "To the ego . . . living means the same as being loved—being loved by the super-ego."[32]

Maurice Bellet gives a full description of this human milieu that surrounds and structures every individual from birth and outside of which the individual cannot attain to full humanness.[33] He sums up this milieu as "the weight of the world" and analyzes the process it follows in terms of an interpretation by "the englobing":

The englobing is constitutive for the subject. . . . It is through it that he can know himself as part of his world, feel himself, define himself, and so on; it renders him the well-known service of "being there" so that he may have a place and means of existing. But the englobing gives being to the subject only in accordance with its own procedure; the subject must adopt a suitable form. Personages, roles and functions; possible images of "myself"; mirrors constantly held up so that one may know who one is. At a deeper level: an index of viable ways, statutes and approaches and of ideals: the man who wishes to be more a man has set before him the "perfection" he is to reach.[34]

As constitutive of the subject, the englobing milieu is "the possible human space."[35] But it locks the subject into itself; it excludes and suppresses "what must be left outside . . . what it cannot bear to see."[36]

To free oneself from it is impossible: it recoups any losses all too easily. It can be transcended only by a regression to what is "prior to it," to what Maurice Bellet calls the "primordial":

In this context the primordial means a reversal. The crossing over is not, of course, a simple transgression of the englobing interpretation; it means the *appearance* of the other, the unforeseen, the more distant —the re-opening signified by the "metaphors" used for the primordial. And the real *limit* is precisely here: in the fact that man is a body, even in his mind (people speak, quite appropriately, of a body of teaching, a body of texts). It is *this* closure, caused by his birth, that he must acknowledge; then the world is *open*, and the walls he has built no longer stand around him.[37]

"The primordial founding is creative. Therefore it excludes. . . . It cannot fail to exclude that which would suppress it, i.e., the process of englobing interpretation *insofar* as this denies the very thing it rightly claims to bring about, viz., the genesis of man."[38]

An odd kind of limit, and different in kind from the limit dear to an englobing interpretation: since it is in no way a barrier, a wall, but is rather space for living. As the end of the will to power, it is potency. Therefore, to go on perceiving it as a prohibition, as a compulsion, is to be really absent from the place where it operates. The primordial limit opens up the greatest possibility and is indeed identical with this.[39]

I see in Maurice Bellet's analysis of the englobing and the primordial (which I have presented all too sketchily), a valuable key enabling the moralist to gain some understanding and practice in the right use of the mores of a human milieu and of the openness of these to what lies beyond a closed, englobing morality.

Bellet's analyses also help in locating the role of law and its proper use in mores and morality.

No society can live without laws, without a code that is promulgated by an authority which possesses its necessary juridical apparatus, its sanctions—and its police.

This is a necessity that affects Christians, not only as members of a political society, but also as members of the ecclesial community. The latter too must have its laws, these being necessitated by the fact that the members are not completely evangelized and that there still remains in them "the law of sin which dwells in my members" (Rom 7:23), or, in other words, pleasure-as-idol and its falsifying power which seems indeed to be present in human nature.[40]

Law is necessary in order "to enter life" (Mt 18:8), and for this reason, "not an iota, not a dot, will pass from the law until all is accomplished" (Mt 5:18): that is, until the end of the "world."

But at this point we should recall that a law of human nature (as "wounded" since the original fall) impels a person to misuse (political and, even more, religious) law so as to find in it a self-satisfaction which bestows a sense of security. At work here is the attraction of the world and a way of life "according to the flesh." "Beware of the leaven of the Pharisees, which is hypocrisy" (Lk 12:1).

This corrupt way of observing the law locks human beings into themselves. Moreover, like every prohibition, it incites rebellion: "If it had not been for the law, I should not have known sin" (Rom 7:7).

In the mythical story of the original sin, it is the prohibition, misleadingly interpreted by the tempter, that awakens in Eve the desire to disobey a divine-authority-that-is-jealous-of-its-rights. "I should not have known what it is to covet if the law had not said, 'You shall not covet.' But sin, finding opportunity in the commandment, wrought in me all kinds of covetousness. Apart from the law, sin lies dead. I was once alive apart from the law, but when the commandment came, sin revived and I died" (Rom 7:7–10).

In this perspective, the terrible accusations which Christ makes against the Pharisees and the teachers of the law reveal their full meaning. These "lawyers" are "without understanding," they are "blind guides" and "hypocrites,"[41] who are destined to be punished in Gehenna. They deserve such accusations because they have turned the law into an absolute: in their eyes, man is for the sabbath (which then becomes an idol), whereas in fact "the sabbath was made for man" (Mk 2:27). The law should lead to God, being "the key of knowledge," but in fact the lawyers have not entered themselves and have tried to prevent others who wished to enter (Lk 11:52). This "hardness of heart" angers Christ: on a sabbath, when he intended to heal a sick man—something not allowed on that day—he "looked around at them with anger" (Mk 3:5).

Behind this legalism lies fear—an ancient fear dating from the sin of Eve and Adam—of the image they have created for themselves of a God who is a spy and a judge. Such a fear is no longer appropriate for those who have trusted in Jesus Christ, since in him they have access to knowledge of the Father and the true nature of his love as the one "who is rich in mercy" and has "made us alive together with Christ" (Eph 2:4–5).

"Do not be afraid," Christ says to Peter when, after the miraculous catch of fish, the latter has cried out, as any good Israelite would: "Depart from me, for I am a sinful man, O Lord" (Lk 5: 8–10). Later on, Peter will understand that the Father's messenger has come for sinners and not for the righteous (Mt 9:13).

This fear is a bad counselor, as the parable of the pounds makes clear. The man who had received only one pound to trade with had not touched it because, as he tells the master, "I was afraid of you, because you are a severe man; you take up what you did not lay down, and reap what you did not sow." The master answers him: "I will condemn you out of your own mouth, you wicked servant!" Everyone knows the sequel: "Take the pound from him, and give it to him who has the ten pounds. . . . To every one who has will more be given, but from him who has not, even what he has will be taken away" (Lk 19:20–26).

The Christian is no longer to fear but to believe in the mercy and love of God. "So it depends not upon man's will or exertion, but upon God's mercy" (Rom 9:16). When we confess our wretchedness to God, we open ourselves to his mercy. That is the point of the parable of the Pharisee and the tax collector, the latter being the most wretched type of individual to be found at that time: a false brother, a revenue agent for the pagan occupying power, and, in addition, a robber of his fellow Jews. Nonetheless he is "justified," while the Pharisee finds self-satisfaction and a false sense of security in the display of his "good works" (Lk 18:9–14).

Such, then, is God's plan:

> And you he made alive, when you were dead through the trespasses and sins in which you once walked, following the course of this world, following the prince of the power of the air, the spirit that is now at work in the sons of disobedience. Among these we all once lived in the passions of our flesh, following the desires of body and mind, and so we were by nature children of wrath, like the rest of mankind. But God, who is rich in mercy, out of the great love with which he loved us, even when we were dead through our trespasses, made us alive together with Christ (Eph 2:1–5).

Justification is a free gift of God. In it he renews man in his own image and likeness and thus enables him to find once again the true

face of the Father who loves his children as, and better than, the
father of the prodigal son loved his child (Lk 15:22–32). Now
we "know the Father" (1 Jn 2:13). "He first loved us" (1 Jn 4:19;
cf. 4:10), "while we were yet sinners" (Rom 5:8). "So we know and
believe the love God has for us. God is love, and he who abides in
love abides in God, and God abides in him" (1 Jn 4:16). "All that I
have heard from my Father I have made known to you" (Jn 15:15).
Did not Christ have the reputation of being "a friend of tax collec-
tors and sinners" (Mt 11:19)?

This revelation of God as love is indeed Good News, for it means
a refashioning both of man himself and of his idea of God. The
knowledge given him is more than an abstract knowledge; it is a
"dwelling," and intimacy. "I made known to them thy name, and I
will make it known, that the love with which thou hast loved me
may be in them, and I in them" (Jn 17:26). There is a "rebirth." In
the new life now given, there is no more sin, for "no one born of
God commits sin" (1 Jn 3:9), while faith in the one the Father has
sent does away with judgment:

> For God sent the Son into the world, not to condemn the world, but
> that the world might be saved through him. He who believes in him is
> not condemned; he who does not believe is condemned already, be-
> cause he has not believed in the name of the only Son of God. And this
> is the judgment, that the light has come into the world, and men loved
> darkness rather than light, because their deeds were evil (Jn 3:17–19).

"The Father judges no one, but has given all judgment to the Son"
(Jn 5:22).[42] In this way, people are freed from fear of God and his
judgment. He is no longer a spy with his eye on human beings: he
loves them in the light which the Son brings to them. There is question no longer of commandments and prohibitions of the law, but of
hearing the word: "If any one hears my sayings and does not keep
them, I do not judge him; for I did not come to judge the world but
to save the world. He who rejects me and does not receive my sayings has a judge; the word that I have spoken will be his judge on the
last day" (Jn 12:47–48). The Spirit of the Father and the Son dwells
in us and frees us from fear and from the law: "If you are led by the
Spirit you are not under the Law" (Gal 5:18); "Christ redeemed us
from the curse of the law" (Gal 3:13), from the curse of God that dis-
missed Adam and Eve from the Garden of Eden and left them "confined under the law" (Gal 3:23).

As captives of the law, the Israelites were, by that very fact, captives of sin, since "the power of sin is the law" (1 Cor 15:56). Those
who are in Christ are freed from the law: "So speak and so act as
those who are to be judged under the law of liberty" (Jas 2:12). In
other words, God no longer judges them by reference to the works of
the law.

This shift also means that we must cease to judge one another (Rom 14:13), since we are all living under the rule of mercy:

> Be merciful, even as your Father is merciful. Judge not, and you will not be judged; condemn not, and you will not be condemned; forgive, and you will be forgiven; give, and it will be given to you; good measure, pressed down, shaken together, running over, will be put into your lap. For the measure you give will be the measure you get back (Lk 6:36–38).

"In passing judgment on [another] you condemn yourself" (Rom 2:1), for you are remaining under the domination of law and applying a measure that can only result in your own condemnation.

The person, then, who puts his or her hope and security in mercy and no longer in works and a "good conscience" is freed from the judgment of not only God, but also of human beings: "Why should my liberty be determined by another man's scruples?" (1 Cor 10:29). St. Paul writes:

> With me it is a very small thing that I should be judged by you or by any human court. I do not even judge myself. I am not aware of anything against myself, but I am not thereby acquitted. It is the Lord who judges me. Therefore do not pronounce judgment before the time, before the Lord comes (1 Cor 4:3–5).

It is in this way that the new law frees from the fear of judgment, whether it be the judgment of God or the judgment of people on one another and on themselves. This new law means faith in the love and mercy of God, as well as an active faith which takes shape in love of neighbor. Love of the brethren is "the fulfillment of the law" (cf. Rom 13:8), a "compendium" of it (cf. Mt 22:40), a touchstone for determining discipleship (Jn 13:35; 21:15–18), and the criterion to be used at the "last judgment" (Mt 25:31–46).

Truly, we are no longer under the rule of law and of salvation through works, but under the rule of love: the love of the Father for his children, the love of Christ for his "friends" (Jn 15:14), and the love of the disciples for one another and for all human beings. The criterion is: love much. This is clear from Christ's response to "a woman of the city, who was a sinner" (Lk 7:37–50). Her sins are forgiven her, "for she loved much." Undoubtedly she was seeking in her passing loves something absolute and was constantly disappointed; but at last she found the true absolute. The rich affection of her heart won out over a strict and rigid observance of the law. One who loves will be given the power to love more and better; one who does not love will be stripped even of what he has. Woe to the dried-up hearts that have been smothered and rendered sterile by the illusory security that comes from the works of the law! That is the lesson Christ reads to a Pharisee who received him as a guest—a lesson that does not seem to have been understood.

> The aim of our charge is love that issues from a pure heart and a good conscience and sincere faith. Certain persons by swerving from these have wandered away into vain discussion, desiring to be teachers of the law, without understanding either what they are saying or the things about which they make assertions (1 Tim 1:5–7).

Obedience to God is, beyond a doubt, fundamental: "As by one man's disobedience many were made sinners, so by one man's obedience many will be made righteous" (Rom 5:19). But this is the obedience of faith and of knowledge of a God who is love (Rom 1:5) and not an accuser.

Whoever believes in this God is also freed from fear. St. Augustine claims that "it is vain to think that one has overcome sin when one has avoided it solely from fear of punishment."[43] Faith in Christ frees us from such fear: We shall "reassure our hearts before him whenever our hearts condemn us; for God is greater than our hearts" (1 Jn 3:19–20).

Faith gives us access to the truth about God and ourselves and thus makes us both "free men" (cf. Jn 8:32) and new men (Col 3:10; etc.). We must cross this threshold if we are to begin to be true disciples of Christ.[44] This does not mean there is no law for us: "not being without law toward God but under the law of Christ" (1 Cor 9:21). Such is the law of the "new covenant, not in a written code but in the Spirit; for the written code kills, but the Spirit gives life" (2 Cor 3:6). The old law has lapsed, and "there is therefore now no condemnation for those who are in Christ Jesus. For the law of the Spirit of life in Christ Jesus has set me free from the law of sin and death. For God has done what the law, weakened by the flesh, could not do" (Rom 8:1–3).

"So . . . the law was our custodian until Christ came, that we might be justified by faith. But now that faith has come, we are no longer under a custodian" (Gal 3:24–25). If the law of the Spirit does not do away with all written law, it retains it only in order to place it at the service of life and thus render its observance possible: "If you love me, you will keep my commandments" (Jn 14:15), and "my commandments" does not exclude the commandments of the Decalogue. But the manner of observing the latter is now completely different. The law is no longer "added [to faith] because of transgressions" (Gal 3:19), for "the law is not laid down for the just but for the lawless and disobedient, for the ungodly and sinners . . ." (1 Tim 1:9).

Since the Christian has been saved by grace and mercy, and not by observance of the law, he now obeys the laws; not in order to gain

self-satisfaction nor as ends in themselves but, rather, as some of the
ways set before him of loving "in deed and in truth" (1 Jn 3:18), that
is, of acting as an "adopted son" and no longer as a slave. "For you
did not receive the spirit of slavery to fall back into fear, but you
have received the spirit of sonship," by reason of which we cry
"Abba! Father!" (Rom 8:15).

"For freedom Christ has set us free; stand fast therefore and do
not submit again to a yoke of slavery," (Gal 5:1), the yoke, that is, of
a law that has been turned into an absolute. As St. Thomas puts it,
"the essential thing in the new law is the grace of the Holy Spirit
which is manifested in faith that works through love [quae manifes-
tatur in fide per dilectionem operante]."[45]

The function of "external" law is to awaken and guide the "interi-
or" man (Rom 7:22) who "is being renewed every day" (2 Cor 4:16).
"Teaching from without has for its purpose to restore the interior
wellspring that directly gives water to the person."[46] "The function
of law is to lead men to virtue, not all at once but by degrees."[47]

The primordially internal nature of the new law does not mean
that it overlooks anything external which might be of help to it,[48]
but these external helps are secondary, says St. Thomas, in regard to
actions (facta), morality (moralia), and the sacraments (sacramen-
ta).[49] "It was not appropriate that the new law should add anything
to the old as far as external actions are concerned."[50]

The moral law is therefore secondary, at least for those who in
deed and in truth live the love which is the fruit of the Spirit, to such
an extent that they are freed from an idolatrous observance of the
written law and from fear. For others, the fear of punishment continues to be real. "He who fears is not perfected in love," for "perfect love casts out fear" (1 Jn 4:18).

This kind of fear, as well as the hope of "reward" in terms of
worldly values (good reputation, wealth, etc.), are "external" and
therefore alienating.[51] To be motivated by such fear and such hope is
to live "according to the flesh,"[52] and to be a slave of idols.

The Septuagint uses the Greek eidōlon to translate about thirty
different Hebrew words: vanity, nothing, lie, emptiness, false god,
and so on, thus giving us a good indication of what the idols, "the
works of human hands," are in which people find satisfaction and
pleasure. The Israelites in the wilderness built themselves a golden
calf as a god (Ex 32:1–6), and, says St. Stephen, they "rejoiced in the
works of their hands" (Acts 7:41).

"Perhaps they only go astray in their search for God and their eagerness to find him" (Wisd. 13:6 JB)? But, alas, they "went after
worthlessness, and became worthless" (Jer 2:5).

Westerners no longer sacrifice to the idols of the Semitic, Greek,
or Roman religions; they are, nonetheless, idolaters because they
find in the works of their hands (progress, economic power, science,

technologies, etc.) that which the idolaters of ancient times found in theirs; consequently, "the whole world is in the power of the evil one" (1 Jn 5:19).

I am convinced that to the degree in which the Western world has become (since the end of the Middle Ages) a world of trade, industry, banking, extensive urbanization, intensive exploitation of natural resources, and wealth, it has increased man's idolatrous concentration on himself. He is more "of the world" than ever before; he is the slave of cupidities that are all the more deceptive as they are more attractive. They do have a certain grandeur about them, but indulgence in them is controlled, as by a kind of fate,[53] by the idol of effective exploitation of nature and human beings. In all this I see the contemporary form of the attraction exercised by the Prince of this world, whose marvels are capable of leading astray, if possible, even the elect (Mt 24:24).

Man is thus alienated into the hands of powers which are in fact idols, and idols all the more deceitful in that they are not called idols and do not have a religious cultus paid to them. They are "idols not to be names" (Wis 14:27).

It is this factual state of affairs that brings out the full value of a morality based on the detached use of pleasure, as I have been describing it here.

I do not believe that the detached use of wealth will undermine all the efforts being made to secure a more equitable distribution of wealth.[54] On the contrary, it can lessen the obstacles which human greed throws in the way of such a distribution. I believe that this morality can liberate us from the alienation into which the world (both capitalist and socialist) is sinking. It alone is capable of dispelling the illusions created by the myth of economic wealth.

How can a Christian stand by, "rose in hand," and be heedless of people's struggles to free themselves from the dehumanizing pressures of a world which the Christian knows hates him (Jn 15:18–19) and to which he no longer wishes to belong insofar as it is a place of satanic illusions, even though he continues to live in its midst? "I do not pray that thou shouldst take them out of the world, but that thou shouldst keep them from the evil one. They are not of the world, even as I am not of the world" (Jn 17:15–16). This world, Christ says, "hates me because I testify of it that its works are evil" (Jn 7:7).

The Christian solution is to live, bear witness, and act (moving from prayer to political, social, and economic involvement), so as to bring about a relativization of all the securities and pleasures people can find and look for in the use of material and affective riches.

The promulgation of national and international laws can be a help, but only if it is joined and even preceded by a liberation of individual and collective mentalities. Such a liberation is a necessry condition for the effective application of laws.

There is here no small problem, and it is one that all civilizations share: the problem of the elite and the masses. Aristotle remarked long ago that

> even when we reach adulthood we must observe certain rules and accustom ourselves to them; for this reason, we will always have need of laws. This means, in short, that we will need them throughout our lives. For the masses obey compulsion rather than a good argument, and respond to punishments rather than to the ideal of moral beauty.[55]

It is this situation that justifies the apparatus of political and moral laws and that sets the moralist a difficult question to which I referred in the historical section of this book.[56] Here is how St. Paul poses the problem: "The law is not laid down for the just but for the lawless" (1 Tim 1:9). There are no prohibitions for the righteous: "All things are lawful for me" (1 Cor 6:12; cf. 10:23).

But this is rather an ideal than a real situation, even among the disciples of Christ insofar as they have not yet become fully subject to the rule of the Spirit. As St. Paul writes to the Corinthians: "I . . . could not address you as spiritual men, but as men of the flesh, as babes in Christ" (1 Cor 3:1).

This Christian "babyhood" is a reality, though somewhat suppressed, in Western political society with its culture and ideology and confusion of politico-ethico-religious laws.

Are we to conclude that the morality of the gospel is reserved to an elite?

My answer would be "Yes," provided we are not talking of an "elite" as measured by the standards of the world. The gospel elite is made up of lowly and poor persons: "Theirs is the kingdom of heaven" (Mt 5:3). It is their lowliness and poverty that opens their ears and their hearts to the word of God.

Those who are wise by the world's standards, the wicked who "receive glory from one another" (Jn 5:44), are blinded and alienated by self-satisfaction with their own images. "Claiming to be wise, they became fools" (Rom 1:22).

The gospel elite, on the other hand, is made up of those who are "foolish" by the world's standards, those who are "wise" with the "secret and hidden wisdom of God" (1 Cor 2:7) which the world accounts as folly: "The foolishness of God is wiser than men, and the weakness of God is stronger than men" (1 Cor 1:25).

The gospels tell us of only a single moment when Christ exults with joy in the Spirit; it occurs as he gives solemn thanks to his Father because it has pleased the latter to reveal the Good News to "babes" (Lk 10:21). One must be little and unencumbered if one is to pass through the narrow gate (Lk 13:24).[57]

The apostles did not belong to the elite of their culture; they were people of small means. When the leaders and elders arrest Peter and John, they perceive them to be "uneducated, common men" (Acts 4:13). The same would be true of the Corinthians to whom Paul could write: "Not many of you were wise according to worldly standards, not many were powerful, not many were of noble birth. . . . God chose what is low and despised in the world, even things that are not" (1 Cor 1:26–28).

The gospel elite is made up not only of canonized saints but of all the obscure who have lived in poverty with respect both to goods and to themselves. "Our Lord's love is revealed as perfectly in the most simple soul that resists His grace in nothing as in the most exalted soul."[58]

This elite of persons who are poor and wise in God's sight has a special name in the Bible: it is called the "remnant"[59] or "the poor of Yahweh" or the "little flock" (Lk 12:32). This remnant is composed of the "elect," who are gratuitously chosen by the Father from among the multitude of those who are called (cf. Mt 22:14).

The aim of gospel morality must therefore be to incite and direct among the "masses" a Christian journey toward the poverty which is openness to the action of the Holy Spirit. And since laws and sanctions are necessary, they must be used in accordance with their true nature, which is to be, not ends in themselves, but servants of people in their search for God.

Chapter 13

Education in Morality Is Education in Pleasure

According to its etymology, the word "educate" means to bring out what is latent or interior or invisible. The newborn child possesses virtualities that need to be "led out" if he or she is to attain to self-awareness; the educational process helps the child to recognize the internal and external laws which foster his or her development or militate against it.

Among these laws, I consider those to be fundamental which control the right and wrong way of seeking happiness or, to put it better, of experiencing pleasure in the way that befits a human being and a disciple of Jesus Christ.

The joys and pains of children are exceptional in their intensity and spontaneity. Childhood is therefore a privileged time for the gradual education of human beings; all the more so since with the passing years the feelings grow dull, and individuals slip into an almost Stoic insensibility[1] or the affective death of boredom[2] or perhaps the generalized lack of desire that used to be familiar to monks and was known as acedia.[3]

Childhood is the age of pleasure; a child's education should therefore be focused on pleasure. Such was Plato's opinion: "The whole purpose of early education will be to see to it that pleasure and liking, pain and dislike, are formed in the souls of the little ones in conformity with right order."[4] The same holds for the education of adolescents: "You should exhort them to the noblest kind of life. To this end you must show them not only that such a life brings a noble reputation, but also that, if one consents to try it and not flee from it in youth, it proves best able to give what we all want: the maximum of pleasure and the minimum of pain throughout a lifetime."[5]

Aristotle refers to Plato on this point and writes: "One must have been led from childhood, as Plato says, to find joy and pain where they are rightly to be found. That is the truest form of education."[6]

From earliest childhood all people seek happiness,[7] but where and how are they to find it? The natural dynamics of the person must be educated. "There is agreement that pleasure especially is connected with our human nature. Consequently, all educators of children use pleasure and pain as rudders with which to steer them to a safe harbor."[8] The reason? "It is accepted that nothing is more important for excellence of character than to find pleasure in the things that merit it and to hate the pains that should be hated."[9]

The pleasure which children experience is intense, fleeting, and marked by impatience because their rational minds are not yet sufficiently developed. Being unable to experience pleasure at this higher level, they are acquainted only with the pleasures of the senses. They look to pleasure for its own sake. "In the youthful years growth entails a kind of intoxication, and youth is the age of pleasure."[10] That is how it is, and it is good. It explains why at that age "bodily pleasures are sought for their own sake, because of their intensity, by persons who are incapable of enjoying other pleasures."[11]

Children and adolescents, therefore, should, as they develop, be helped to become conscious of a desire for pleasures of a different quality. The Greeks spoke of becoming *kalokagathos*; modern philosophers talk of transcendence; in this book I have preferred to speak of an openness to the beyond of pleasure.

Especially in this first stage, education must involve a discipline:

> There is need to "discipline" that which desires what is evil, and that which is in the midst of its stage of development. Where are these two things more clearly present than in appetite and in a child? For children too live at the mercy of appetite, and the desire for pleasure predominates in them. If therefore a child is not docile and submissive to authority, this desire will become excessive; for the desire for pleasure is insatiable, and everything stimulates it in the case of a being that is as yet irrational; moreover the indulgence of an appetite intensifies its innate strength, and if these appetites are strong and excessive in number they can reach the point of excluding reflection. They must therefore be moderate and few in number and must at no point contradict the rule. Then the person is what we call "docile," that is, "disciplined" or temperate. Just as a child must conform his life to the program set down for him by his tutor, so the appetitive power must conform its life to the rule; in both cases the rule proposed is moral beauty. The temperate person desires what he ought, as he ought, and when he ought; and that is precisely what the rule prescribes.[12]

There is thus no question of forbidding the child and adolescent all pleasure, but only of helping him to discover the way that will lead him to full maturity, that is, to success in experiencing life's pleasures according to their true nature and in a liberating "poverty."

It is good that a child should experience the pleasures proper to his or her age, however "bodily" these may be. Even for an adult, a minimum of these pleasures is a vital necessity. According to Aristotle, they are a cure for sadness[13] and contribute to repose of soul. And St. Thomas writes: "Just as bodily fatigue is dispelled by bodily rest, so fatigue of soul is dispelled by rest for the soul. The soul's rest comes through pleasure."[14] For both Aristotle and St. Thomas, this restoration of the rational part of the human person through sensible pleasure is the object of the virtue they call eutrapelia.[15]

It is by helping children to a *proper* experience of the pleasures of their age that there is some hope of opening them to the pleasures of adulthood. This course of action also avoids making children feel an irrational sense of guilt, especially since, even without any stirring of guilt feelings by clumsy teachers, certain pleasures are felt to be shameful and enjoyed only in secret.[16]

A discipline which does not inculcate guilt feelings is necessary if the child is to be led little by little to emancipation from the egocentric use of pleasure. This task is a difficult one, because "pleasure has grown up with all of us from our earliest childhood; consequently it is hard to rub off this passion and rid ourselves of it, so ingrained is it in our vital activity."[17]

The intemperate individual is one who has not rid himself of the child's way of taking pleasure. His behavior is "childish"[18] because it is proper to a child to take pleasure for pleasure's sake and as one who is locked into the present moment, without any openness to the beyond of pleasure. As Baudelaire observed:

> The love of pleasure binds us to the present. A care for our salvation links us to the future.
>
> He who binds himself to pleasure—that is, to the present—seems to me like a man rolling down a slope, trying to cling to bushes, and uprooting them and carrying them with him in his fall.[19]

The purpose of education, then, is to help the young to a discovery of "spiritual" pleasures. If they do not succeed in finding these, they will stop at "bodily" pleasures. No one can do without all pleasure for a long time, and those who are unable to enjoy spiritual pleasures will turn to, or stop at, carnal ones.[20]

The aim, therefore, must be to help the young discover and appreciate the pleasures of moral beauty, the beauty of the "virtuous." Those who do not succeed in making this kind of "pleasure" predominant in their lives are out of harmony with themselves: they desire one thing and have a rational wish for another. There you have the very definition of the "incontinent,"[21] those who "being unable to enjoy a pleasure that is pure and worthy of a human being, take refuge in bodily pleasures."[22] They are "surfeited with repentance."[23]

This moral education in pleasure requires a rule, a scale of values: "We must take note of the things to which we are most inclined (for nature disposes us one way in regard to one thing and another way in another); we can determine this from the pleasure and pain we feel."[24] But Aristotle adds: "Finally and above all we must be on guard against the pleasant and pleasure, for we are not impartial judges in regard to it."[25]

Here is where the educator and moralist have a role to play. Their function is not to impose their personal set of values without any discussion. Rather, they are to adopt the maieutic of Socrates and awaken those in their charge to discernment, to a critical approach, and to the free acceptance of the primacy of moral beauty, that is, of the detached and liberating use of pleasures.

This is not possible without discipline and the formulation of prohibitions: "Education must inhibit, forbid and suppress, and this it has abundantly seen to in all periods of history. But we have learnt from analysis that precisely this suppression of instincts involves the risk of neurotic illness. . . . Thus education has to find its way between the Scylla of non-interference and the Charybdis of frustration."[26]

If desire is to be successfully satisfied, it must obey a law which is constitutive for it: the law of castration and radical prohibition:

> In psychoanalysis this word [castration] signifies an interdiction of desire as regards the ways of obtaining pleasure (I would say: an interdiction of the instinct); this interdiction harmonizes and promotes both the one desiring, who is thus brought into unity with the law that humanizes him, and the desire itself, for which the interdiction opens the way to greater pleasures.[27]

Along the same lines, Denis Vasse observes that when a person

> tries to obtain total possession of the object, he finds that he is dispossessed both of the object and of his own appetite for it. At this point he finds repose and glimpses the truth about his own being. If this be the case, then renunciation *cannot* be prior to love but is its fruit and act. Renunciation does not come *before* desire for the other—be he neighbor or God—*it is its act*.[28]

Interdiction and renunciation play a role in the education of desire, especially in freeing it of its illusions.

Desire seems to promise a complete satisfaction which it never delivers. St. Augustine commented that "in whatever direction I turn, hardly have I tasted joy, even the most eagerly desired, when it loses its savor for me."[29] Desire is thus the "seducer of the whole world" wherein people find themselves ensnared.

Interdiction and renunciation educate desire, but only if they are not formulated as categorical imperatives, as arbitrary manifestations of an absolute authority that is pitiless and beyond comprehension. It is when interdiction and renunciation are formulated in the latter way that they seem to cause and foster a neurotic guilt. Or at least it is then that we get fixed moral norms, supposedly changeless and universal, in which the subject takes shelter as within a ring of defenses in order there to doze away in the false security of a good conscience or in a "security in sin—sin redeemed and ransomed,"[30] or in the infantile security of submission and limited ambition.[31]

The person's attitude is then one of affective sclerosis,[32] of resignation, of stereotyped relations with others and with reality.

> In neuroses, defensive compromises force the individual to enter into fixed relations with reality, relations in which objects present themselves to him in stereotyped ways. By reason of conflicts or counterinvestments, encounter and the experience of satisfaction bring into action only ridiculous guardians of energy. From the moment when the subject is freed from this system of neurotic subjection to a certain kind of reality, another kind of "reality" is presented to him—that of chance, encounter, discovery: situations in which a pleasure can arise that is analogous to that of growing awareness. These are so many circumstances which favor an unforeseen release from systems of investment that seemed carefully safeguarded against any change whatsoever.[33]

Between the Scylla of noninterference and the Charybdis of frustration, a way must be sought that leads to the complete truth of desire and pleasure as I have tried to analyze these.

By its internal dynamism, desire is "the promise of a pleasure that will surpass all pleasures hitherto known and will lay hold of the human being, whatever the cost. Pleasure is not at all a bad counselor."[34] True enough—provided there be also an awareness of all that can be infantile, insidious, and even neurotic about pleasure, as well as all the illusions it can foster; provided too that pleasure be open to its beyond[35] and that the insecurity the subject will experience pleases him.

> Desire, for a human being, is truly desire only if it is accompanied by insecurity. There must be risk if there is to be desire, for desire is never repetitive. It contains a kind of necessity; one enters the spiral of the known, but there a strong desire springs up that leads beyond the known. In such a situation there is necessarily a risk. And the keener the desire and the more it touches on what is essential to the

person who expresses himself in it, that is, the more his desire is a present expression of his dynamism while at the same time being connected with the source of its subject, then the more the subject will be ignorant of what dwells in him and where he is going and what it is that is calling him. Desire calls for fulfillment. This fulfillment cannot be a repetition, for then it would be a habit; then the unknown that is being sought would simply be a repetition. Desire makes itself known to a human being only because he knows there is risk in it. Humanly speaking, therefore, desire is accompanied by a feeling of insecurity.[36]

This risky search for the unknown—not for a pleasure hitherto unknown but for what is beyond it—needs to be regulated by the reality principle; this is the role of the intellect. "Our only way of controlling our instincts is with our minds,"[37] says Freud. He is saying nothing new, for Aristotle had already commented: "A person is said to be in control, or not be in control, of his passions according as his reason is or is not in control. Is this not as much as to say that our reason is ourselves?"[38]

"Where id was, there ego shall be,"[39] that is, there intellect shall be and, consequently, regulation of the id by the reality principle. It is through this process that there is growth from the "pleasure-ego" to the "reality-ego" in the three stages which Freud sketched out: the "original reality-ego" (the ego identifying itself with what is pleasurable), the "purified pleasure-ego," and the "final reality-ego."[40]

Analytic treatment depends on this rational and realistic kind of control: "There is no doubt that the resistance of the conscious and unconscious ego operates under the sway of the pleasure principle: it seeks to avoid the unpleasure which would be produced by the liberation of the repressed. Our efforts, on the other hand, are directed towards procuring the toleration of that unpleasure by an appeal to the reality principle."[41]

"In point of fact it [the non-neurotic ego] behaves like the physician during an analytic treatment: it offers itself, with the attention it pays to the real world, as a libidinal object to the id, and aims at attaching the id's libido to itself."[42]

In this way the individual reaches maturity where, "having renounced the pleasure principle and having adapted himself to reality, he seeks his object in the outer world."[43]

Neuroses and psychoses originate in a rejection of the external world or in a revolt against it.[44] Maturation and health are characterized by affective investment in the world outside the subject, not so that a person may lose him or herself in it, but rather that he or she may find themselves there as they move from the "primary narcissism" to the "secondary narcissism."[45]

This maturity is reached only by stages, but "each stage in the development must offer enough satisfaction for the child to feel that the next stage will offer still other satisfactions, but at the same time not so much pleasure that his interest in and curiosity about new pleasures will be dulled. Education can be summed up as the effort to maintain that kind of balance."[46]

In a quite different perspective, yet one I think somewhat convergent with that of psychoanalysis, St. Thomas bases the moral life on a finality that is chosen and experienced, and thus on pleasure (in the broad sense which I have been giving this term).[47] The child is finalized by the search for pleasure for himself, and he attains adulthood by gradually changing to a finality in the order of moral beauty (the *kalokagathos* of the Greeks). This change itself becomes possible in the degree that his rational intellect and intelligent affectivity develop. The first deliberation regarding himself and the choice of this fully human finality is, in St. Thomas' view, the decisive moment in the moral life:

> Once the person begins to have the use of reason . . . the first thing that occurs to him to think about is deliberation regarding himself. And if he orders himself to the right end, he will obtain, through grace, the remission of original sin. But if he does not order himself to the right end, then, to the degree that he is capable of discernment at this age, he will sin mortally by not doing what lies in his power.[48]

It is impossible to throw into better relief the choice of a finality for human life and thus its morality. If the choice is good, it is made with pleasure, just as each subsequent stage brings pleasure: "Anyone who wants to make progress must have spiritual pleasure,"[49] both as hoped for and as already enjoyed. The source of moral action is the "ultimate" (absolute) end which is happiness,[50] and law must keep this same end in view.[51] For "the useful is not as pleasing as the beautiful and not as worthy of being loved."[52] Education exercises its most fruitful function when it awakens and purifies the taste for moral beauty. Once again, this does not mean that education neglects the law and its prohibitions; it means only that these are not turned into absolute imperatives and allowed to become a source of fear. St. Paul's advice to the Ephesians was: "Fathers, do not provoke your children to anger."[53]

In short, education in morality is an education in taste, an education in pleasure that is experienced according to its full truth. "It is of no little importance for our actions that we experience joy and sadness in season and out of season."[54] With the good sense of a native of Marseilles, Marcel Pagnol gives us César's answer to his dying friend Honoré when the latter confesses his sins:

> Honoré: Well, yes, I committed that sin. And the worst thing about it is that I enjoyed committing it.

César: Of course! If sins made us suffer when we committed them, we'd all be saints.[55]

When all is said and done, moral progress is entirely a matter of learning to taste the quality of pleasures, so that "good things will be sought with greater eagerness"[56] and, as a result, we will advance from pleasure to better pleasure, since pleasure "is not in us in the static manner of a thing we possess."[57] Rather, pleasure energizes and modifies the subject himself for better or for worse. "When a man passes from virtue to vice, he becomes different," for "according to a man's character, so does the end appear to him."[58]

The choice of an end is a choice of a kind of love and a kind of pleasure. It presupposes renunciations which are freely accepted because what is renounced is loved less than that for the sake of which the renunciations are chosen.[59]

At the same time, this makes it possible for the person not to become alienated in the pleasures found in material or affective riches. In fact, according to St. Thomas, sin consists precisely in making such things our end. He never tires of saying that such riches are not evil in themselves; everything depends on the use we make of them, as St. Paul urged long ago: we should "use the world as though we used it not."[60] That person is morally good who delights in that kind of use of the world. "Tell me *where* you find pleasure (or hope to find) and *how* you live, and I will tell you what kind of person you are." Education is education in taste, in "good taste."[61]

For the acquisition of a virtuous character, nothing is more important than to enjoy the things we ought to enjoy and to hate the things we ought to hate. For pleasant and hateful things press permanently on us, throughout our lives, and they have great weight, that is, great influence, on virtue and the happy life, for men choose what is pleasant and try to escape what is painful.[62]

We must remind ourselves here that this kind of moral success is impossible for human beings, especially as regards "poverty of spirit," but that, on the other hand, everything is possible to God (Mk 10:27). This is why St. Paul prayed "always" for the Thessalonians, asking God to "fulfil every good resolve" (2 Thess 1:11). He was echoed by St. Augustine, who offered this advice: "When evil pleases us and the good has no attraction for us, we must ask God to give us back the taste for the good."[63]

When we envisage the moral person as one who shows good taste in the way he or she experiences pleasure, we turn morality into a wisdom, that is, a knowledge that brings a savor with it, a *sapida sapientia* in the language of St. Thomas.[64] That, in fact, is the original sense of the Latin verb *sapere*.

Morality is of course a science and must be enriched with all possible contributions from the human sciences, but it is a practical science, a science of action. The thing that qualifies it to be elevated to the dignity of "wisdom" is its being lived out in such a way that it bases its most certain judgments on what St. Thomas calls "knowledge by connaturality."[65] In its highest form it is a gift of the Holy Spirit and, specifically, the gift which tradition calls the gift of wisdom.

A simply human morality is also a wisdom, because it means "living happily and nobly."[66] Buffon was correct in saying that a writer's literary style is "the man himself."[67] This is even truer of the moral life. Each person has his or her own style of living, loving, feeling pleasure,[68] and giving pleasure.[69]

We are dealing here with more than a science: we are dealing with a wisdom and an art of living,[70] and when morality is this it has reached its perfect form.

Abbreviations

CP	*Collected Papers* of Freud
DC	*Documentation catholique*
DTC	*Dictionnaire de théologie catholique*
ETL	*Ephemerides Theologicae Lovanienses*
LumVie	*Lumière et vie*
PG	*Patrologia Graeca*
PL	*Patrologia Latina*
RFP	*Revue française de psychanalyse*
RSPT	*Revue des sciences philosophiques et théologiques*
RSR	*Recherches de science religieuse*
SC	*Sources chrétiennes*
SE	*Standard Edition* of the Collected Works of Freud
ST	St. Thomas Aquinas, *Summa Theologica*
VS	*Vie spirituelle*
VSS	*Vie spirituelle: Supplément*
VC	*Verbum Caro*

NOTES

Introduction

1. *A Season in Hell*, tr. by L. Varese (Norfolk, Conn.: New Directions, 1945), p. 71.

2. Sigmund Freud, *Civilization and Its Discontents*, tr. by J. Strachey (New York: Norton, 1961), p. 91.

3. Cf. Jean Delumeau, *La Peur en Occident, XIVᵉ–XVIII² Siècles* (Paris: Fayard, 1978). This will be the subject of Chapters 4 and 5 in this book.

4. Cf. Henry Ey, P. Bernard, and Ch. Brisset, *Manuel de Psychiatrie* (Paris: Masson, 1960), pp. 460–524. "Schizophrenie," in Laplanche and Pontalis, *Vocabulaire de la Psychanalyse* (Paris: Presses Universitaires de France, 1967). Benjamin B. Wolman, *Vectoriasis Praecox or the Group of Schizophrenias* (Springfield, Ill.: Charles C. Thomas, 1966); Eva P. Lester and Catherine La Roche, "Schizophreniform Psychosis of Childhood: Therapeutic Considerations," *Comprehensive Psychiatry* Vol. 19 (1978), 153–59.

5. Roger Bastide, *The Sociology of Mental Disorder*, tr. by J. McNeil (New York: McKay, 1972), p. 77.

6. Sigmund Freud, "The Loss of Reality in Neurosis and Psychosis," *Collected Papers* (5 vols.; New York: Basic Books, 1969), 2:277–82. [Henceforth: *CP* with volume and page.]

7. Sigmund Freud, *An Outline of Psychoanalysis*, tr. by J. Strachey (New York: Norton, 1949), p. 115.

8. Ibid., p. 118.

9. Lester and La Roche, art. cit.

10. Cf. Erik Erikson, *Identity and the Life Cycle: Selected Essays* (Psychological Issues, vol. 1, no. 1; New York: International Universities Press, 1959), p. 63.

11. Laplanche and Pontalis, art. cit.

12. Sigmund Freud, "The Unconscious," *CP* 4:136.

13. E. Bleuler, *Dementia praecox oder Gruppe der Schizophrenien* (Leipzig and Vienna, 1911), cited by Laplanche and Pontalis, art. cit.

14. Sigmund Freud, "The Unconscious," *CP* 4:128.

15. Ey et al., op. cit., p. 468.

16. Cf. especially Ey et al., ibid., and Wolman, op. cit., pp 199–205.

17. George Devereux, *Basic Problems of Ethnopsychiatry*, tr. by B. M. Gulati and G. Devereux (Chicago: University of Chicago Press, 1980), p. 201.

18. Ibid., p. 216; "I hold that the quasi-restitutional function of the modern patient's adoption of the schizophrenic model and his tendency to 'stabilize' his illness—to make it chronic and malignant—are due to the fact that this pattern is rooted in the ethnic character and is reinforced by social pressures" (p. 221).

19. Ibid., p. 200.

20. Cf. La Société désorientée (Recherches et débats, no. 89, Paris: Desclée De Brouwer, 1978).

21. Maurice Bellet, La Théorie du Fou (Paris: Desclée De Brouwer, 1977), especially pp. 242–43.

22. Cf. Devereux, op. cit., pp. 185–236.

23. Cf. Delumeau, op. cit.

24. Dr. Francis Pasche brings this out when he characterizes "Judeo-Christian orthodoxy" by its opposition to the gnostic mentality, in his A Partir de Freud (Paris: Payot, 1969), pp. 129–56.

25. Cf. Paul Vignaux, "Nominalisme," DTC 11:783.

26. Sigmund Freud, An Outline of Psychoanalysis, p. 106.

27. Sigmund Freud, "The Unconscious," CP 4:136.

28. Ibid.

29. Sigmund Freud, New Introductory Lectures on Psychoanalysis, tr. by J. Strachey (New York: Norton, 1965), p. 166.

30. Sigmund Freud, "Narcissism: An Introduction," CP 4:54, and "Psychology and Religious Origins" [a Preface to Theodor Reik's Ritual (London, 1931)], CP 5:94. Cf. Totem and Taboo: Resemblances between the Psychic Lives of Savages and Neurotics, tr. by A. A. Brill (New York: Vintage Books, n.d.), p. 96.

31. Sigmund Freud, New Introductory Lectures on Psychoanalysis, p. 175.

32. Sigmund Freud, "The Resistances to Psycho-Analysis," CP 5:168.

33. Sigmund Freud, New Introductory Lectures on Psychoanalysis, p. 155.

34. Sigmund Freud associates this "God Logos" with the goddess Ananke̅ (Necessity), an association he finds in one of his favorite authors, the Dutch writer Multatuli, whose real name was E. D. Dekker (d. 1887). Freud refers to this "divine pair" in "The Economic Problem of Masochism," CP 2:265, and in The Future of an Illusion, tr. by W. D. Robson-Scott, rev. by J. Strachey (Garden City, N.Y.: Doubleday Anchor Books, 1961), p. 88. Cf. what Freud says about submission to Ananke̅, the law of nature, in his Leonardo da Vinci and a Memory of His Childhood, tr. by A. Tyson (New York: Norton, 1964), pp. 86–87.

35. [The author here cites Freud, "Why War? A Letter to Einstein," but I cannot find the passage in this letter, in CP 5:273–87.—Tr.]

36. Bastide, op. cit., p. 205.

37. Pasche, op. cit., pp. 152–53.

38. Cf. Henri de Lubac, Corpus Mysticum (Paris: Aubier, 1944); Albert Plé, "Pour une Mystique des Mystères," VSS, no. 23 (November, 1952), 377–96, and "Les Mystères de Dieu," VS, 72 (1945), 209–26. For St.

Thomas, the "mystery of God" is the humanity of Jesus Christ (*ST* 2-2, 1, 8c).

39. Bastide, op. cit., pp. 204–8.

40. René Descartes, *A Discourse on Method*, Part 2, in *A Discourse on Method and Selected Writings*, tr. by J. Veitch (New York: Dutton, 1951), p. 15.

41. Bastide, op. cit., p. 204.

42. I can only hope that economist François Perroux will have a large readership and a great deal of influences for his efforts in preaching an economy based on gift; cf. *Economie et Société: Contrainte, Echange, Don* (Paris: Presses Universitaires de France, 1960), and "Richesse et Pauvreté au XXᵉ Siècle: Questions Posées aux Chrétiens," in *L'Eglise Invitée au Courage* (Paris: Centurion, 1964).

43. Sigmund Freud, *An Outline of Psychoanalysis*, p. 109.

44. Cf. Mircea Eliade, *Occultism, Witchcraft, and Cultural Fashions* (Chicago: University of Chicago Press, 1975); etc.

45. Sigmund Freud, Note found on his worktable after his death, *SE* 23:300.

46. Sigmund Freud, *New Introductory Lectures on Psychoanalysis*, p. 80.

47. Albert Camus, *The Rebel: An Essay on Man in Revolt*, tr. by A. Bower (New York: Vintage Books, 1956), p. 32.

48. André Gide, *The Fruits of the Earth and the New Fruits*, tr. by D. Bussy (New York: Knopf, 1949), p. 221.

49. *ST* 1-2, 106, 4c.

Chapter 1

1. The reader interested in a biblical study of joy and the beatitudes may consult Jacques Dupont, *Les Béatitudes* (2 vols.; Paris: Gabalda, 1969); Nelly Beaupère, *Saint Paul et la Joie* (Paris: Cerf, 1973); Augustin George, "Le Bonheur Promis par Jésus," *LumVie*, no. 52 (April–May, 1961), 36–58; Sandro Spinsanti, "Les Bonheur des Béatitudes," *VC*, no. 103 (1972–73), 4–31; Pierre-Jean Labarrière, "L'Homme des Béatitudes," *Christus*, no., 63 (June 1969), 352–65; etc.

2. But there are related terms such as *chara* (joy: 140 times), *agalliasis* (exultation: 16), *euphrainein* (to rejoice: 16), *hilaros* (cheerful: 2), *asmenōs* (gladly, with pleasure: 1), *oninasthai* (have pleasure or joy of: 1). The idea of happiness therefore occurs 231 times in the New Testament. It is already present in the Old Testament, especially in connection with Yahweh's election of Israel: "Happy are you, O Israel! Who is like you, a people saved by the Lord . . . !" (Deut 33:29). Cf. Pietro Dacquino, "Human Joy and the Hereafter in the Biblical Books," in Christian Duquoc (ed.), *The Gift of Joy* (Concilium 39; New York: Paulist, 1968), pp. 17–32.

3. Lk 1:45; 10:23; 11:28; Mt 13:16; 16:17; Jn 20:29; Rom 15:13; Phil 1:25; Rev 1:3.

4. Jn 3:29; 16:22.

5. Jn 15:11; 16:24; 17:13.

6. 1 Thess 1:6.

7. Rom 12:12; Tit 2:13.

8. Gal 5:22; Rom 12:8; 1 Cor 13:6.

9. 1 Thess 1:6; Acts 8:39; 11:23; 13:48; 16:34.

10. Acts 2:46; cf. Lk 14:15; Rev 19:9.

11. Lk 1:45-55; 11:27.

12. Lk 1:44; 3:29.

13. Even in quite specific problems Paul has recourse to the principle of happiness; with regard to widows, for example, he writes: "But in my judgment she is happier if she remains as she is" (1 Cor 7:40).

14. Mt 5:10; Acts 5:41; 2 Cor 1:5; 1 Pet 3:14; 4:14; Jas 4:12. Cf. Hans Urs von Balthasar, "Joy and the Cross," in Duquoc (ed.), *The Gift of Joy* (n. 2), pp. 83-96.

15. Cf. Karel Vladimir Truhlar, "The Earthly Cost of the Beatitudes," in *The Gift of Joy*, pp. 33-44; André Manaranche, "Le bonheur, problème politique," *Christus*, no. 63 (June, 1969), 308-22.

16. Cf. A.-J. Festugière, "La Doctrine du Plaisir des Premiers Sages à Epicure," *RSPT* 25 (1936), 242-43.

17. Plato, *Timaeus* 68a, 90a-d; cf. A.-J. Festugière, *Contemplation et vie contemplative chez Platon* (Paris: Vrin, 1936), pp. 268-334.

18. Aristotle, *Topics* 112a36.

19. Cf. Festugière, "La Doctrine du Plaisir," p. 242.

20. Ragnar Holte, *Béatitude et Sagesse: Saint Augustin et le Problème de la Fin de l'Homme dans la Philosophie Ancienne* (Paris: Etudes Augustiniennes, 1962), p. 15.

21. Cf. especially the passages in Plotinus (*Enneads* VI, 7) on the imperturbable, blissful contemplation of the One, the divine, as beyond every "form."

22. Cf. Jean Daniélou, *Platonisme et Théologie Mystique* (Théologie 2; Paris: Aubier, 1944); A.-J. Festugière, *L'enfant d'Agrigente* (Paris: Cerf, 1941); J. Arnou, "Platonisme des Pères," *DTC* 12:2258ff.

23. Cf. Vernon J. Bourke, *History of Ethics* (Garden City, N.Y.: Doubleday, 1968), pp. 47-108 passim; Etienne Gilson, *La Philosophie au Moyen Age* (Paris: Payot, 1944), especially on Latin Platonism in the fourth century, pp. 115-38, etc.

24. Cf. Bourke, op. cit. (especially on Platonic ethics at Cambridge, pp. 116-19, 136-43); D. P. Walker, *The Ancient Theology: Studies in Christian Platonism from the Fifteenth to the Eighteenth Century* (London: Duckworth, 1973).

25. For the texts, cf. Maurice Solovine, *Epicure: Doctrines et maximes* (Paris: Hermann, 1965). The translation of the texts is taken, whenever possible, from Cyril Bailey's version in Whitney J. Oates (ed.), *The Stoic and Epicurean Philosophers* (New York: Random House, 1940; Modern Library edition, 1957).

26. *Letter to Herodotus* (Oates, p. 3).

27. Marcus Aurelius, *Meditationes* IX, 41 (Oates,pp. 559–60).

28. Cited by Aetios of Amida IV, 3, 11 (Solovine, p. 38).

29. Sextus Empiricus, *Hypotyposes Pyrrhonicae* 11, 9 (Solovine, p. 144).

30. Cicero, *Academica* 14, 45 (Solovine, p. 144).

31. Sextus Empiricus, op. cit., 1, 203 (Solovine, p. 146).

32. *Letter to Menoecius* (Oates, p. 31).

33. Athenaeus, *Deipnosophistae* XII, 546 (Oates, p. 50, no. 59).

34. *Letter to Menoecius* (Oates, pp. 31–32).

35. Ibid. (Oates, p. 32).

36. Diogenes Laertius X, 135 (Oates, p. 44).

37. Cf. *Principal Doctrines*, no. III: "The limit of quantity in pleasures is the removal of all that is painful" (Oates, p. 35).

38. *Principal Doctrines*, no. II (Oates, p. 35).

39. *Herculaniensia* I, 148 (Solovine, p. 151).

40. *Letter to Menoecius* (Oates, p. 32).

41. Fragments of *Epicurus' Exhortation*, no. XLIV (Oates, p. 42).

42. Ibid., no. LXXVII (Oates, p. 44).

43. Ibid., no. XXI (Oates, p. 41).

44. This was doubtless due to the fact that the Fathers of the Church, from Clement of Alexandria to St. Augustine (all of them more or less Platonists and Stoics), rejected Epicureanism with contempt and indignation. Epicurus was to have hardly any influence during the Renaissance, despite Lorenzo Valla (1406–1457) and Gassendi (1592–1655); cf. Bourke, op. cit., pp. 114 (Valla) and 129 (Gassendi).

45. The French translation is from R. Antoine Gauthier and Jean-Yves Jolif, *L'Ethique à Nicomaque* (Louvain: Editions Universitaires, 1958). "I shall not cite the *Magna Moralia*, which is usually only a commentary on the *Nicomachean Ethics*," says A.-J. Festugière in his *Aristote: Le Plaisir* (introduction, translation, and notes; Paris: Vrin, 1936), p. 11. On the subject with which I am dealing here, cf. Jean Vanier, *Le Bonheur, Principe et Fin de la Morale Aristotélicienne* (Paris: Desclée De Brouwer, 1965), and R. A. Gauthier, *La Morale d'Aristote* (Paris: Presses Universitaires de France, 1958).

46. Even though they seek different pleasures, all human beings seek the same pleasure, "for all beings have something divine in them" (1099b11).

47. Speaking of happiness, Aristotle says: "Were we to possess it alone, it would make our life worth living and free us from every need" (1097b14–15).

48. Cf. "The noble and good things in life are rightly obtained by those who act" (1098b35). "In matters of feeling and action theories are less reliable than facts" (1172a32); etc.

49.   By contemplation, Aristotle means not mysticism, but the activity of the intellect, the knowledge that is an end in itself (cf. 1177b18–25).

50.   "Perfection" in the language of Aristotle is synonymous with completion. A French person of our day might speak of *épanouissement* (literally, a "blossoming out").

51.   "Each activity has its own proper pleasure" (1175b25).

52.   Following Plato, Aristotle distinguishes between pleasures involving pain and pleasures not involving pain, the latter being pleasures by their nature, such as pleasure in the supreme good.

53.   "No one would think of encouraging us to do what is not in our power or what we do not do voluntarily. Of what use would it be for a person to let himself be persuaded that he is not really hot or sick or hungry, when he is? He continues to suffer nonetheless" (113b24). "Those who do something under compulsion and against their will feel pain in doing it" (1110b11).

54.   "Others, on the contrary, regard it [pleasure] as thoroughly bad, either because they are convinced that pleasure is indeed bad or because they think it better for the conduct of human life to call pleasure bad. Since the majority of people are inclined to pleasure and to becoming slaves of pleasure, these thinkers believe they must urge them in the opposite direction so that they will at least reach a just mean" (1172a20).

55.   Aristotle justifies the pleasures of play and amusement: "The relaxation gotten from amusement is a necessary part of life" (1128b1). He is speaking of the virtue of eutrapelia.

56.   This "rule" is not a law in the sense in which moralities based on duty use the term. The rule here is the just mean.

57.   "We must be courageous not because we are forced to it but because it is noble" (1116b1), "for the very beauty of its act is the end which virtue sets before itself" (1115b12).

58.   *La Morale d'Aristote,* p. 75.

59.   Cf. 1095b24–32, and *Politics,* 1324a29–31.

60.   Cf. Vanier, op. cit., pp. 146–61.

61.   "Happiness is to be found in leisure" (1177b4).

62.   Cf. Gauthier, op. cit., p. 51.

63.   Especially after the condemnation of various "Aristotelian" theses by Stephen Tempier, bishop of Paris, in 1277.

64.   Bourke, op. cit., gives useful information on the (limited) influence of Aristotle through the centuries; cf. the Index under "Aristotle."

65.   R. Minnerath, *Les Chrétiens et le Monde (Ier et IIe siècles)* (Paris: Gabalda, 1973), p. 157.

66.   In addition to the standard works on St. Augustine—especially those of Etienne Gilson, *The Christian Philosophy of St. Augustine,* tr. by L. E. M. Lynch (New York: Random House, 1960), and H. I. Marrou, *St. Augustine and His Influence Through the Ages,* tr. by P. Hepburne-Scott (New York: Harper, 1957), and *Saint Augustin et la Fin de la Culture Antique* (Paris: Brocard, 1958)—there are two valuable books on the problem of happiness in St. Augustine: Ragnar Holte (n. 20), and Aimé Becker, *De l'Instinct du Bonheur à l'Extase de la Béatitude: Théologie et Pédagogie du Bonheur dans la Prédication de Saint Augustin* (Paris: Lethielleux, 1968).

67. *De civitate Dei* VII, 1—7 (*PL* 41:193-200).

68. *Sermo 150* (*PL* 38:807-14).

69. *Sermo* 150, 5 and 10 (*PL* 38:809-10 and 813-14).

70. Cf. Holte, op. cit., p. 195.

71. Ibid., pp. 51ff.

72. *De Trinitate* XIII, 5 (*PL* 42:1020).

73. *Epistula* 130 (*PL* 33:497).

74. *De magistro* 14, 46 (*PL* 32:1220).

75. Cf. Becker, op. cit., pp. 34-39, 285ff.

76. *De vita beata* 1, 5 (*PL* 32:962).

77. Cf. Becker, op. cit., p. 289.

78. *De vita beata* 2, 11 (*PL* 32:965).

79. Holte, op. cit., p. 220.

80. *Sermo* 150, 9 (*PL* 38:812). Cf. *De civitate Dei* XII, 1 (*PL* 41:349): "Although not every creature can be happy . . . yet the creature that can cannot be so by its own power, since it was created from nothing, but only by the power of him who created it."

81. *Sermo* 123, 5 (*PL* 38:686). Cf. *Sermo* 128, 9 (*PL* 38:717): "It is the Spirit of God in you that resists what is opposed to you. For you refused to turn to God, you fell, you broke like a vessel that slips from a person's hand and is shattered. And it is because you have broken yourself that you are your own enemy and opposed to yourself. Destroy this antagonism and you will regain the integrity of your being."

82. Cf. Holte, op. cit., pp. 97-98.

83. *De Genesi adversus Manichaeos* I, 20. 31 (*PL* 34:188).

84. Holte, op. cit., p. 50, remarks that "for the Platonists the virtues practiced in the sensible world are of inferior rank, and the development of the Platonic tradition shows a persistent tendency to exclude them completely from the *telos*."

85. *Confessions* X, 30-35.

86. *De Doctrina Christiana* I, 3 (*PL* 34:20).

87. *In Evangelium Joannis Tractatus* 26, 4 (*PL* 35:1608-9).

88. *Sermo 96*, 1 (*PL* 38:585).

89. *Confessions* XIII, 9-10.

90. *De Civitate Dei* XV, 22 (*PL* 41:467).

91. *De musica* VI, 11, 29 (*PL* 32:1179).

92. *De Doctrina Christiana* I, 27 (*PL* 34:29).

93. *Contra Faustum Manichaeum* XXII, 28 (*PL* 42:419).

94. *Enarrationes in Psalmos* 101, 2 (PL 37:1296).

95. *Epistula ad Macedonium* 155, 12 (PL 33:671).

96. *Enarrationes in Psalmos* 39, 3 (PL 36:424).

97. Ibid., 7, 40 (PL 36) [?]. Cf *Sermo* 61 (PL 38:411): "God holds back what he does not wish to give you immediately, in order that you may learn to desire great things with a great desire."

98. Cf. Holte, op. cit., pp. 211ff.; Becker, op. cit., pp. 285–98; and F. Cayré "Frui et Uti," *Année Théologique* 9 (1949), 50.

99. *De Doctrina Christiana* I, 3, 3 (PL 34:20).

100. *Enarrationes in Psalmos* 118, serm. 32, 2 (PL 37:1563).

101. For a discussion of the gratuitousness of love, I refer to Becker's fine pages in his tenth chapter, "Eudaimonia et Agapè."

102. *Contra Faustum Manichaeum* XXII, 22 (PL 42:415).

103. Cf. Holte, op. cit., pp. 306ff.

104. *Contra Faustum Manichaeum* XXII, 27 (PL 42:418).

105. *De Doctrina Christiana* I, 35, 39 (PL 34:34).

106. Holte, op. cit., pp. 257–58.

107. *Contra Secundinum Manichaeum* 17 (PL 42:592–93).

108. Holte, op. cit., p. 289.

109. *De Libero Arbitrio* III, 15, 44 (PL 32:1292–93).

110. Holte, op. cit., p. 332.

111. Ibid., p. 336, citing *De Genesi ad litteram* II, 5, 6.

112. *De Spiritu et Littera* 14, 26 (PL 44:217).

113. Cf. Holte, op. cit., p. 275.

114. Cf. especially A.-D. Sertillanges, "Notes doctrinales," in *La Béatitude* (Paris: Editions de la Revue des Jeunes, 1936), pp. 263–321, and his *La Philosophie Morale de Saint Thomas d'Aquin* (Paris: Aubier, 1942); Etienne Gilson, *Saint Thomas d'Aquin* (Les moralistes chrétiens; Paris: Gabalda, 1941); Jacques Maritain, *Neuf Leçons sur les Notions Premières de la Philosophie Morale* (Paris: Téqui, 1951); S. Pinckaers, *Le Renouveau de la Morale* (Tournai: Casterman,1964); A. Plé, *Vie Affective et Chasteté* (Paris: Cerf, 1964); etc.

Chapter 2

1. The "moralizing" approach introduced the practice of translating the Hebrew *tob* and *ra* as "good" and "evil." In fact, the Hebrew words can just as well be translated as "beautiful" and "ugly" or "happy" and "unhappy." The word *tob* originally designates persons and objects that rouse agreeable feelings or a euphoria of the entire person: a good meal, a beautiful girl, people who do good deeds, or, in short, anything that brings happiness or facilitates the life of body or mind. Cf. "Good and Evil," in X. Léon-Dufour (ed.), *Dictionary of Biblical Theology*, rev. ed. tr. by P. J. Cahill and E. M. Stewart

(New York: Seabury, 1973), p. 213. The *Modern Concordance to the New Testament,* edited by M. Darton (Garden City, N.Y.: Doubleday, 1976), gives 157 occurrences of *kalos* ("beautiful") in the sense of "good." Modern English usage hardly allows this kind of fidelity to the Hebrew and Greek texts; it is a fidelity excluded by the legalist mentality at work in the moralities of duty.

2. Dominique Barthélmy, *God and His Image: An Outline of Biblical Theology,* tr. by A. Dean (New York: Sheed & Ward, 1966).

3. Ibid., p. 21, n. 2, observes that these words, which in a more literal translation would read "not eat of all the trees," are a Hebraism meaning "not at all."

4. Ibid., p. 26 (all three citations).

5. Ibid., pp. 31–32.

6. Note how man discovers his mortality: far from God (whom he fears), he murders his brother and fears to be condemned in turn.

7. Barthélemy, op. cit., p. 32.

8. Gérard Siegwalt, *La Loi, Chemin du Salut* (Neuchâtel: Delachaux and Niestlé, 1971), p. 271.

9. When the Septuagint (LXX) translated Torah by the Greek word *Nomos* (Law), it may have facilitated the legalistic conception of the covenant, but it cannot be held responsible for this conception. Cf. Laurent Monsengiwo Pasynia, *La Notion de Nomos dans le Pentateuque Grec* (Rome: Pontifical Biblical Institute, 1973).

10. Siegwalt, op. cit., p. 162.

11. The flight from insecurity shows both in the possession of wealth (Lk 16:14: "The Pharisees, who were lovers of money, heard all this, and they scoffed at him") and in the quest of honors and of admiration from those who saw their good works (Mt 6:1–8; 23:5–7; etc.).

12. J. Murphy O'Connor, in *L'Existence Chrétienne selon Saint Paul,* has brought out the fact that the moral life is a response to a call. He writes: "The claim to know God's will through a series of precepts is characteristic of the person who turns in on himself and is full of vanity" (pp. 115–16). Christ says to the Pharisees: "How can you believe, who receive glory from one another . . .?" (Jn 5:44).

13. Cf. below, Chap. 11, *The Narcissistic Pleasures of Right Action.*

14. Cf. M. Van Molle's three articles in *VSS,* no. 84 (February,1968), pp. 105–27; no. 86 (September, 1968), pp. 394–424; no. 88 (February, 1969), pp. 101–24.

15. Ibid., no. 88 (February, 1969), p. 113. The "worship of the Rule" is found in every age, even the twentieth century, which has seen the publication of a book with this title.

16. Sigmund Freud, *The Ego and the Id,* tr. by J. Strachey (New York: Norton, 1960), p. 76. Cf. Antoine Vergote, "La Peine dans la Dialectique de l'Innocence, de la Transgression et de la Réconciliation," in E. Castelli (ed.), *Le Mythe de la Peine* (Paris: Aubier, 1967).

17. Cf. G. X. Kaufmann, "Normes, Effondrement des Normes et le Problème de la Liberté en Perspective Sociologique," *VSS,* no. 90 (September,

1969), pp. 330–44; Helmut Schelsky, *Sociologie de la Sexualité*, tr. from German by M. Camhi (Paris: Nouvelle Revue Française, 1966); Abel Jeannière, *The Anthropology of Sex*, tr. by J. Kernan (New York: Harper & Row, 1967); etc.

18. Sigmund Freud, *Civilization and Its Discontents*; Charles Odier, *Les Deux Sources Consciente et Inconsciente de la Vie Morale* (Boudry, Switz.: La Baconnière, 1947); etc.

19. Henri Bergson, *The Two Sources of Morality and Religion*, tr. by R. Ashley Audra and C. Brereton (New York: Holt, 1935), especially the first chapter.

20. M.-D. Chenu, "The Renewal of Moral Theology: The New Law," *Thomist* 34 (1970), 9–10. VSS, no. 90 (September, 1969), p. 295.

21. As St. Thomas says (*ST* 1–2, 106, 1c), the power (*virtus*) that is at work in the new law is entirely the grace of the Holy Spirit that is given to those who believe in Jesus Christ.

22. Sigmund Freud, *The Ego and the Id*, p. 52. Cf. *Totem and Taboo*, p. 192; and *Moses and Monotheism*, tr. by K. Jones (New York: Vintage Books, 1939), p. 156: "To return to ethics . . . what . . . appears mysterious, grandiose, and mystically self-evident owes its character to its connection with religion, its origin in the will of the father."

23. *Moses and Monotheism*, p. 152.

24. Jean-Pierre Vernant, *Mythe et Pensèe Chez les Grecs* (Paris: Maspero, 1971), pp. 79–94.

25. *Moses and Monotheism*, pp. 139–40.

26. Joseph Moingt, "Le Dieu de la Morale Chrétienne," *RSR* 62 (1974), 641.

27. Cf. Claude Gérest, "The Spirituality of Authority in the Eleventh and Twelfth Centuries," in F. Böckle and J.-M. Pohier (eds.), *Power and the Word of God* (Concilium 90; New York: Herder & Herder, 1973), pp. 77–88.

28. Cited by Philippe Erlanger, "La Prise de Pouvoir par Louis XIV," *Historia*, no. 242 (January, 1967), p. 72.

29. Cited by Orest Ranum, *Les Parisiens au XVIIᵉ Siècle* (Paris: Armand Colin, 1973), p. 178.

30. Moingt, art. cit., p. 641.

Chapter 3

1. Joseph Moingt, "Le Dieu de la Morale Chretienne," *RSR* 62 (1974), 640.

2. Pierre de Labriolle, *History and Literature of Christianity from Tertullian to Boethius*, tr. by H. Wilson (New York, Knopf, 1925), p. 91.

3. Ibid., p. 78.

4. Cf. Philippe Delhaye, *Le Décalogue et sa Place dans la Morale Chrétienne* (Brussels: Pensée Catholique, 1963), pp. 124ff.

5. Justin Martyr, *Dialogus cum Tryphone* XI, 3 (*PG* 6:493).

6. Irenaeus of Lyons, *Adversus Haereses* I, 4, 16.

7. Augustine, *Contra Faustum Manichaeum* XV, 8 (*PL* 42:312).

8. Cf. Cyrille Vogel, *Le Péché et la Pénitence dans l'Eglise Ancienne* (Paris: Cerf, 1966).

9. Cf. Delhaye, op. cit., pp. 125–30.

10. They were following St. Augustine in particular who had written: "Here, briefly and in general terms, is my understanding of virtue: Virtue is the charity by which that which should be loved is loved [*qua id quod diligendum est diligitur*]" (*Epistula* 167, 4, 15 [*PL* 33:709).

11. The Greek provenance of this concept is obvious.

12. Vernon J. Bourke, *History of Ethics* (Garden City, N.Y.: Doubleday, 1968), p. 62.

13. Marcus Aurelius, *Meditations*, tr. by M Staniforth (Penguin Classics L140; Baltimore: Penguin Books, 1964), V, 3, p. 78. Cf. Cicero, *De Finibus* III, 7, 20, and Marcus Aurelius, *Meditations* X, 6.

14. J. von Arnim, *Stoicorum Veterum Fragmenta* (4 vols.; Leipzig, 1903–24), I, no. 184.

15. Cf. A.-J. Festugière, *La Révélation d'Hermès Trismégiste* 2 (Paris: Gabalda, 1949), p. 350: "If one wanted to sum up the spirit of Stoicism in a single word, I think the word would have to be 'consent.' Stoicism is a mystique of consent."

16. Marcus Aurelius, *Meditations* VI, 44. Cf. IX, 28: "If that whole be God, then all is well" (p. 144).

17. Ibid., V, 1; VII, 57; X, 28.

18. Ibid., VII, 19; VIII, 34.

19. Ibid., VII, 22.

20. Ibid., V, 10. (p. 82).

21. Ibid., XII, 3.

22. Ibid., VIII, 27 (p. 128).

23. Ibid., IV, 41 (p. 73); XII, 33.

24. Ibid., III, 3 (p. 55).

25. Ibid., XI, 19 (p. 175).

26. Diogenes Laertius, *Vitae Philosophorum* VIII, 10, and Cicero, *Tusculanae Disputationes* IV, 1.

27. Marcus Aurelius, *Meditations* IV, 3 (p. 64).

28. Ibid., XI, 2 (p. 166); cf. XI, 16.

29. Ibid., VIII, 43; cf. IV, 3; V, 19; VIII, 40; V, 26.

30. Ibid., XII, 22 (p. 181); cf. XII, 25; XII, 8.

31. The only or principal virtue is strength or nerve or manliness: ibid., XI, 18 and 23.

32. Ibid., X, 12 [This sentence is omitted in the Staniforth translation and is here translated from Plé's text—Tr.]; cf. VII, 67 and 68; X, 6; VI, 51; XI, 16.

33. Ibid., II, 16 (p. 51).

34. Ibid., V, 27 (p. 87); cf. XII, 26; II, 13 and 16; X, 8.

35. Ibid., IV, 49 (p. 75).

36. A.-J. Festugière, op. cit., p. 283. Cf. G. Germain, *Epictète et la spiritualité stoïcienne* (Paris: Seuil, 1964).

37. Marcus Aurelius, *Meditations* XII, 32 (p. 187).

38. Ibid., X, 33 (p. 161).

39. Ibid., XI, 13 (pp. 170-71).

40. Ibid., IX, 1 (p. 137).

41. Ibid., VI, 10 (p. 92).

42. Festugière, op. cit., p. 267.

43. Ibid., pp. 266, 331-32.

44. Michel Spanneut, *Le Stoïcisme des Pères de l'Eglise, de Clément de Rome à Clément d'Alexandrie* (Paris: Seuil, 1957), pp. 49-53.

45. Ibid., p. 432. Cf. p. 266: "Ancient Stoicism provided Christianity with a series of concepts and theories; contemporary Stoicism [contemporary with the early Church] dictated its practical morality, even down to the very words used."

46. Ibid., p. 260.

47. Cf. Léontine Zanta, *La Renaissance du Stoïcisme au XVIe Siècle* (Paris: Champion, 1914), and Bourke, op. cit., pp. 32-39, 129-30, 163.

48. La Fontaine, *Le Philosophe Scythe* XII, 20.

Chapter 4

1. Cf. Régine Pernoud, *Pour en Finir avec le Moyen Age* (Paris: Seuil, 1977).

2. Cf. Jean Gimpel, *The Medieval Machine: The Industrial Revolution of the Middle Ages* (New York: Holt, Rinehart and Winston, 1977; Baltimore: Penguin Books, 1977, which is cited here).

3. Ibid., p. 57.

4. Cf. Jean Leclercq, *The Love of Learning and the Desire for God*, tr. by C. Misrahi (New York: Fordham University Press, 1961).

5. Régine Pernoud, *Histoire de la Bourgeoisie Française 1. Des Origines aux Temps Modernes* (Paris: Seuil, 1960), p. 96.

6. Ibid., p. 117.

7. Ibid., p. 426.

8. Ibid., p. 119.

9. Ibid., pp. 124–25.

10. Michel Mollat, *Genèse Médiévale de la France Moderne, XIVᵉ–XVᵉ Siècles* (Paris: Arthaud, 1977), p. 233.

11. Gimpel, op. cit., p. 211.

12. Michel Mollat, "Le Sentiment de la Mort dans la Vie et la Pratique Religieuse à la Fin du Moyen Age," *VSS*, no. 77 (May, 1966), p. 219. Cf. Pierre Chaunu, *Le Temps des Réformes* (Paris: Fayard, 1975), Chapter 1.

13. Heinz Zahrnt, *Dans l'Attente de Dieu* (Tournai: Casterman, 1970), p. 52.

14. Emmanuel Le Roy Ladurie, *Le Territoire de l'Historien* (Paris: Gallimard, 1973), p. 154.

15. P. Ourlac, in Fliche et Martin (eds.), *Histoire de l'Eglise* XIV:521.

16. Nicholas of Cusa, cited by Zahrnt, op. cit., p. 35.

17. Johan Huizinga, *The Waning of the Middle Ages*, tr. by F. Hopman (1924; Baltimore: Penguin Books, 1955, which is cited here), p. 30.

18. Cited ibid., p. 35; cf. Nicolas de Clemanges, *Le Traité de la Ruine de l'Eglise*, ed. by A. Coville (Paris: E. Droz, 1936).

19. Cf. above, Introduction.

20. Huizinga, op. cit., pp. 26–27.

21. In regard to the obsession with death, some remarks of Freud deserve to be cited here. One of his patients (the "rat-man") "had a quite peculiar attitude toward the question of death. He showed the deepest sympathy whenever any one died, and religiously attended the funeral; so that among his brothers and sisters he earned the nickname of 'bird of ill omen.' In his imagination, too, he was constantly making away with people so as to show his heartfelt sympathy for their bereaved relatives." The thoughts of these obsessed persons, Freud continues, "are unceasingly occupied with other people's length of life and possibility of death; their superstitious propensities have, to begin with, had no other content and have perhaps no other source whatever. But these neurotics need the help of the possibility of death chiefly in order that it may act as a solution of conflicts they have left unsolved": "Notes upon a Case of Obsessional Neurosis," *CP* 3:370–71.

22. Cf. Huizinga, op. cit., chapter 11: "The Vision of Death"; Mollat, art. cit.; Philippe Ariès, *Western Attitudes toward Death: From the Middle Ages to the Present*, tr. by P. M. Ranum (Baltimore: Johns Hopkins University Press, 1974).

23. Huizinga, op. cit., p. 33.

24. Cf. ibid., p. 148.

25. Cf. ibid., Chapter 11. Cf. Roman Jacobson, "Les Mystères Burlesques au Moyen Age," *Critique*, March, 1974, p. 287, on the "funeral games" in Subcarpathian Russia: "In the room in which the dead person was laid out . . . the young people gathered in the evening and indulged in frightening and barbaric games with the corpse. For example, they would drag him by the feet and urge him to stand up. They would pass a piece of straw or fir-twig under his nose and tickle him to make him laugh, and all this in the

presence of his family. They would tie a string to the dead man's hand and, while the psalter was being read, the young men would pull on the string and make the dead man's hand move. They would place the body on a bench, attach a cord to leg or arm, and pull it while shouting: 'He's getting up! He's getting up!' "

26. Huizinga, op. cit., p. 24.

27. *Acta Sanctorum* I:485–94.

28. Huizinga, op. cit., p. 193.

29. Cf. ibid., chapters 20 and 21.

30. Gimpel, op. cit., pp. 200–4.

31. Pernoud, *Histoire de la Bourgeoisie Française* I:311. Jacques Coeur was condemned in 1453.

32. Huizinga, op. cit., pp. 44–50.

33. One saying had it that "On a day when you see Christopher's face you will not die a violent death" (cited in Mollat, art. cit., p. 227).

34. Especially sins of "the flesh." Gerson was the first, as far as I know, to regard masturbation as a more serious sin than sexual relations outside of marriage. Jean de Varennes called for the stoning of adulterers and denied the validity of the ordination of "unworthy" priests. Cf. Huizinga, op. cit., pp. 196–97. Cf. Jos van Ussel, *Histoire de la Répression Sexuelle* (Paris: Robert Laffont, 1972).

35. Pernoud, op. cit., pp. 136–37.

36. Ibid., p. 169.

37. Ibid., p. 206.

38. Mollat, op. cit. (n. 10), pp. 206–13.

39. Ibid., pp. 66–68, 74–75, 137–41, 220–28, 233–35.

40. We see the lords rebelling especially in 1440 (the Praguerie), 1465 (the Ligue de Bien Public), etc. The Estates General of 1357, composed of delegates from the three orders, already claimed the right to assemble on its own authority in order to decide on war, taxes, and the appointment of royal councillors; cf. Mollat, op. cit., p. 67.

41. Ibid., p. 145.

42. Ibid., p. 146.

43. Pernoud, op. cit., p. 414.

44. Mollat, op. cit., p. 127.

45. Pernoud, op. cit., pp. 352–53.

46. Ibid., pp. 244ff.

47. The Jacquerie (1358), Wat Tylor in England (1381), the Maillotins (Paris), Harelle (Rouen), and Tuchins (Languedoc) in 1382, Caboche (Paris) in 1413, and so on.

48. Pernoud, op. cit., p. 238; cf. ibid., p. 116.

49. Ibid.

50. It is not easy to get access to the texts of Occam. The reader may fall back on several studies devoted to him: Louis Vereecke, "L'Obligation Morale selon Guillaume d'Occam," *VSS*, no. 45 (1958); Paul Vignaux, "Occam, III–IV," *DTC* 11:876–90, and *Nominalisme du XIVᵉ Siècle* (Montreal: Institut d'Etudes Médiévales, 1948); Georges de Lagarde, *Naissance de l'Esprit Laïque au Déclin du Moyen Age* (rev. ed.; Louvain: Nauwelaerts and Paris: Editions Béatrice-Nauwelaerts, 1956–70), vols. 4–5; Maurice Gandillac, "Ockham et la 'Via Moderna,'" in Fliche et Martin (eds.), *Histoire de l'Eglise* XIII, pp. 417–38. On the present state of Occam studies, cf. William J. Courtenay, "Nominalism and Late Medieval Thought: A Bibliographical Essay," *Theological Studies* 33 (1972), 721–30.

51. The voluntarism of Henry of Ghent (Henricus Gandavensis) may have prepared the way for Occam. Cf. Vernon J. Bourke, *History of Ethics* (Garden City, N.Y.: Doubleday, 1968), p. 104.

52. Occam, *I Sent.* II, 7, cited in Gandillac, art. cit., p. 427, n. 1.

53. Lagarde, op. cit., 5:46–47.

54. Vereecke, art, cit., p. 134.

Chapter 5

1. Jacques Soustelle, *Les Quatre Soleils* (Paris: Plon, 1967), p. 247.

2. Michel Mollat, *Genèse Médiévale de la France Moderne* (Paris: Arthaud, 1977), Preface.

3. Soustelle, op. cit., p. 271.

4. As Régine Pernoud has clearly shown in her *Pour en Finir avec le Moyen Age* (Paris: Seuil, 1977).

5. Cf. Erik H. Erikson, *Young Man Luther: A Study in Psychoanalysis and Society* (New York: Norton, 1958).

6. The disciples of St. Thomas did not put up any resistance to the common outlook, but interpreted their master as a legalist.

7. Joseph Moingt, "Le Dieu de la Morale Chrétienne," *RSR* 62 (1974), 653.

8. Jean Delumeau, *Naissance et Affirmation de la Réforme* (Nouvelle Clio 30; Paris: Presses Universitaires de France,1965); idem, *Catholicism Between Luther and Voltaire: A New View of the Counter-Reformation*, tr. by J. Philadelphia: Westminster, 1977); and idem, *Le Christianisme va-t-il Mourir?* (Paris: Hachette, 1977).

9. Orest Ranum, *Les Parisiens du XVIIᵉ Siècle* (Paris: Armand Colin, 1973), p. 269.

10. Bernard Plongeron, "Napoleon I and Political Ethics," in F. Böckle and J.-M. Pohier (eds.), *Power and the Word of God* (Concilium 90; New York: Herder and Herder, 1973), pp. 66–76.

11. Raymond Deniel, *Une Image de la Famille et de la Société sous la Restauration* (Paris: Editions ouvrières, 1965).

12. Voltaire, *Dialogues.*

13. Cf. P. Haubtmann, *P. J. Proudhon: Genèse d'un Anti-théiste* (Paris: Mame, 1969), p. 161.

14. Friedrich Nietzsche, *The Will to Power*, tr. by W. Kaufmann and R. J. Hollingdale (New York: Random House, 1967), no. 253, p. 147.

15. Nineteenth century theologians no longer dared remind people of the positions of St. Thomas (which were commonly held in the thirteenth century) on property: that it may be justly acquired and kept, but that its use must take the common good into consideration.

16. Cf. Jean Tonneau, "Propriété," *DTC* 13:757–846.

17. Pernoud, *Histoire de la Bourgeoisie Française* I:356.

18. Whereas in the Middle Ages first the slaves, then the serfs, were gradually emancipated. It was the sixteenth century that brought slaves on the scene again: the blacks of Africa who were brought in chains to America. The first convoy of slaves was in 1517 (cf. Pernoud, op. cit., p. 366). We all know how the "whites," in their greed for gold, treated the Indians of North and South America.

19. Philippe Ariès, "Religion Populaire et Réformes Religieuses," in *Religion Populaire et Réforme Liturgique* (Paris: Cerf, 1975), p. 86.

20. Immanuel Kant, *Critique of Practical Reason*, tr. by T. A. Abbott, in *Kant* (Great Books of the Western World 42; Chicago: Encyclopaedia Britannica, 1952), p. 310.

21. Ibid., p. 303.

22. Immanuel Kant, *Fundamental Principles of the Metaphysic of Morals*, tr. by T. A. Abbott, in *Kant*, p. 254.

23. Ibid., p. 260.

24. *Critique of Practical Reason*, p. 303.

25. Immanuel Kant, *Opus Posthumum* (in the French tr. of Gibelin), p. 23.

26. Ibid., p. 12.

27. Ibid., p. 8.

28. Ibid., p. 45.

29. *Critique of Practical Reason*, pp. 330–31.

30. Immanuel Kant, *The Doctrine of Virtue*, tr. by M. J. Gregor (New York: Harper Torchbooks, 1964), p. 35.

31. *Critique of Pure Reason*, tr. by J. M. D. Meiklejohn, in *Kant*, p. 236.

32. Cf. R.-A. Gauthier, "Eudémonisme," *DTC* 4:166.

33. Cf. *Critique of Pure Reason*, pp. 113–15.

34. Cf. *Critique of Practical Reason*, p. 360. Cf. the well-known passage: "Two things fill the mind with ever new and increasing admiration and awe, the oftener and the more steadily we reflect on them: *the starry heavens above and the moral law within*" (ibid.).

35. Eric Weil, *Philosophie Morale* (2nd ed.; Paris: Vrin, 1969), p. 101.

Chapter 6

1. 1 Jn 3:11; cf. Deut 6:5; Lev 19:18.

2. The moralities of duty have given the word "commandment" the sense of strict and legalistic obligation, but this restricts and distorts the meaning of the Greek word *entolē*. The same holds for the words "justice" (or "uprightness") and "law." *Entolē* is indeed a commandment, but in the form of teaching or instruction (1 Thess 4:1), and is thus fairly close in meaning to "ways" (*hodoi*) or "principles of life" (1 Cor 4:17).

3. On the proper meaning of "world" and "flesh," cf. below [pp 262–64 of French; 243–46 of English].

4. Rom 6:6; Eph 4:22; Col 3:9.

5. Friedrich Nietzsche, *Thus Spoke Zarathustra*, tr. by W. Kaufmann (New York: Viking, 1966); Part III, no. 12: "On New and Old Tablets," p. 199. Nietzsche has another remark that applies especially to the moralists of duty: "Moral judgments and condemnations constitute the favorite revenge of the spiritually limited against those less limited—also a sort of compensation for having been ill-favored by nature—finally an opportunity for acquiring spirit and *becoming* refined—malice spiritualized": *Beyond Good and Evil*, tr. by W. Kaufmann (New York: Random House Vintage Books, 1966), no. 219, p. 147.

6. Sigmund Freud, *Moses and Monotheism*, pp. 139–40. Cf. also has *Civilization and Its Discontents* and his *Group Psychology and the Analysis of the Ego*, tr. by J. Strachey (New York: Liveright, 1967), chapter 5 (pp. 25–31).

7. Gérard Mendel, *Pour Décoloniser l'Enfant* (Paris: Payot, 1971), p. 245.

8. G. Defois et al., *Le Pouvoir dans l'Eglise* (Paris: Cerf, 1973), p. 65.

9. Ibid., p. 98.

10. Many examples of this view of things may be found in Raymond Deniel, *Une Image de la Famille et de la Société sous la Restauration* (Paris: Editions ouvrières, 1965).

11. Defois et al., op. cit., p. 98.

12. Ibid., p. 16.

13. Ibid., p. 77.

14. Ibid., p. 75.

15. Louis Althusser, "Idéologie et Appareils Idéologiques," *La Pensée*, June, 1970, p. 24. Cf. E. Duval, "L'idéologie," *VSS*, no. 106 (September, 1973), p. 283; A. Dumas, "Fonction de l'Eglise," in his *Prospective et Prophétie* (Paris: Cerf, 1972).

16. Cf. Paul Tillich, *Morality and Beyond* (New York: Harper & Row, 1963), p. 74: "Only conscientiousness is always demanded. This correponds to the Protestant, especially the Lutheran, evaluation of works. It is the expression of the activistic element of the *bougeoisie* and is identical with the bourgeois adaptation to the technical and psychological demands of the economic system. Duty is what serves bourgeois production." The Lutheran bougeoisie is not the only group to which this description applies.

200

17. Friedrich Nietzsche, *La Volonté de Puissance* (Paris: Nouvelle Revue Française, 1935), p. 120. [The order of entries and even, it seems, the overall content are different in the French translation and in the Kaufmann–Hollingdale version. I have not been able to find all the cited passages in the English version and have had to translate some from Plé's French text.—Tr.]

18. Roger Mehl, "Universalité et Párticularité du Discours de la Théologie Morale," *RSR* 59 (1971), 370. In its document "La Parole de l'Eglise en Matière Éthique," the Lyons Theological Commission sees as "doubtful in our day the claims of a moral discourse that seeks to be universal. Any moral discourse is but one phase in a search for universality; if it does not view itself in this light, it becomes atemporal, centralistic, and in the final analysis ineffective": *DC* 71 (1974), 528. Cf. Bishop Matagrin: "In the past, obeying God meant applying a creed and a moral code to the circumstances of everyday life. Today it means, above all, being faithful to the God who calls us, by finding a response that is inspired by faith and love": *Jacques Duquesne Interroge Mgr Matagrin* (Paris: Le Centurion, 1973), p. 85.

19. Charles Péguy, *Note Conjointe sur M. Descartes*, in *Oeuvres Complètes* (Paris: Nouvelle Revue Française), 9:102–3.

20. Sigmund Freud, *Moses and Monotheism*, p. 156.

21A. One might add, with a celibate clergy especially in mind, the sacredness of the archaic Mother that has been projected onto the Church; cf. A. Plé, "Révolte Contre la Mère?" *Le Supplément*, September, 1970, pp. 311–32.

21B. Cf. Philippe Delhaye, "La Charité Reine des Vertus," *VSS*, no. 41 (1957), 135–71.

22. Sigmund Freud, *Group Psychology and the Analysis of the Ego*, pp. 25–31. Cf. Wilfried R. Bion, *Experiences in Groups and Other Papers* (New York: Basic Books, 1969); Jean-Pierre Deconchy, *L'orthodoxie Religieuse* (Paris: Editions ouvrières, 1971); etc.

23. Moral obligation is endogenous. Cf. Jean Tonneau, *Absolu et Obligation en Morale* (Paris: Vrin, 1965).

24. Sören Kierkegaard, *Either/Or* (2 vols.; Princeton: Princeton University Press, 1949), vol. 2, tr. by W. Lowrie, p. 213.

25. Arthur Vermeersch, *De Castitate et Vitiis Contrariis* (Rome: Gregorian University Press, 1921), p. 256, no. 258.

26. *ST* 1–2, 71, 4c; etc.

27. Cf. A. Motte, "The Obligation to Follow a Vocation," in *Vocation*, tr. by W. Mitchell (London: Blackfriars, 1952), pp. 18–36.

28. Cf. Pierre Cotel and Emile Jombart, *Cathechism of the Vows*, tr. by W. H. McCabe (New York: Benziger, 1924), p. 36. This book was originally published in 1862 and came to be widely used by religious men and women, thanks to later editions that were "harmonized with the Code of Canon Law." These words are from Emile Jombart's 1919 edition, the one translated into English. Jombart is careful "to effect a clear-cut distinction between canonico-moral questions, which involve obligations imposed under pain of sin, and ascetical questions which deal with perfection" (pp. 12–13). Thus morality is, on the one hand, absorbed by law and, on the other, cut off from "asceticism" (from which any mystical perspective is expressly excluded).

29. St. Thomas, *ST* 1-2, q. 55.

30. Heribert Jone, *Moral Theology*, translated and adapted by Urban Adelmann (Westminster, Md.: Newman, 1948), p. 276, no. 388.

31. Cf. J.-M. Pohier, "Psychologie Contemporaine et Requêtes de la Foi," *VSS*, no. 82 (1967), 395-412. Appealing to St. Thomas, Pohier regards Christian action as one of the theological loci, or sources, for moral thought.

32. Aristotle, *Nicomachean Ethics*, 1112a29-32.

33. R.-A. Gauthier and J.-Y. Jolif, *L'Ethique à Nocomaque: Commentaire* (Louvaine Editions universitaires, 1959), p. 25.

34. "Does not all formal thinking make claims that are all the more absolute as the thinking is empty of existential content? Nothing is more radically absolute than an affirmation about purely abstract being": Antoine Vergote, "L'accès à Dieu par la conscience morale," *ETL* 37 (1961), 485. Vergote concludes that "the absolute is not written into moral precepts" and that "in Kantian formalism we see an absolutist ambition of the spirit which no positivism can justify" (p. 491).

35. Arthur Rimbaud, "First Communions," VIII and IX, in *Complete Works, Selected Letters*, tr. by W. Fowlie (Chicago: University of Chicago Press, 1966), p. 101.

36. Friedrich Nietzsche, *The Will to Power*, no. 141, p. 91.

37. Emmanuel Mounier, *Traité du Caractère* (Paris: Seuil, 1947), p. 509.

38. There is no object without a subject; the two are inseparable. The will of the subject cannot be excluded from moral evaluation. Cf. St. Thomas, *ST*, 1-2, pp. 18-19.

39. Sigmund Freud, *Civilization and Its Discontents*, p. 91.

40. Sigmund Freud, "Thoughts on War and Death," *CP* 4:299.

41. Montaigne, *Essays*, III, 13: "Of Experience," in *The Complete Works of Montaigne*, tr. by D. M. Frame (Stanford, Calif.: Stanford University Press, 1958), p. 856.

42. Cf. Eliane Amado Levi-Valensi, *Le Temps dans la Vie Morale* (Paris: Vrin, 1968).

43. Sigmund Freud, *Civilization and Its Discontents*, p. 81, n. 1.

44. Sigmund Freud, *The Ego and the Id*, p. 76.

45. E. R. Dodds, *The Greeks and the Irrational* (Berkeley and Los Angeles: University of California Press, 1959), p. 75.

46. For "the aggressiveness of conscience keeps up the aggressiveness of the authority" (*Civilization and Its Discontents*, p. 75), and "the prevention of an erotic satisfaction calls up a piece of aggressiveness against the person who has interfered with the satisfaction, and . . . this aggressiveness has itself to be surpassed in turn" (ibid., p. 85). "An evil impulse—a death wish— is always at the basis of the formation of a prohibition" (*Totem and Taboo*, p. 95).

47. Dénis Vasse, *Le Temps du Désir* (Paris: Seuil, 1969), p. 144.

48. Cf. A. Hesnard, *L'Univers Morbide de la Faute* (Paris: Presses Universitaires de France, 1949), and *Morale sans Péché* (ibid., 1954).

49. Paul Ricoeur, " 'Morale sans Péché ou Péché sans Moralisme," *Esprit,* August–September, 1954, p. 308.

50. Gregory Zilboorg, "Le Sentiment de Culpabilité," *VSS,* no. 63 (1962), 540.

51. Ricoeur, art. cit., p. 311.

52. Sigmund Freud, "On Narcissism: An Introduction," *CP* 4:30–59.

53. A. Green, "Le Narcississme Moral," *RFP,* May–June, 1969, p. 354.

54. Ibid., p. 348.

55. Ibid., pp. 362 and 346.

56. A. Plé, *Freud et la Morale* (Paris: Cerf, 1969), chapter 4.

57. Green, art. cit., p. 358.

58. Ibid., p. 346.

59. The superego represents tradition. Cf. Janine Chasseguet-Smirgel, "Essai sur l'Idéal du Moi," *RFP,* September–December, 1973, p. 760.

60. Antoine Vergote, *L'Interprétation du Langage Religieux* (Paris: Seuil, 1974), pp. 196–97.

61. Chasseguet-Smirgel, art. cit., p. 770.

62. Sigmund Freud, "The Economic Problem in Masochism," *CP* 2:266–77.

63. Cf. Freud, *Civilization and Its Discontents,* p. 91.

64. Friedrich Nietzsche, *On the Genealogy of Morals,* tr. by W. Kaufmann (New York: Random House Vintage Books, 1967).

65. Friedrich Nietzsche, *Beyond Good and Evil,* no. 186, p. 98. Cf. *La Volonté de Puissance,* pp. 115, 119, etc.

66. Cf., e.g., Aristotle, *Nicomachean Ethics,* 1094b14, and in the commentary of Gauthier-Jolif (n. 33), pp. 10–12.

67. Cf. C. T. Frey Wehrlin, *Tiefenpsychologie und Ethik,* cited in Groeger, "La Monogamie a-t-Elle un Avenir?" *Dialogue,* no. 37, p. 6: "All present morality comes from the past and is thus unsuited for resolving really current problems."

68. Green, art. cit., p. 355.

69. Freud is one of the great revealers of this mask of rationalizations. Cf. Karl Stern, *The Flight from Woman* (New York: Farrer, 1965).

70. Friedrich Nietzsche, *La Volonté de Puissance,* p. 133.

71. Friedrich Nietzsche, *Beyond Good and Evil,* no. 187, p. 99.

72. Karl Marx, *The Holy Family,* cited in Michel Verret, *Les Marxistes et la Religion. Essai sur l'Athéisme Moderne* (Paris: Editions sociales, 1965), p. 142.

Chapter 7

1. Charles Odier, *Les Deux Sources Consciente et Inconsciente de la Morale* (Boudry, Switz.: La Baconnière, 1963).

2. A. Hesnard, *L'Univers Morbide de la Faute* (Paris: Presses Universitaires de France, 1949), and *Morale sans Péché* (ibid., 1954).

3. Paul Tillich, *Morality and Beyond* (New York: Harper & Row, 1963), p. 77.

4. Jacques Maritain, *La Philosophie Morale* 1 (Paris: Gallimard, 1960), p. 548.

5. I may mention "situation morality," the efforts of Romano Guardini to do justice to "the vibrant nobility, greatness and beauty of the good" (*Morale au-delà des Interdits* [Paris: Cerf, 1970], p. 8), and, along personalist lines, Bernhard Häring, *Morality Is For Persons.* (New York: Farrar, 1971); etc.

6. This is the line taken in existentialism, from Kierkegaard to Jean-Paul Sartre. Cf. Francis Jeanson, *Le Problème Morale et la Pensée de Sartre* (Paris: Seuil, 1965); Simone de Beauvoir, *The Ethics of Ambiguity*, tr. by B. Frechtman (New York: Citadel, 1964).

7. Cf. the Note issued by the Office of Doctrinal and Pastoral Research (of the Permanent Committee of the French Episcopate), June, 1968, in *DC* 66 (1969), 24–35. Cf. also Pierre Rémy, *Foi Chrétienne et Morale* (Paris: Le Centurion, 1973); Pinto de Oliveira, *Autonomie. Dimensions Éthiques de la Liberté* (Fribourg: Editions Universitaires, and Paris: Cerf, 1978); etc.

8. Cf. Jean-Marie Domenach, "Pour en Finir avec l'Aliénation," *Esprit*, December, 1965, pp. 1058–83; and Paul Ricoeur, "Aliénation," *Encyclopaedia Universalis.*

9. André Gide, *The Fruits of the Earth*, p. 12.

10. Cf. the list of moral systems based on pleasure, in A.-D. Sertillanges (ed.), *La Béatitude: Somme Théologique* (Paris: Editions de la Revue des Jeunes, 1936), p. 282; René LeSenne, *Traité de Morale Générale* (Paris: Presses Universitaires de France, 1942), on the moralities of pleasure (pp. 378–90) and the moralities of feeling (pp. 425–46).

The credit goes to Giovanni Blandino, S.J., for calling attention to the morality of pleasure; cf. G. Blandino et al., *L'etica della Felicità* (Bologna: Edizione di Etica, 1968). Without making any pretense at a complete bibliography I call the reader's attention to Jean Vanier, *Le Bonheur, Principe et Fin de la Morale Aristotélicienne* (Paris: Desclée De Brouwer, 1965); Nelly Beaupère, *Saint Paul et la Joie* (Paris: Cerf, 1973); and, of course, the three volumes of Jacques Dupont's *Les Béatitudes* (Paris: Gabalda, 1969). A quick review of the subject can be found in *Oui au Bonheur* (Sémaines des Intellectuels Catholiques, 1970; Paris: Desclée De Brouwer, 1970).

From a more spiritual than moral point of view: Michael Muller, *La Joie dans l'Amour de Dieu* (Paris: Aubier, 1935); Pie-Aymon Reggio, *La Joie* (Paris: Cerf, 1958); *Christus*, no. 63 (June, 1969): *Etre Heureux*; S. Pinckaers, *La Quête du Bonheur* (Paris: Téqui, 1979).

11. Kant was not the first to separate happiness and morality, at least "in this world." Malebranche had already written in his *Traité de Morale*, Part II, Chapter 2: "Happiness is the reward of merit and therefore cannot be the foundation of it."

12. Friedrich Nietzsche, *The Will to Power*, no. 296, p. 167.

13. Friedrich Nietzsche, *The Anti-Christ*, tr. by R. J. Hollingdale in *Twilight of the Idols and The Anti-Christ* (Penguin Classics; Baltimore: Penguin, 1968), no. 11, p. 122.

14. Albert Camus, "Nuptials," in his *Lyrical and Critical Essays*, tr. by E. C. Kennedy (New York: Knopf, 1969), p. 70.

15. Georges Dubal, *Moi et les Autres* (Neuchâtel: Delachaux and Niestlé, 1960), p. 22.

16. Friedrich Nietzsche, *Beyond Good and Evil*, no. 168, p. 92.

17. Gal 5:21; Rom 14:1; etc.

18. Phil 3:1; 4:4; 2 Cor 12:11; 1 Thess 5:16.

19. The verb *syn-chairein* (to rejoice together) is used seven times in the New Testament: Lk 1:58; 15:6, 9; 1 Cor 12:26; 13:6; Phil 1:17, 18.

20. Aristotle, *Nicomachean Ethics* 1155b8.

21. *ST* 2-2, 152, 1c.

22. Ibid., 1-2, 5, 1c.

23. *In 2 Corinthios*, lect. 5, on 13:11.

24. Aristotle, *Eudemian Ethics* 1214b10. Cf. *Nicomachean Ethics* 1119a10: "If a person does not take pleasure in anything and makes no distinction between various acts as far as degree of pleasure is concerned, he is far from human."

25. St. Augustine, *De Civitate Dei* VIII, 8 (*PL* 41:232).

26. Sigmund Freud, *A General Introduction to Psychoanalysis*, tr. by J. Riviere (New York: Boni and Liveright, 1924; New York: Pocket Books, 1952),p. 365.

27. For the psychiatric viewpoint, cf. Henry Ey, *La Conscience* (Paris: Presses Universitaires de France, 1963), pp. 336–66.

28. Paul Ricoeur sees a disparity between pleasure and happiness, while J.-M. Pohier sees an opposition. Cf. Paul Ricoeur, *Fallible Man*, tr. by C. Kelbley (Chicago: Gateway Editions, n.d.), p. 191, and J.-M. Pohier, *Le Chrétien, le Plaisir et la Sexualité* (Paris: Cerf, 1974), pp. 28–37.

29. Pohier, op. cit., p. 67; cf. pp. 29–30.

30. Ibid., p. 30.

31.. Cf. below, Part II, Chapter 9.

32. Bergson, *The Two Sources of Morality and Religion*, p. 101.

33. *ST* 2-2, 77, 7c.

34. *ST* 1-2, 3, 3 ad 2.

35. Jean Trémolières, *Diététique et Art de Vivre* (Paris: Seghres, 1976), p. 35.

36. Ibid., p. 225.

37. For St. Thomas, *delectatio* is a passion (1-2, 31). He reserves the word *gaudium* for the joy flowing from the activities of the mind, but he notes that "every object of pleasure can also be an object of joy for beings endowed with reason" (1-2, 31, 3c). This does not eliminate the sensible and passional character of the *delectatio* experienced by beings endowed with reason. St. Thomas often speaks of "spiritual pleasures [*delectationes spirituales*]" (e.g., 2-2, 141, 4 ad 4).

38. Cf. the works of Heath, Olds, and others. Cf. Robert G. Heath (ed.), *The Role of Pleasure in Behavior* (a symposium of twenty-two authors) (New York: Harper & Row, 1964).

39. In their own ways, economics and politics are beginning to concern themselves with the "well-being" of the population and are going in for statistics on the "gross national happiness."

40. According to St. Thomas, pleasures and pains are the principal passions; cf. *De Veritate* 26, 5.

41. *ST* 1-2, 34, 1c: "Pleasures, being connected with actions, have a greater affinity with these than do desires, which precede them in time."

42. Jacques Dupont, *Les Béatitudes* 2:324-38.

43. St. Paul speaks of the "blessed God" of the gospel (1 Tim 1:11; 6:15).

44. In this second case, the Greeks spoke of *eutychia*, which means both good fortune and happiness, *tychē* being what humans receive (of happiness and misfortune) by the will of the gods.

45. Aristotle, *Nicomachean Ethics* 1099b11.

46. Ibid., 1140a19.

47. Ibid., 1133b21-24.

48. Ibid., 1100b3.

49. Dupont, op. cit., 2:330.

Chapter 8

1. *Nicomachean Ethics* 1153b25.

2. *De Trinitate* XIII, 5, (PL 43:1020); cf. *Epistula* 130 *ad Probam* (PL 33: 493-507); *De Moribus Ecclesiae Catholicae* 3, 4 (PL 32:1312); etc.

3. *ST* 1-2, 5, 8c; cf. 5, 5, ad 1; etc.

4. *Essays* I, 20: "That to Philosophize Is to Learn to Die," tr. in Frame, op. cit., p. 56.

5. *Pensées*, Brunschvicg no. 425, in *Pascal: Pensées*, tr. by A. J. Krailsheimer (Baltimore: Penguin, 1966), no. 148.

6. *Critique of Practical Reason*, tr. by T. A. Abbott, in *Kant* (Great Books of the Western World 42; Chicago: Encyclopaedia Britannica, 1952), p. 300.

7. "Those who deny that their basic motivation is the search for pleasure are unconscious folk who would long since have vanished from the biosphere if what they said were true": Henry Laborit, *Eloge de la Fuite* (Paris: Laffont, 1974), p. 114.

8. Sigmund Freud, *Civilization and Its Discontents*, p. 23.

9. Igor Caruso, "L'Ambivalence dans la Société de Bien-être," *Bulletin de Psychologie*, March 30, 1963.

10. Poll conducted by SOFRES (Société Française d'Enquêtes par Sondages) and published in *Nouvel Observateur*, September 3-9, 1973, pp. 37-47.

11. Helmut Schelsky, *Sociologie de la Sexualité* (Paris: Nouvelle Revue Française, 1966), p. 201.

12. Henri Bergson, *Mind-Energy: Lectures and Essays*, tr. by H. W. Carr (London: Macmillan, 1920), p. 23.

13. *Nicomachean Ethics* 1175a20.

14. Ibid., 1099a12.

15. Ibid., 1175a10–20.

16. *Pensées*, Brunschvicg 425, Krailsheimer 148.

17. André Malraux, *Les Chênes qu'on Abat* (Paris: Gallimard, 1971), p. 120.

18. Antoine Vergote, "L'accès à Dieu par la Connaissance Morale," *ETL* 37 (1961), 495.

19. *ST* 1–2, 5, 3c. This is the theme of *Contra Gentiles* 3:48.

20. *Civilization and Its Discontents*, p. 23. Cf. ibid., p. 39: "Present-day man does not feel happy in his God-like character." The *Standard Edition* of Freud's complete works publishes some notes found on a separate sheet of paper (*SE* 23:300); in one such note, dated August 3 (1939? Freud died on September 23 of that year), Freud remarks that "there is always something lacking for complete discharge and satisfaction—*en attendant toujours quelquechose qui ne venait point* [always waiting for something which never came]." This theme of the "lack" has been taken up by Jacques Lacan and, in a different perspective, by D. W. Winnicott, *Playing and Reality* (New York: Basic Books, 1971); etc.

21. *Civilization and Its Discontents*, p. 24.

22. Ibid., p. 52. Cf. Freud's "Contributions to the Psychology of Love," *CP* 2:213–16.

23. Letter to Marie Bonaparte, in *Letters of Sigmund Freud*, selected by E. Freud and tr. by T. and J. Stern (New York: Basic Books, 1960), no. 290, p. 436.

24. Sigmund Freud, *Civilization and Its Discontents*, p. 24. Cf. "On Transience," *CP* 5:79–82; Y.C.J. Paret, "Essai sur le Bonheur," *RFP*, July–August, 1974, pp. 561–608.

25. Sigmund Freud, *Group Psychology and the Analysis of the Ego*, p. 47.

26. Sigmund Freud, *Civilization and Its Discontents*, p. 26.

27. Ibid. Cf. *Beyond the Pleasure Principle*, tr. by J. Strachey (New York: Liveright, 1950), pp. 86–87, etc.

28. Sigmund Freud, *Group Psychology and the Analysis of the Ego*, p. 47.

29. Sigmund Freud, "Negation," *CP* 5:184. This theme of the "lost object" has often been studied by psychoanalysts; cf. especially nos. 7–8 (1972) of the periodical *Topique*.

30. *Three Contributions to the Theory of Sex*, tr. by A. A. Brill in A. A. Brill (ed.), *The Basic Writings of Sigmund Freud* (New York: Random House, 1938), p. 614.

31. "Negation," *CP* 5:184.

32. *Three Contributions to the Theory of Sex,* p. 614. Cf. Gide's words in *The Fruits of the Earth*: "Nathaniel, I will speak to you of drunkenness. Nathaniel, often the simplest quenching of my thirst was enough to intoxicate me. I was already so drunk beforehand with desires. And what I looked for on the road first of all was not so much an inn as my hunger" (p. 106).

34. Sigmund Freud, *Beyond the Pleasure Principle,* p. 47.

35. Ibid., p. 50.

36. Ibid., p. 87.

37. Aristotle, *Politics* 1267b3–5.

38. Pascal, *Pensées,* Brunschvicg 82, Krailsheimer 44.

39. *Civilization and Its Discontents,* p. 92.

40. Ibid., p. 11.

41. *Thus Spoke Zarathustra,* Part III, no. 5: "On the Virtue That Makes Small," p. 169.

42. Ibid., p. 170.

43. Sigmund Freud, *Beyond the Pleasure Principle,* p. 56.

44. Sigmund Freud, *Civilization and Its Discontents,* p. 36.

45. Cf. ibid., p. 87.

46. "Civilized man has exchanged a portion of his possibilities of happiness for a portion of security" (ibid., p. 62).

47. Sigmund Freud, *An Outline of Psychoanalysis,* p. 110.

48. St. Augustine, *Confessions* X, 28, 39.

49. Voltaire, *Candide, Zadig, and Selected Stories,* tr. by D. M. Frame (New York: New American Library, 1961), p. 99.

50. Oscar Wilde, *Lady Windermere's Fan,* Act 3.

51. St. Bernard, *Treatise on the Love of God,* chapter 7, nos. 19 and 21.

52. Sören Kierkegaard, *Either/Or,* 2:164.

53. Ibid., 2:185.

54. Charles Baudelaire, *Elevation,* tr. by Roy Campbell, in *The Flowers of Evil,* selected and edited by Marthiel and Jackson Mathews (rev. ed.; New York: New Directions, 1962), p. 11.

55. Friedrich Nietzsche, *Beyond Good and Evil,* no. 224, p. 153.

56. Charles Baudelaire, *Recollection,* tr. by Robert Lowell, in *The Flowers of Evil,* p. 201.

57. Sigmund Freud, "Instincts and Their Vicissitudes," *CP* 4:82.

58. Sigmund Freud, "Contributions to the Psychology of Love," *CP* 4:215.

59. Charles Baudelaire, *My Heart Laid Bare,* no. XIX, in *My Heart Laid Bare, and Other Prose Writings,* tr. by N. Cameron (New York: Vanguard, 1951), p. 181.

60. Cf. Michael Balint, *Problems of Human Pleasure and Behaviour* (London: Hogarth Press, 1957); Daniel Wildocher, "L'Économie du Plaisir," *Nouvelle Revue de Psychanalyse,* no. 3 (Spring, 1971), pp. 161–75.

61. Sigmund Freud, *Beyond the Pleasure Principle*, p. 56.

62. Ibid., p. 7.

63. Sigmund Freud, *A General Introduction to Psychoanalysis*, p. 330.

64. Sigmund Freud, *Civilization and Its Discontents*, p. 31; "Instincts and Their Vicissitudes," *CP* 4:60–83, *passim*.

65. "Instincts and Their Vicissitudes," *CP* 4:70. Cf. *Civilization and Its Discontents*, p. 68: "But even where it [sadism] emerges without any sexual purpose, in the blindest fury of destructiveness, we cannot fail to recognize that the satisfaction of the instinct is accompanied by an extraordinarily high degree of narcissistic enjoyment, owing to its presenting the ego with a fulfillment of the latter's old wishes for omnipotence."

66. Sigmund Freud, "The Moses of Michelangelo," *CP* 4:257.

67. Sigmund Freud, "A Disturbance of Memory on the Acropolis," *CP* 5:305.

68. Sigmund Freud, "On Transience," *CP* 5:79.

69. Sigmund Freud, *Moses and Monotheism*, p. 149.

70. Sigmund Freud, *Civilization and Its Discontents*, p. 90. Cf. *Moses and Monotheism*, p. 150.

71. Friedrich Nietzsche, *Beyond Good and Evil*, no. 198, p. 109.

72. Sigmund Freud, "Formulations Regarding the Two Principles in Mental Functioning," *CP* 4:18.

73. Cited by A.-J. Festugière, "La Doctrine du Plaisir des Premiers Sages à Epicure," *RSPT* 25 (1936), 243.

74. The expresssion is Festugière's in his *L'Idéal Religieux des Grecs et l'Evangile* (Paris: Gabalda, 1932), p. 62.

75. St. Paul was already obliged to do battle against the gnostics and especially those who forbade marriage; cf. 1 Tim 4:3.

76. Cf. G. Bardy, "Apatheia," *Dictionnaire de Spiritualité* 1:727–46.

77. Raymond Polin, *Le Bonheur Considéré Comme l'un des Beaux-Arts* (Paris: Presses Universitaires de France, 1965), pp. 64–65.

78. Ibid., p. 82.

79. *Alain on Happiness*, tr. by R. E. and J. E. Cottrell (New York: Ungar, 1973), pp. 234, 236.

80. Denis Vasse, "Le Plaisir et la Joie," *LumVie*, no. 114 (1973), 85. This may be the case in a purely "economic" conception of pleasure, but is this the only conception, even in Freud?

81. François Laplantine, "Les idéologies contemporaines du plaisir," *LumVie*, no. 114 (1973), 64.

82. *Bhagavad-Gita* II, 47, tr. in R. C. Zaehner, *The Bhagavad-Gita* (Oxford: Clarendon Press, 1969), p. 51.

83. Sigmund Freud, *Civilization and Its Discontents*, p. 91.

84. The term is Alain's: "The egoist is sad because he is waiting for happiness" (*Alain on Happiness*, p. 243).

85. A. Green, in a paper read at the 30th Congress of Romance-Language psychoanalysts (1970), published in *RFP*, September, 1970, pp. 1–111.

Chapter 9

1. Sigmund Freud, *An Outline of Psychoanalysis*, p. 113.

2. *Nicomachean Ethics* 1175a24–28.

3. R. de Saussure, "Métaphysique du Plaisir," *RFP*, November-December, 1958, p. 659.

4. Sigmund Freud, "The Economic Problem in Masochism," *CP* 2:256.

5. It is symptomatic that the word "quality" is not an entry in the *Vocabulaire de la Psychanalyse* of Laplanche and Pontalis. But there is a reference to it in the article "Principe du Plaisir."

6. Sigmund Freud, "Analysis Terminable and Interminable," *CP* 5:329.

7. This use of the idea of "purity" is oddly close to Aristotle's: "The pleasures of thought are purer than the pleasures of the senses" (*Nicomachean Ethics* 1175a36). I would very much like to know what it is that Freud thinks these "finer and Higher" pleasures are "purified" from.

8. Sigmund Freud, "Instincts and Their Vicissitudes," *CP* 4:78.

9. Sigmund Freud, *Civilization and Its Discontents*, p. 26.

10. Sigmund Freud, *The Ego and the Id* [I have not been able to find the cited words in the English translation.—Tr.]

11. Aristotle, *The Soul* 421a25.

12. *ST* 1, 76, 5c.

13. Ibid., 2–2, 141, 4c.

14. Sigmund Freud, "The Dynamics of the Transference," *CP* 2:319.

15. Aristotle, *Nicomachean Ethics* 1174a16–18. Cf. J.-M. Pohier, *Le Chrétien, le Plaisir et la Sexualité* (Paris: Cerf, 1974), p. 31: "The fascination of pleasure is due in large part to the equivocal position it allows us to maintain regarding the possibility of satisfying desire. Man will turn pleasure into an absolute."

16. Friedrich Nietzsche, *Thus Spoke Zarathustra*, Part IV, no. 19: "The Drunken Song," p. 322.

17. Cf. Gauthier and Jolif, *Ethique à Nicomaque: Commentaire* 2:810.

18. Plato, *Phaedrus* 255b.

19. Cf. Yvonne Pellé-Douel, "Notes, sur l'Érotisme," in *Sexologie* (Paris: Presses Universitaires de France, 1971), p. 8.

20. Georges Bataille, *Death and Sensuality: A Study of Eroticism and the Taboo*, tr. by M. Dalwood (New York: Walker, 1962), p. 31.

21. Sigmund Freud, *Civilization and Its Discontents*, p. 11: "A sensation of 'eternity,' a feeling as of something limitless, unbounded—as it were, 'oceanic.' "

22. Published in *SE* 23:300.

23. Sigmund Freud, *New Introductory Lectures on Psychoanalysis*, p. 74.

24. Sigmund Freud, *An Outline of Psychoanalysis*, p. 108; "Psychanalyse et Médicine," in *Ma Vie et la Psychanalyse* (Paris: Nouvelles Revue Française, 1950), p. 112; *Inhibitions, Symptoms and Anxiety*, in *SE* 20:140.

25. Sigmund Freud, *An Outline of Psychoanalysis*, p. 109.

26. Denis Vasse, "Le Plaisir et la Joie," *LumVie*, no. 114 (1973), 99.

27. Georges Bataille, op. cit., p. 16 and passim.

28. Ibid., p. 19.

29. Ibid., p. 119. Bataille refers to the Bacchic festivals: "In the upside down world of feast-days the orgy occurs at the instant when the truth of that world reveals its overwhelming force. Bacchic violence is the measure of incipient eroticism whose domain is originally that of religion" (p. 117).

30. Ibid., p. 135.

31. Charles Baudelaire, *Fusées* III, tr. ibid., p. 127.

32. Cf. Freud, *The Future of an Illusion*, tr. by W. D. Robson-Scott, rev. by J. Strachey (Garden City, N.Y.: Doubleday Anchor Books, 1964), p. 25: "Those precepts [of civilization] themselves were credited with a divine origin; they were elevated beyond human society and were extended to nature and the universe."

33. Cf. Freud, *Civilization and Its Discontents*, p. 26: "The irresistibility of perverse instincts, and perhaps the attraction in general of forbidden things finds an economic explanation here."

34. Georges Bataille, op. cit., p. 140.

35. Ibid., pp. 141–42.

36. Cf. ibid., p. 31; Pellé-Douel, art. cit., p. 11.

37. Cf. *Either/Or*, 2:161.

38. Charles Baudelaire, *My Heart Laid Bare*, no. LV, in op. cit., p. 193.

39. Sigmund Freud, "On Narcissism: An Introduction," *CP* 4:58: "As in childhood, to be his own ideal once more, also where sexual tendencies are concerned, is the ideal that man strives to attain." And Freud, "Notes upon a Case of Obsessional Neurosis," *CP* 3:315: "The unconscious, I [Freud] explained [to the "Rat-man"] *was* the infantile" in us. Elsewhere Freud calls attention to the desire for "the immortality of the ego which is so relentlessly assailed by reality" ("On Narcissism: An Introduction," *CP* 4:49).

40. *ST* 1–2, 34, 1, ad 2; 1–2, 4, 2, ad 2. St. Thomas characterizes sins of intemperance as childish (2–2, 142, 2c).

41. Friedrich Nietzsche, *Beyond Good and Evil*, no. 175, p. 93.

42. Sigmund Freud, *Civilization and Its Discontents*, p. 30.

43. St. Augustine, *De Civitate Dei* XIV, 9 (*PL* 41:415).

44. Ibid. (*PL* 41:417).

45. Ibid. (*PL* 41:413). Cf. *In Epistolam Primam S. Joannis Tractatus* X, 6 (*SC* 75:426–27): "These pleasures [fleshly pleasures] are eating, drinking, lewdness, gaming, and hunting; these sumptuous vanities are the source of all evils. Does this mean we fail to recognize them as pleasurable? Who will deny that we find them attractive? But we love God's law even more."

46. Aristotle, *Nicomachean Ethics* 1107b7; 1119a5. Aristotle shows good sense when he observes that "pleasure has grown up with all of us from our earliest childhood; consequently it is difficult to rub off this passion and rid ourselves of it, so ingrained is it in our vital activity" (1105a1).

47. St. Thomas, *Summa Theologiae* 2-2, 142, 1; etc. Against the Stoics: 1-2, 24, 2, ad 3; etc. "There can be no happiness without concomitant sensible pleasure" (1-2, 4, 1c).

48. Rom 1:31; 2 Tim 3:3.

49. Phil 3:1; 4:4; 2 Cor 13:11; 1 Th 5:16.

50. Gal 5:22; Acts 13:52; Rom 14:17; 15:13; etc.

51. St. Augustine, *In Epistolam Primam S. Joannis Tractatus* X, 7 (*SC* 75: 428-29).

52. Cf. Françoise Dolto, "Au Jeu du Désir, les dés sont Pipés et les Cartes Truquées," *Bulletin de la Société Française de Philosophie*, 1972, no. 4, p. 132.

53. Charles Baudelaire, *My Heart Laid Bare*, no. XLII, in op. cit., p. 189.

54. Sigmund Freud, "Instincts and Their Vicissitudes," *CP* 4:65.

55. Sigmund Freud, "On Narcissism: An Introduction," *CP* 4:33.

56. Sigmund Freud, *A General Introduction to Psychoanalysis*, p. 428 Cf. "On Narcissism: An Introduction," *CP* 4:41-42: "The mechanism of disease and symptom-formation in the transference neurosis, the passage from introversion to regression, is to be connected with a damming-up of the object-libido."

57. Sigmund Freud, "On Narcissism: An Introduction," *CP* 4:30-31.

58. Ibid., pp. 47-48.

59. Sigmund Freud, *Totem and Taboo*, p. 117.

60. Sigmund Freud, *Three Contributions to the Theory of Sex*, in *The Basic Writings of Sigmund Freud*, p. 598.

61. Ibid., p. 597.

62. Cf. especially the following publications (in the order of their original appearance): "Formulations Regarding the Two Principles in Mental Functioning" (1911), *CP* 4:13-21; "On Narcissism: An Introduction" (1914), *CP* 4:30-59; "Instincts and Their Vicissitudes" (1915), *CP* 4:60-83; and especially *Beyond the Pleasure Principle* (1920).

63. Sigmund Freud, "The Economic Problem in Masochism" *CP* 2:257.

64. Sigmund Freud, "Some Character-Types Met With in Psycho-Analytic Work," *CP* 4:319.

65. Sigmund Freud, *Totem and Taboo*, p. 117.

66. Sigmund Freud, "Formulations Regarding the Two Principles of Mental Functioning," *CP* 4:18.

67. Sigmund Freud, "Psychanalyse et médicine," in *Ma vie et la psychanalyse*, pp. 151-52.

68. In one of his very last works, *An Outline of Psychoanalysis* (published after his death, in 1940), Freud writes: "The activity of the other agencies of the mind is able only to modify the pleasure principle but not to nullify it; and it remains a question of the greatest theoretical importance, and one that has not yet been answered, when and how it is ever possible for the pleasure principle to be overcome" (p. 109).

69. Cf. Freud, "The Loss of Reality in Neurosis and Psychosis," *CP* 2:279: "Neurosis and psychosis are both of them an expression of the *id* against the outer world, of its 'pain,' unwillingness to adapt itself to necessity, to *anankē*." And cf. *Beyond the Pleasure Principle*, p. 6: "The pleasure principle long persists, however, as the method of working employed by the sexual instincts, which are so hard to 'educate,' and, starting out from these instincts, or in the ego itself, it often succeeds in overcoming the reality principle, to the detriment of the organism itself."

70. Sigmund Freud, *The Future of an Illusion*, p. 81.

71. Sigmund Freud, "Analysis Terminable and Interminable," *CP* 5:352.

72. Denis Vasse, *Le Temps du Désir*, pp. 28–29.

73. Cf. Freud, *An Outline of Psychoanalysis*, p. 106: "Reality will always remain 'unknowable.' "

74. Cf. Vasse, op. cit., p. 64: "It is given to the human person to transform the relation of consumption, in which he has his origin and without which he perishes, into a relation of communion in which differences are not destined to disappear as they do in eating, but can attain fulfillment in the form of inalienable freedoms. When consumption can become a sign of communion, man appears on the scene."

75. D. W. Winnicott, *Playing and Reality* (New York: Basic Books, 1971), p. 2.

76. Cited by J.-B. Pontalis in his Preface to the French translation of Winnicott's book: *Jeu et Réalité* (Paris: Gallimard, 1976), p. XII.

77. Ibid.

78. Paul Ricoeur, *Fallible Man*, p. 197.

79. Charles Baudelaire, *Hymn to Beauty*, tr. by Dorothy Martin in *The Flowers of Evil*, p. 30.

80. Ricoeur, op. cit., p. 192.

81. Pohier, op. cit., p. 34.

82. Charles Baudelaire, *The Abyss*, tr. by Jackson Mathews, in *The Flowers of Evil*, pp. 193–94.

83. Maurice Bellet, *La Théorie du Fou* (Paris: Desclée De Brouwer, 1977), p. 35.

84. Aristotle, *Nicomachean Ethics* 1175a20.

85. St. Thomas often says that "truth is in the intellect" and "goodness is in things" (cf. *De Veritate* 21, 1c); that the movement of desire has reality for its goal (*ST* 1-2, 40, 2c and 6, ad 2), whereas the movement of knowledge terminates in the knowing subject (*De Veritate* 1, 2c).

86. *ST* 1-2, 1, 8c. Cf. 1-2, 2, 6, ad 1: "It is one and the same thing to desire the good and to desire pleasure which is nothing but a resting in the good."

87. *ST* 1-2, 2, 6, ad 1.

88. *ST* 1-2, 6, 1c; 2, 6c.

89. *ST* 1-2, 1, 1 ad 2. "Pleasure is a completion that accompanies seeing, and not a completion that makes the seeing more perfect in its kind" (1-2, 4, 2, ad 4), because appetite does not of itself possess a faculty by which to grasp its object (1-2, 3, 4).

90. *ST*, 1-2, 4, 2, ad 2. Cf. 1-2, 34, 1, ad 2.

91. Cf. J. Vanier, op. cit., pp. 256-65. This aspect of the moral good appears in the etymology of the Greek word *aretē*, "virtue." Karl Kerenyi, "Le Mythe de l'Arétè," in E. Castelli (ed.), *Démythisation et Morale* (Paris: Aubier, 1965), observes: "*Aretē* can be regarded as etymologically derived from *areskein*, 'to please': it is that which pleases—a feminine noun and an abstract one, but more feminine than abstract in character" (p. 29). Kerenyi also notes that the Latin *virtus*, on the contrary, reflects "the virile character of the death-dealing male" (p. 28).

92. A.-D. Sertillanges, *Saint Thomas d'Aquin* (Paris: Alcan, 1922), 2:231.

93. Aristotle, *Nicomachean Ethics* 1104b30: "The objects worthy of choice are three in number: the beautiful, the useful, and the pleasant." Cf. St. Thomas' commentary on this passage, and *ST* 1, 5, 6c, ad 2; etc.

94. *Nicomachean Ethics* 1174a1-7.

95. *ST* 1-2, 34, 4c: "Since, as I said, pleasure crowns an action after the manner of an end, the action cannot be perfectly good unless there is also pleasure in the good, for the goodness of a thing depends on its end. Thus the goodness of pleasure is in a way a cause of the goodness of the action. Cf. 1-2, 33, 4; 32, 1, ad 3. Cf. *Nicomachean Ethics* 1175a10-20, and St. Thomas' commentary on the passage.

96. Cf. *Nicomachean Ethics* 1099a17 and 1173b28-30, and St. Thomas' commentary on these passages, as well as *ST* 1-2, 34, 4c; 59, 3c; etc.

97. Cf. St. Thomas Aquinas, *In Ethica Nicomachea* X, lect. 6: "Those who feel no pleasure in virtuous actions will be unable to persevere in them."

98. *ST* 1, 95, 2, ad 3. And cf. the very shrewd observation: "The remedy for fatigue of soul as for fatigue of body is rest. It is pleasure that gives rest to the soul. Its fatigue must therefore be remedied by allowing it some pleasures that will lower the tension of the mind" (2-2, 168, 2c). Cf. also 2-2, 141, 6, ad 2. Also Aristotle, *Nicomachean Ethics* 1119a11-20; etc.

99. Anne Frank, *The Diary of a Young Girl*, tr. by B. M. Mooyaart (Garden City, N.Y.: Doubleday, 1952; New York: Simon and Schuster Pocket Books, 1953 [which is cited here]), p. 150, entry dated March 7, 1944. Anne would be fifteen years old on June 12 of that year.

100. Ibid., pp. 150-51.

101. Ibid., p. 151.

102. St. Thomas has a fine commentary on these texts. Cf. also *ST* 2-2, 23, 5; 26, 4, ad 3; 27, 3; etc.

103. Cf. St. Thomas' observation that sinners love themselves in the wrong way because they "think that the most important part of them is their sensual and corporeal nature" (in which the pleasure principle is in control),

whereas "the good, having a true knowledge of themselves, love themselves in a truthful way," that is, not making love of their own life their unqualified end (2-2, 126, 1c et ad 3).

104.   St. Thomas often adverts to this theme of self-love as the root and model of love for others: "One behaves toward others in the same way that one behaves toward oneself" (*ST* 1-2, 99, 1, ad 3; cf. 2-2, 25, 4; etc.).
He also bases this argument on the idea of unity: "Friendship implies a certain union. Dionysius says that 'love is a unifying force.' But every individual, in relation to himself, has his own unity which is superior to the union he can have with another. And just as unity is the principle of union, so the love one has for oneself is the form and root of friendship. It can be said that we have friendship with others when we are for them what we are for ourselves" (2-2, 25, 4c; cf. *In III Sent.*, d. 29, 1, 5, ad 2).

105.   *In III Sent.*, d. 29, 1, 5, ad 3.

106.   This theme has become increasingly popular ever since Maurice Nédoncelle's *La Réciprocité des Consciences. Essai sur la Nature de la Personne* (Paris: Aubier, 1942). Cf. especially Olivier du Roy, *La Réciprocité. Essai de Morale Fondamentale* (Paris: Epi, 1970). And cf. J.-C. Sagny, *Conflit, Changement, Conversion* (Paris: Cerf and Desclée, 1974), p. 26: "Reciprocity defines the world of human beings to such an extent that it serves as an adequate characterization of it."

107.   Cf. Freud, *Civilization and Its Discontents*, p. 41.

108.   Ibid., p. 26.

109.   Sigmund Freud, *The Future of an Illusion*, p. 89.

110.   Sigmund Freud, *Civilization and Its Discontents*, p. 90.

111.   Francis Pasche, "L'art et le syndrome," *RFP*, May–June, 1977, p. 473.

112.   Ibid., p. 473, n. 1. Freud did not analyze esthetic pleasure. In his opinion, "psychoanalysis, unfortunately, has scarcely anything to say about beauty" (*Civilization and Its Discontents*, p. 30).

113.   Denis Vasse, *Le Temps du Désir*, p. 64.

114.   *ST* 1, 60, 5c. Cf. *In Epistulam ad Romanos*, ch. 5, lect. 3: "Just as the various members of the body are parts of the person, so all human beings are parts and, as it were, members of human nature." And cf. *ST* 2-2, 47, 10, ad 2: "One who seeks the common good of the many seeks thereby his own good."

115.   *ST* 1-2, 109, 3c.

116.   *ST* 1, 6, 1, ad 2.

117.   *ST* 1-2, 2, 8c.

118.   *Contra Gentiles* 3:50. Cf. *ST* 1-2, 2, 7c: "Happiness is something of the soul, but that which produces it is independent of the soul."

119.   *Compendium Theologiae* 104.

120.   Aristotle, *Physics* 187b.

121.   St. Thomas, *Contra Gentiles* 3:49.

122.   *ST* 2-2, 47, 3, ad 2.

123.   St. Thomas, *Contra Gentiles* 3.49.

124. *ST* 1, 12, 4c.

125. Cf., among many other texts, this one from St. John of the Cross, *Spiritual Canticle*, second redaction, strophe 1, tr. by E. Allison Peers (Westminster, Md.: Newman; Garden City, N.Y.: Doubleday Image Books, 1961): "Be thou never willingly satisfied with that which thou understandest of God, but rather with that which thou understandest not of Him; and do thou never rest in loving and having delight in that which thou understandest and feelest concerning God" (p. 248).

126. St. Augustine, *In Epistolam Primam S. Joannis* tractatus IV, 6 (*SC* 75:230–31).

127. St. Thomas, *ST* 1–2, 109, 3c.

128. St. Thomas, *In 2 Corinthios*, ch. 3, lect. 2. The temptation springs from the infinite character of the desire (cf. *ST* 1–2, 30, 4; *In I Sent.*, 1, 4, 1, ad 2).

129. For St. Thomas, "order" is a relation, a structured dynamism, an end. Cf. *ST* 1, 11, 3c; 116, 2, ad 3; 2-2, 153, 2c; 161, 5c; etc.

130. *ST* 1, 93, 4c.

131. St. Thomas, *Contra Gentiles* 3:57.

132. St. Thomas, *ST* 2-2, 2, 3c. The theme of the human person as *capax Dei* and of the natural desire for God has given rise to many controversies. Cf. A.-D. Sertillanges (ed.), *Somme Théologique: La Béatitude*, pp. 305–15; A. Motte, in *Bulletin thomiste* 9 (1932), 651–75.

133. Gaston Bachelard, *The Poetics of Space*, tr. by M. Jolas (New York: Grossman, 1964; Boston: Beacon, 1969), p. 222.

Chapter 10

1. Cf. St. Thomas, *De Veritate* 26, 5c.

2. Aristotle, *Nicomachean Ethics* 1096a33–34.

3. Cf. St. Thomas, *ST* 1–2, 2, 2, ad 1.

4. Ibid., 1–2, 34, 4, ad 3.

5. Cf. St. Thomas, *Contra Gentiles* 2:26: "The ultimate completion of an act is the pleasure it affords."

6. Aristotle, *Nicomachean Ethics* 1153a12; etc.

7. Aristotle, *The Soul* 433a9–22. It is worth noting that one of Freud's great achievements was to have shown that psychic life is dynamic or finalized.

8. Ibid., 433a10.

9. Gauthier-Jolif, *Ethique à Nicomaque: Commentaire*, p. 577.

10. Aristotle, *Nicomachean Ethics* 1102a28. Gauthier and Jolif translate *logos* here as "rule," since the *logos* regulates desire.

11. Aristotle, *The Soul* 433a22–25. Cf. Gauthier-Jolif, op. cit., p. 211.

12. Aristotle, *The Soul* 433b5–12.

13. Aristotle, *Metaphysics* 1072a29–30.

14. St. Thomas, *ST* 1–2, 25, 2c; cf. 1–2, 11, 3, ad 3.

15. St. Thomas, *Contra Gentiles* 3:17, Cf. Aristotle, *Nicomachean Ethics* 1101b.

16. Sigmund Freud, *Civilization and Its Discontents*, p. 23. Cf. *A General Introduction to Psychoanalysis*, p. 366, etc.

17. Sigmund Freud, "Instincts and Their Vicissitudes," *CP* 4:65.

18. Sigmund Freud, *Civilization and Its Discontents*, p. 25.

19. Cf. Freud, "Instincts and Their Vicissitudes," *CP* 4:78: "Let us for the moment define loving as the relation of the ego to its source of pleasure."

20. Sigmund Freud, *The Origins of Psychoanalysis: Letters to Wilhelm Fliess*, tr. by E. Mosbacher and J. Strachey (New York: Basic Books, 1954), p. 384.

21. R. de Saussure, "Métaphysique du Plaisir," *RFP*, November-December, 1958, p. 341.

22. St. Thomas, *ST* 1–2, 35, 4, ad 2.

23. Ibid., 1–2, 2, 4c.

24. Ibid., 1–2, 108, 1, ad 2.

25. Eliane Amado Lévy-Valensi, *Voies et Pièges de la Psychanalyse*, pp. 197–98.

26. Aristotle, *Nicomachean Ethics* 1097b14–15. Cf.: "Happiness is therefore something final and independent, since it is, to begin with, the end to which all our objects and actions are ordered" (1097b20).

27. Ibid., 1139a31.

28. Ibid., 1139b4. The primordial importance of this reflective wish and of choice is clearly brought out by St. Thomas in his study of the virtue of prudence (*ST* 2–2, pp. 47–56) and more recently by Emmanuel Mounier, *Traité du Caractère* (Paris: Seuil, 1947), 2:395–467, and Olivier du Roy, *La Réciprocité. Essai de Morale Fondamentale* (Paris: Epi, 1970).

29. Aristotle, *Nicomachean Ethics* 1106b36. The famous "just mean" is to be understood as the "measure" that is appropriate in passions and actions (110bb14–35); it is a mean "not in the object" but "relative to us," a "relative mean" (1106a27, b7). The mean is an "extreme in the order of excellence and of the good in relation to us" (1107a8).

30. Sigmund Freud, *Civilization and Its Discontents*, p. 30. [The French translation of Freud which the author is using has here: "in what particular fashion he can *become happy*."—Tr.]

31. Sigmund Freud, "Psychanalyse et Médicine," in *Ma Vie et la Psychanalyse*, pp. 151–52.

32. Jean Trémolières, *Diététique et Art de Vivre* (Paris: Sghers, 1975), p. 275.

33. Sigmund Freud, *A General Introduction to Psychoanalysis*, p. 360. Freud also speaks of the phases of the Oedipus complex as following a "schedule"; cf. "The Passing of the Oedipus-Complex," *CP* 2:270.

34. Sigmund Freud, *Civilization and Its Discontents*, p. 71.

35. Andre Gide, *The Fruits of the Earth*, p. 12.

36. Erich Fromm, the psychoanalyst, has entitled one of his books *Escape from Freedom* (New York: Rinehart and Winston, 1972 [1941]). In his *Absolu et Obligation en Morale* (Paris: Vrin, 1965), Jean Tonneau observes (pp. 16–17) that the temptation to conceive the form of morality as an absolute —*absolutus*, i.e., detached, separated, without connections—springs from the desire to escape "indetermination and uncertainty," which are a source of anxiety. He cites a number of texts from St. Thomas, including this one: "In the order of action choice follows on a judgment of reason. But in this order great uncertainty is normal because our actions have to do with contingent singulars which by reason of their variability are uncertain" (*ST* 2–2, 14, 1c).

37. St. Thomas, *ST* 2–2, 186, 6, ad 3.

38. Ibid., 1–2, Prologue.

39. Ibid., 1–2, 108, 1, ad 2.

40. Ibid., 2–2, 19, 4c; cf. 2–2, 183, 4c. And cf. G. Dubal, *Moi et les Autres* (Neuchâtel: Delachaux et Niestlé, 1960), p. 148, n. 11: "The idea of freedom is connected with the Indo-European root *frei:* to have pleasure, to love, to be liberated"; "Free, or Liberated, from the Latin *liberare*, is another name for Bacchus."

41. St. Thomas, *In 2 Corinthios*, ch. 3, lect. 5; cf. *ST* 1–2, 107, 1, ad 2 and ad 3; 2–2, 44, 1, ad 2; *Contra Gentiles* 4:22.

42. Jacques Henriot, *Existence et Obligation* (Paris: Presses Universitaires de France, 1967), p. 406.

43. Ibid., pp. 156–57.

44. Ibid., p. 162.

45. Ibid., p. 165.

46. Ibid., p. 171.

48. Jean Tonneau has clearly brought out this position of St. Thomas; cf. his *Absolu et Obligation en Morale*. Moral obligation is the obligation imposed by the *dictamen rationis. (ST* 1–2, 108, 2, ad 1; cf. 1–2, 19, 3, ad 3).

49. *ST* 1–2, 90, 1, ad 1.

50. Ibid., 1–2, 21, 1c.

51. Ibid., 1–2, 71, 6c.

52. Ibid., 1, 113, 1, ad 2.

53. Ibid., 2–2, 19, 2, ad 2.—"Natural law . . . derives its force from nature and from the written law" (2–2, 60, 5c).

54. Ibid., 1–2, 71, 2, ad 4; 1–2, 106, 1, ad 2.

55. Ibid., 1–2, 90, 1c.

56. Ibid., 1–2, 99, 1c.

57. Ibid., 1–2, 21, 4, ad 3.

58. Ibid., 1–2, 99, 2–3.

59. Ibid., 1, 113, 1, ad 1; 1-2, 96, 2, ad 3; 2-2, 8, 3, ad 3.

60. Ibid., 1-2, 90, Prologue.

61. Ibid., 1-2, 106, 1c.

62. How can we fail to think here of Freud's statement: "My love is something valuable to me which I ought not to throw away without reflection. It imposes duties on me for whose fulfillment I must be ready to make sacrifices" (*Civilization and Its Discontents*, p. 56).

63. Amado Lévy-Valensi, op. cit., pp. 230-31.

61. Henry Ey, *La Conscience*, pp. 351-52.

62. Amado Lévy-Valensi, op. cit., p. 331.

66. Ibid., p. 367. Cf. p. 338: "Psychology implies an ethic that locates the subject's effort in a time of responsibility, consistency, development, and self-transcendence."

67. Ibid., p. 269.

68. Vasse, *Le Temps du Désir*, pp. 40-41.

69. Ibid., p. 39.

70. Amado Lévy-Valensi, op. cit., p. 334.

71. Ibid., p. 336.

72. This is at the basis of Freud's discoveries but also of anthropology. Cf. Claude Lévi-Strauss, *The Elementary Structures of Kinship*, tr. by H. H. Bell, J. R. v. Sturmer, and R. Needham (Boston: Beacon, 1969).

73. Sigmund Freud, *Totem and Taboo*, p. 117.

74. Sigmund Freud, *A General Introduction to Psychoanalysis*, p. 354. Cf. "Mourning and Melancholia," *CP* 4:152-70; "A Distortion of Memory on the Acropolis," *CP* 5:302-13.

75. Sigmund Freud, " 'Civilized' Sexual Morality and Modern Nervousness," *CP* 2:89.

76. Chassegut-Smirgel, art. cit., pp. 782-83.

77. Cf. Amado Lévy-Valensi, op. cit., especially p. 324; Vasse, *Le Temps du Désir*; Roland Sublon, *Le Temps de la Mort* (Strasbourg: Cerdic, 1975); Jean Bergeret, "La Notion du Plaisir," *LumVie*, no. 114 (1973), 53-54.

78. Sigmund Freud, *Beyond the Pleasure Principle*, p. 56.

79. Sigmund Freud, *Moses and Monotheism*, p. 152.

80. Sigmund Freud, *Civilization and It Discontents*, p. 24.

81. Sigmund Freud, "Thoughts on War and Death," *CP* 4:317.

82. Letter to Oskar Pfister, March 6, 1910, in *Psychoanalysis and Faith: The Letters of Sigmund Freud and Oskar Pfister*, tr. by E. Mosbacher (New York: Basic Books, 1963), p. 35.

83. Sigmund Freud, "The Loss of Reality in Neurosis and Psychosis," *CP* 2:279.

84. Vasse, *Le Temps du Désir*, p. 92.

85. Cf. F. X. Kaufmann, "Normes, Effondrement des Normes et Problème de la Liberté en Perspective Sociologique," *VSS*, no. 90 (September, 1969), 330-44.

86. Sigmund Freud, *Civilization and Its Discontents*, p. 36.

87. Ibid., p. 43.

88. Ibid., p. 44.

89. Ibid., ch. 8 (pp. 81-92).

90. Ibid., p. 81.

91. Cf. Ibid., p. 52.

92. Ibid., p. 87.

93. Ibid., p. 62.

94. Ibid., p. 24.

95. Ibid., pp. 55-56. For an analysis of these libidinal bonds in collective life, cf. *Group Psychology and the Analysis of the Ego*, ch. 7, on identification (pp. 37-43).

96. J.-C. Sagne, "La Loi, la Réciprocité et le Don," *VSS*, no. 108 (February, 1974), 13; reprinted in his *Conflit, Changement, Conversion* (Paris: Cerf, 1974).

97. Paul Valéry, *Oeuvres* (Pléïade edition) 2:40.

98. Friedrich Nietzsche, *Beyond Good and Evil*, no. 188, p. 100.

Chapter 11

1. André Gide, *L'Immoraliste* (Pocket Book ed.), p. 115.

2. Idem, *The Fruits of the Earth*, tr. by D. Bussy (New York: Knopf, 1949), p. 33.

3. Idem, *The New Fruits*, in *The Fruits of the Earth*, p. 222.

4. Senator Brongersma, "L'Homophile à Visage Découvert," *Arcadia*, January, 1974, pp. 23-24.

5. Aristotle, *Nicomachean Ethics* 1105a4.

6. Ibid., 1113a29-33.

7. Ibid., 1097b24.

8. St. Thomas, *ST* 1-2, 34, 4c.

9. Aristotle, *Nicomachean Ethics* 1107b31.

10. Ibid., 1103a3.

11. Ibid., 1102b28.

12. Ibid., 1102b13-24.

13. St. Augustine, *De civitate Dei* XIV, 26 (*PL* 41:433). See also *De Genesi Ad Litteram* IX, 10 (*PL* 34:395-96). Augustine's view of the flesh even makes him hopeful that before "sin" "the man's seed might have been communicated to his wife while leaving her virginity intact": *De Civitate Dei* XIV, 26 (*PL* 41:434).

14. *De Civitate Dei* XIV, 26 (*PL* 41:434): *Libidinis Morbum.*

15. Ibid., XIV, 16 (*PL* 41:425).

16. On Julian of Eclanum and his dispute with Augustine, cf. François Refoulé, "Julien d'Eclane, Théologien et Philosophe," *RSR* 52 (1964), 42–84, 233–47; Peter Brown, *Augustine of Hippo: A Biography* (Berkeley and Los Angeles: University of California Press, 1967), pp. 381–97.

17. For a history of the various opinions found in the tradition, cf. Joseph E. Kerns, *The Theology of Marriage: The Historical Development of Christian Attitudes toward Sex and Sexuality in Marriage* (New York: Sheed & Ward, 1964), especially the chapter entitled "If Adam Had Not Fallen."

18. St. Thomas, *ST* 1, 98, 2, ad 3.

19. St. Thomas, *In Aristotelis De Anima*, Lib. II, lect. 19.

20. St. Augustine, *Contra Julianum* V, 28 (PL 44:801).

21. *Quaedam deformitas immoderatae concupiscentiae* ("a certain disfigurement due to immoderate desire"): *ST* 1, 98, 2c; cf. 1–2, 56, 4c.

22. St. Thomas, *De malo* 4, 2, ad 1.

23. Cf. Françoise Dolto, *The Jesus of Psychoanalysis: A Freudian Interpretation of the Gospel*, tr. by H. R. Lane (Garden City, N.Y.: Doubleday, 1979), p. 17: ". . . the unconscious, where desire has its source, where it departs on the search for what it is lacking."

24. St. Thomas, *ST* 1–2, 55, 4, ad 5.

25. Sigmund Freud, *New Introductory Lectures on Psychoanalysis*, p. 80.

26. It is characteristic of the temperate person to desire what is suitable, and as and when it is suitable (Aristotle, *Nicomachean Ethics* 1119b18; St. Thomas, *ST* 1, 95, 2, ad 3; 2–2, 141, 6, ad 3). The function of virtue is to "introduce order" into love (*ST* 1–2, 55, 1, ad 4), and not to suppress the passions but to order them. Morality fulfills and completes desire by ordering it to the "reasonable" good, to the good-beautiful (ibid., 1–2, 59, 4c; 58, 2c). This happy ordering is healthy and beautiful (ibid., 1–2, 55, 2, ad 1). It is the function of reason to order things in view of an end (ibid., 1–2, 90, 1c).

27. Ibid., 1–2, 17, 1c.

28. The comparison is Aristotle's (*Politics* I, 3), and St. Thomas takes it over (*ST* 1, 81, 3, ad 2; 1–2, 56, 4, ad 3; 58, 2c). The resistance of the passions to the ascendancy (*imperium*) of the intellect is an effect of original sin: "As a result of its own rebellion against God, reason sees the flesh in turn rebelling against it" (ibid., 2–2, 153, 2, ad 2); consequently, each of our powers is "left to its own independent movement," ibid., 1–2, 82, 4, ad 1).

29. St. Thomas, *De Caritate*, 5, ad 3; 3, ad 18.

30. St. Thomas, *De Veritate* 15, 2, ad 9.

31. Aristotle, *Nicomachean Ethics* 1119a34–b18; St. Thomas, *ST* 2–2, 151, 1c.

32. St. Thomas speaks of a *vis motiva* (*ST* 1, 81, 3c).

33. St. Thomas, *De Virtutibus in Communi* 4c; *In III Sent.*, d. 23, q. 1, a. 1c.

34. St. Thomas speaks of a *materia circa quam* (*ST* 1-2, 55, 4c; 59, 4, ad 1; 2-2, 152, 1c). Cf. Aristotle, *Nicomachean Ethics*, 1152b1-7. St. Thomas, ibid., 1-2, 60, a. 5c: "The good of man, which is the object of love, desire and pleasure." It is on this basis that St. Thomas determines the object of the moral virtues (2-2, q. 58, a. 1c).

35. *ST* 1-2, 59, 4, ad 1.

36. Ibid., 1-2, 55, 1c.

37. Ibid., 2-2, 125, 2c.

38. Cf. St. Thomas, *In Ethica Nicomachea* VII, lect. 12 in fine, on 1153a34.

39. Prov 2:13-14.

40. Aristotle, *Nicomachean Ethics* 1176a24.

41. Ibid., 1099a17.

42. Ibid., 1173b28-30.

43. Ibid., 1114a31.

44. Ibid., 1114b1-20.

45. Ibid., 1168b34; 1169a5.

46. Ibid., 1139a24.

47. Ibid., 1139b4.

48. Ibid., 1176a10-23.

49. St. Thomas, *ST* 2-2, 32, 1, ad 1. Conversely, the pleasure derived from wrong action is the criterion of deliberate sin and vice: "One who sins because of passion commits the sin with a certain remorse and sorrow, while one who sins by free choice rejoices in the commission of the sin" (*In 2 Corinthios*, ch. 13, lect. 2).

50. *ST* 1-2, 34, 4c; cf. ibid., 59, 3c, and Aristotle, *Nicomachean Ethics* 1151b34.

51. *ST* 1-2, 34, 4.

52. Aristotle, *Nicomachean Ethics* 1175a20.

53. *ST* 1-2, 27, 3c.

54. Ibid., 1-2, 55, 2, ad 3.

55. Pierre Teilhard de Chardin, *On Happiness*, tr. by R. Hague (New York: Harper & Row, 1973), pp. 22-24.

56. Sigmund Freud, *The Future of an Illusion*, p. 22.

57. Chasseguet-Smirgel, art. cit., p. 872.

58. Aristotle, *Nicomachean Ethics* 1098b35.

59. Freud, *Civilization and Its Discontents*, pp. 26-27.

60. Ibid., p. 90.

61. Cf. Aristotle, *Nicomachean Ethics* 1115b12: "The beauty of its own act is the end virtue proposes to itself"; and 1116a6: "It is therefore for the beauty of his action that the courageous man stands fast."

62. Sigmund Freud, "On Narcissism: An Introduction," *CP* 4:50–57.

63. Sigmund Freud, *Moses and Monotheism*, pp. 149–50.

64. Ibid., p. 150.

65. Ibid., p. 109.

66. Sigmund Freud, *Civilization and Its Discontents*, p. 68.

67. Sigmund Freud, "On Narcissism: An Introduction," *CP* 4:57.

68. Chasseguet-Smirgel, art. cit., p. 776–77.

69. Ibid., pp. 904ff.

70. Madame Chasseguet-Smirgel asks (ibid., p. 876): "Why does the regulation of our 'self-esteem' depend so often on others?"

71. Sigmund Freud, *Civilization and Its Discontents*, p. 85.

72. Ibid., p. 26.

73. Georges Bataille, op. cit., p. 127, citing Baudelaire *Fusées* III.

74. Ibid., p. 105.

75. Chasseguet-Smirgel, art. cit., p. 813.

76. Sigmund Freud, "On Narcissism: An Introduction," *CP* 4:47.

77. Sigmund Freud, *Beyond the Pleasure Principle*, p. 44.

78. Sigmund Freud, *An Outline of Psychoanalysis*, p. 20.

79. Cf. Olivier du Roy, *La Réciprocité. Essai de Morale Fondamentale* (Paris: Epi, 1970), p. 6: "The ultimate truth of this morality consists in aiming beyond law and legality at encounter and reciprocity." Cf. also the special issue of *Christus*, no. 82 (April, 1974), on the new morality; etc.

80. From Hegel down to Husserl, Heidegger, Jaspers, and Jean-Paul Sartre, this relational component of the subject has been developed from all angles. Cf. especially Martin Buber, *I and Thou*, tr. by R. G. Smith, (2nd ed.; New York: Scribner's, 1958); Maurice Nédoncelle, *La Réciprocité des Consciences* (Paris: Aubier, 1942); Maxime Chastaing, *L'Existence d'Autrui* (Paris: Presses Universitaires de France, 1951); F. J. J. Buytendijk, *Phénoménologie de la Rencontre* (Paris: Desclée De Brouwer, 1952); Victor Jankélevitch, "Le Prochain et le Lointain," in *La Présence d'Autrui* (Paris: Presses Universitaires de France, 1957); more recently, J. Gouvernaire, "Des Interdits à la Relation," *Christus*, no. 82 (April, 1972), 176–88. Cf. also A. J. Voelke, *Les Rapports avec Autrui dans la Philosophie Grecque* (Paris: Vrin, 1961).

81. Sigmund Freud, *The Interpretation of Dreams*, tr. by J. Strachey, in *SE* 4:250.

82. Ibid., *SE* 4:255.

83. Ibid., *SE* 4:84.

84. Sigmund Freud, *Civilization and Its Discontents*, p. 87.

85. Sigmund Freud, *Group Psychology and the Analysis of the Ego*, p. 35.

86. Sigmund Freud, *A General Introduction to Psychoanalysis*, pp. 453–54.

87. Sigmund Freud, "Instincts and Their Vicissitudes," *CP* 4:79.

88. Sigmund Freud, *Group Psychology and the Analysis of the Ego*, p. 47. In his "Contributions to the Psychology of Love" Freud speaks of two currents of feeling: "To ensure a fully normal attitude in love, two currents of feeling have to unite—we may describe them as the tender, affectionate feelings and the sensual feelings. . . . Of these two currents affection is the older. It springs from the very earliest years of childhood" (*CP* 4:204).

89. Sigmund Freud, *Group Psychology and the Analysis of the Ego*, p. 72.

90. Sigmund Freud, "The Passing of the Oedipus-Complex," *CP* 2:273.

91. Sigmund Freud, *Three Contributions to the Theory of Sex*, in *The Basic Writings of Sigmund Freud*, p. 617, n. 2.

92. François Chirpaz, "Dimensions de la Sexualité," *Etudes* 330 (1969), 420. The same author writes in *Esprit*, November, 1969, p. 1839: "The essential ethical concern is to keep a human presence in the sexual act and to allow that to appear which seeks expression through it. The ethical concern must not come after the fact in an effort to give sexuality a moral standing; it must allow the meaning that is in the act to appear and to humanize and, in short, to make possible an encounter between the two persons." This describes the experience of some couples, such as Gérard and Anne Philipe: "We wanted to set fire in each other to that which is least ready to be kindled. Once our love was born we constantly explored and illumined one another. We were surrendered to one another" (*Le Temps d'un Soupir* [Paris: Le Livre du Poche, 1972], p. 119).

93. Mt 6:43–48.

94. Michel Adam, *La Calomnie, Relation Humaine* (Paris: Le Centurion, 1968).

95. Lk 6:28.

96. Mt 7:12. Ancient Chinese wisdom, for its part, taught that "what I do not wish others to do unto me, I also wish not to do unto them'" Confucius, *Sayings* V, 12, tr. by J. R. Ware (New York: New American Library, 1955), p. 40.

97. Maurice Bellet, "L'inadmissible," *Christus*, no. 82 (April, 1974), p. 250.

98. Piera Castoriadis-Aulagnier, "A Propos de la Réalité: Savoir ou Certitude," *Topique*, May 13, 1974, p. 13.

99. Roger Garaudy, in *Le Monde*, September 8, 1972.

100. Cf. S. Lebovici, "A Propos de la Lecture des Textes Freudiens sur le Narcissisme," *RFP*, September-December, 1965, p. 489: "The sexual instincts which from the outset required an object, and the needs of the ego instinct which are never capable of autoerotic satisfaction, naturally complicate this stage of the primary narcissism and open the way to a complicated development which has this stage for its point of departure."

101. Francis Pasche, "L'Anti-narcissisme," *RFP*, September-December, 1965, p. 507.

102. Sigmund Freud, "Instincts and Their Vicissitudes," *CP* 4:78–79.

103. Eduardo R. Colombo, "A Propos du Concept de Réalité dans la Théorie Psychanalytique," *Topique*, May 13, 1974, p. 62.

104. Sigmund Freud, *A General Introduction to Psychoanalysis*, p. 348:
"Such development [i.e., the development of the libido] involves two dangers; first, that of inhibition, and secondly, that of regression." Ibid., p. 428:
"The withdrawal of object-libido into the ego is certainly not pathogenic. . . . But it is quite a different matter when a definite, very forcible process compels the withdrawal of the libido from its objects. The libido that
has then become narcissistic can no longer find its way back to its objects,
and this obstruction in the way of the free movement of the libido certainly
does prove pathogenic. It seems that an accumulation of narcissistic libido
over and above a certain level becomes intolerable. We might well imagine
that it was this that first led to the investment of objects, that the ego was
obliged to send forth its libido in order not to fall ill of an excessive accumulation of it."

105. Cf. A. Green, "Le Narcissisme Moral," *RFP*, May–June, 1969, p. 357:
"The narcissistic wound inflicted by the impossibility of experiencing and
thus transcending omnipotence brings with it an excessive dependence on
the maternal object as a source of security."

106. Cf. Freud, *Civilization and Its Discontents*, p. 68: "Even where it
[sadism] emerges without any sexual purpose . . . the satisfaction of the instinct is accompanied by an extraordinarily high degree of narcissistic enjoyment, owing to its presenting the ego with a fulfilment of the latter's old
wishes for omnipotence."

107. Cf. S. Nacht, "Le Narcissisme, Gardien de la View," *RFP*,
September–December, 1965, p. 532: "A destructive response to frustration,
which then permeates the child himself, because he is unable to express
himself against an 'other' distinct from himself, becomes precisely what I
am calling organic primary masochism."

108. Sigmund Freud, *A General Introduction to Psychoanalysis*, p. 356.

109. Cf. Freud, "On Narcissism: An Introduction," *CP* 4:43: "The libido
that is liberated by frustration does not remain attached to objects in phan-
tasy, but returns to the ego: . . . . megalomania."

110. Sigmund Freud, *A General Introduction to Psychoanalysis*, p. 353.
Cf. Chasseguet-Smirgel, art. cit., pp. 735–930.

111. Sigmund Freud, *A General Introduction to Psychoanalysis*, p. 354.

112. Ibid.

113. Cf. Chasseguet-Smirgel, art. cit., p. 783: "Access to reality and the existence of the ego and the secondary processes are possible only in the absence of a total satisfaction of our desires, such as union with the mother
would bring us."

114. Cf. Freud, *The Ego and the Id*, p. 44: "The character of the ego is a
precipitate of abandoned object-cathexes and . . . contains the history of
these object-choices."

115. P. Luquet, "Introduction à la Discussion sur le Masochisme Secon-
daire," *RFP*, September–December, 1965, p. 522.

116. Cf. Francis Pasche, "L'Anti-narcissisme," *RFP*, September–December,
1965, pp. 503–19.

117. Luquet, art. cit., p. 524. Luquet remarks that under these conditions
"the ego functions have been autonomized." Cf. Freud, *The Ego and the Id*,
p. 44.

118. Cf. Nacht, art. cit., p. 530: "By itself a lack which the individual feels interiorly as essential can trouble the primary narcissism and sap the strength of this guardian of life. If something the individual feels to be essential is lacking to him, he sees the cohesion needed for existence as crumbling. He no longer loves himself, he no longer loves his life, and he ceases to cling to it. The primary narcissism is extinguished and the gates are opened to the enemy."

119. In the article cited in n. 98, pp. 5–6: "Every experience of pleasure *in the register of the I* implies that the statement which designates the latter as subject or object of an affect is for it a source of identificational pleasure." Cf. Chasseguet-Smirgel, art. cit., p. 770: "A certain narcissistic investment of the instincts is inherent in the integration of the latter into the person, that is, in their acceptance by the ego or their 'egotization' " (with a reference to B. Grunberger, "Etude sur la Relation Objectale Anale," in *Le Narcissisme* [Paris: Payot, 1959]).

120. Cf. Freud, *The Interpretation of Dreams*, in *SE* 4:566: "The bitter experience of life must have changed this primary thought-activity into a more expedient secondary one."

121. Sigmund Freud, *Beyond the Pleasure Principle*, p. 44.

122. Cf. ibid., pp. 43–88; *Civilization and Its Discontents*, p. 59: "Instinctual passions are stronger than rational interest"; *The Future of an Illusion*, ch. 10; etc.

123. Sigmund Freud, "Repression," *CP* 4:84.

124. Sigmund Freud, *The Interpretation of Dreams*, in *SE* 4:552.

125. Sigmund Freud, *New Introductory Lectures on Psychoanalysis*, p. 89.

126. Sigmund Freud, *Civilization and Its Discontents*, p. 56: "My love is something valuable to me which I ought not to throw away without reflection. It imposes duties on me for whose fulfillment I must be ready to make sacrifices."

127. Sigmund Freud, "Some Character-Types Met With in Psycho-Analytic Work," *CP* 4:319. And cf. "Formulations Regarding the Two Principles in Mental Functioning," *CP* 4:18: "A momentary pleasure, uncertain in its results, is given up, but only in order to gain in a new way an assured pleasure coming later."

128. Sigmund Freud, "Instincts and Their Vicissitudes," *CP* 4:78.

129. Sigmund Freud, *Civilization and Its Discontents*, p. 26.

130. Sigmund Freud, *Beyond the Pleasure Principle*, p. 21. Cf. Saussure's remark in his "Métaphysique du Plaisir," *RFP*, November–December, 1958, p. 662: "The more the id and the superego are in opposition to the ego, the less will the pleasure of any one of these instances correspond to that of the others." St. Thomas had already observed: "It can happen that a person experiences certain bodily pleasures in which he does not find joy from the standpoint of reason" (*ST* 1–2, 31, 3c).

131. Cf. Gide, *The Fruits of the Earth*, p. 220: "My happiness is to increase other people's. To be happy myself I need the happiness of all."

132. Daniel Lagache, "Vues Psychanalytiques sur le Bonheur," in *Les Conditions du Bonheur* (Rencontres Internationales de Genève; Boudry: La Baconnière, 1961), pp. 74–75.

133. Cf. Freud, "Analysis Terminable and Interminable," *CP* 5:354, 351–52: "To secure the best possible psychological conditions for the functioning of the ego" makes a cure possible, thanks to a "relationship between analyst and patient [that] is based on a love of truth, that is, on an acknowledgment of reality, and that . . . precludes any kind of sham or deception."

134. Sigmund Freud, "Formulations Regarding the Two Principles in Mental Functioning," *CP* 4:14.

135. Michael Balint, *Thrills and Repressions* (International Psychoanalytical Library 54; London: Hogarth Press, 1959), p. 65.

136. Jacques Lacan, *Ecrits* (Paris: Seuil, 1966), p. 181.

137. This is what the Father says at the moment of Jesus' baptism (Mt 3:17) and at the Transfiguration (Mt 17:5). Cf. Mt 12:18 (where Is 42:1 is cited) and 2 Pet 1:17.

138. Jn 8:29.

139. Lk 2:14.

140. Lk 12:32; cf. Mt. 11:26.

141. Eph 1:5.

142. Phil 2:13.

143. Eph 1:9.

144. Col 1:10.

145. 2 Cor 5:9.

146. Rom 15:2.

147. Cf. Rom 12:2; 14:18; 1 Cor 7:32; etc.

148. Gal 1:10; Eph 6:6; 1 Thess 2:4; etc.

Chapter 12

1. The time is not long past when the professor of canon law taught the moral theology courses in seminaries and scholasticates.

2. For St. Thomas, the basic rule for moral acts is the rule of rational intelligence as energized and finalized by the affectivity that enriches it, namely, the will (cf. *ST* 1-2, 90, 1c), and the rule of human nature (*Contra Gentiles* 3:129).

3. Cf. Jean Carbonnier, *Droit Civil* (Paris: Presses Universitaires de France, 1962), 1:12.

4. Aristotle, *Politics* II, 5.

5. St. Augustine, *Epist.* 36 (*PL* 33:136): "Mos populi Dei, vel instituta majorum pro lege tenenda sunt." St. Thomas will repeat this (*ST* 2-2, 79, 2, ad 2; cf. 2-2, 10, 12c; etc.)

6. Aristotle, *Nicomachean Ethics* 1095a7.

7. Ibid., 1179a12-20. Cf. this typically Aristotelean remark: "Theories must be required to fit the matter to which they are applied" (1103b34). Cf. the commentary of Gauthier and Jolif, First part, pp. 12–25.

8. Ibid., 1143b11–13.

9. Ibid., 1113b29–32.

10. Ibid., 1106b36.

11. Cf. "Orthodoxie et Orthopraxie," *VSS*, no. 118 (September, 1976), and L. Boisset, "Demain, la Théologie," ibid., no. 124 (February, 1978), 121–53.

12. The reader need only consult St. Thomas' commentary on the *Nicomachean Ethics* at the passages I have been citing.

13. The last of the ten "theological sources" (*Loci Theologici*) of Melchior Cano (1562) includes history, documents, and oral tradition. Cf. Ambroise Gardeil, "Lieux théologiques," *DTC* 9:717.

14. Cf. Gaston Bouthoul, *Les Mentalités* (Paris: Presses Universitaires de France, 1958); Mircea Eliade, *Occultism, Witchcraft, and Cultural Fashions* (Chicago: University of Chicago Press, 1975), Chapter 1 on cultural fashions.

15. Roland Barthe, *Système de la Mode* (Paris: Seuil, 1967).

16. Salaried work for women, the "advancement of women," the changing distribution of authority (and household tasks) between husband and wife, and so on, have led to changes in French law.

17. Cf. Helmut Schelsky, *Sociologie de la Sexualité* (Paris: Nouvelle Revue Française, 1966); Abel Jeannière, *The Anthropology of Sex*, tr. by J. Kernan (New York: Harper and Row, 1967); Jos van Ussel, *Histoire de la Répression Sexuelle* (Paris: Laffont, 1975).

18. E.g., Marie Cardinal, *La Clé sur la Porte* (Paris: Grasset and Fasquelle, 1972); *Autrement Dit* (ibid., 1977).

19. Cf., e.g., Joseph Spae, *Les Chrétiens vus du Japon* (Paris: Cerf, 1978).

20. Philippe Warnier, *La Foi d'un Chrétien Révolutionnaire* (Paris: Fayard, 1975), p. 43.

21. Cf. especially E. Schillebeeckx and B. van Iersel (ed.), *Revelation and Experience* (Concilium 113; New York; Seabury, 1979); François Refoulé, "Jésus Comme Référence à l'Agir des Chrétiens," in *Ecriture et Pratique Chrétienne* (Paris: Cerf, 1978), pp. 197–236; C. J. Pinto de Oliveira, *La Crise du Choix Moral dans la Civilisation Technique* (Fribourg, Switz.: Editions Universitaires, and Paris: Cerf, 1968); Gérard Fourez, *Choix Éthiques et Conditionnement Social* (Paris: Le Centurion, 1979).

22. Henri Bergson, *The Two Sources of Morality and Religion*, p. 56.

23. Cf. Michel Mollat, *Genèse Médiévale de la France Moderne* (Paris: Arthaud, 1977), p. 165: "The knight's aim was to do deeds of prowess which would win him renown among his peers and the ladies of the nobility."

24. Charles Baudelaire, *My Heart Laid Bare*, no. V, in *My Heart Laid Bare, and Other Prose Writings*, p. 177. Cf. Albert Camus's analysis of "The Dandies' Rebellion," in his *The Rebel: An Essay on Man in Revolt*, tr. by A. Bower (New York: Vintage Books, 1956), pp.47–54.

25. There is also a "clerical" milieu which obeys the same laws of social pressure and fashions. Cf. Serge Bonnet, *A Hue et à Dia* (Paris: Cerf, 1973). Whence the current "fashion" of "declergification" and the danger of "ecclesiocentrism" which is noted by J.-P. Bagot, *Le risque de la Bible* (Paris: Cerf, 1974), pp. 65ff.

26. Stendhal, *The Red and the Black*, tr. by C. J. Scott-Moncrieff, last sentence of Chapter 1.

27. M. Souchon, "Ethique de la Communication," *RSR* 62 (1974), 541–62.

28. Sigmund Freud, *Group Psychology and the Analysis of the Ego*, p. 16.

29. Ibid., p. 7.

30. The Latin word *norma* means: a (carpenter's) square, a rule, model, example.

31. Cf. Jean-Pierre Deconchy, *L'Orthodoxie Religieuse* (Paris: Editions Ouvrières, 1971); Hervé Carrier, *Psychosociologie de l'Appartenance Religieuse* (Rome: Gregorian University Press, 1960).

32. Freud, *The Ego and the Id*, p. 77.

33. Maurice Bellet, *La Théorie du Fou* (Paris: Desclée De Brouwer, 1977).

34. Ibid., pp. 242–43.

35. Ibid., p. 203.

36. Ibid., pp. 239–40.

37. Ibid., pp. 240–41.

38. Ibid.

39. Ibid., p. 242.

40. The anger that drives to homicide and the desire that drives to adultery seem in a way to be natural (*nobis a natura inesse*): St. Thomas, *ST* 1–2, 108, 3, ad 1.

41. Cf. Mt 23:2–3: "The scribes and the Pharisees sit on Moses' seat; so practice and observe whatever they tell you, but not what they do; for they preach but do not practice."

42. Judgment (*krisis*) is a discernment or distinguishing and not primarily a "judgment" in the juridical sense of a condemnation, as people only too often interpret it because they are afraid and are living with the anxiety of guilt instead of acknowledging that they are sinners and throwing themselves on the Father's mercy, which is the only hope of salvation.

43. St. Augustine, *Epist.* 145, 4 (*PL* 33:593).

44. In his *Table Talk*, Luther describes as follows the moment when he discovered the gospel: "At that point I made a distinction between the justice of the law and the justice of the gospel. Until then I did not realize the difference between the law and the gospel; I put them on the same level and read the gospel of Christ as though I were reading the law of Moses. But when I discovered the true difference between them and realized that the law and the gospel are two different things, then I understood the scriptures" (*Tischreden* 5, 55, 18).

45. St. Thomas, *ST* 1–2, 108, 1c.

46. St. Augustine, *De Genesi ad Litteram* II, 5, 6 (*PL* 34) [I cannot find the cited words in Augustine's text.—Tr.].

47. St. Thomas, *ST* 1–2, 96, 2, ad 2.

48. Ibid., 1–2, 108, 1, ad 1.

49. Ibid., 1–2, 108, 2c; 106, 2, ad 1; etc.

50. Ibid., 1–2, 8, 2c and ad 3.

51. Ibid., 1–2, 107, 1, ad 2; 108, 1c; cf. *Contra Gentiles* 4:22.

52. Ibid.

53. Economic growth seems to be increasingly uncontrolled and uncontrollable and to be leading to a widespread catastrophe. Cf. the appeal issued by the Club of Rome, and Donella H. Meadows et al., *The Limits of Growth: A Report for the Club of Rome's Project on the Predicament of Mankind* (sponsored by the Massachusetts Institute of Technology) (New York: New American Library, 1964). Cf. André Bieler, *Le Developpement Fou. Le Cri d'Alarme des Savants et l'Appel des Eglises* (Geneva: Labor et Fides, 1974). The experts seem to have no sense of irony when they draw up statistics for "Gross National Happiness."

54. Cf. Paul VI, Encyclical Letter *Populorum Progressio.*

55. Aristotle, *Nicomachean Ethics* 1180a4.

56. Cf. above, [Part I, Ch. 5, 1st section].

57. This point does not emerge clearly enough in the debate between Jean Daniélou and J.-P. Jossua after the publication of the former's book, *Prayer as a Political Problem*, tr. by J. P. Kirwan (New York: Sheed and Ward, 1967). Cf. "Christianisme de masse ou d'élite," *Verse et Controverse*, no. 4 (1st quarter, 1968).

58. St. Thérèse of Lisieux, *Story of a Soul*, tr. by J. Clarke (Washington, D.C.: Institute of Carmelite Studies, 1975), p. 14.

59. Cf. especially Albert Gelin, *The Poor of Yahweh*, tr. by K. Sullivan (Collegeville, Minn.: Liturgical Press, 1964); J. Dupont, B. Rigaux, et al., *La Pauvreté Évangélique* (Paris: Cerf, 1971).

Chapter 13

1. In a letter to Lou Andreas-Salomé on May 10, 1925 (when he was sixty-nine years old) Freud wrote: "A crust of indifference is slowly creeping up around me; a fact I state without complaining. It is a natural development, a way of beginning to be inorganic. The 'detachment of old age,' I think it is called. It must be connected with a decisive turn in the relationship of the two instincts postulated by me. The change taking place is perhaps not very noticeable; everything is as interesting as it was before, neither are the ingredients very different; but some kind of resonance is lacking; unmusical as I am, I imagine the difference to be something like using the pedal or not. The never-ceasing tangible pressure of a vast number of unpleasant sensations must have accelerated this otherwise perhaps premature condition, this tendency to experience everything *sub specie aeternitatis*": Sigmund Freud and Lou Andreas-Salomé, *Letters*, tr. by W. E. Robson-Scott (New York: Harcourt Brace Jovanovich, 1972), p. 154.

2. Cf. Baudelaire's poem on boredom, *The Ruined Garden*, tr. by Robert Lowell, in *The Flowers of Evil*, p. 19:
Time and nature sluice away our lives.
A virus eats the heart out of our sides,
digs in and multiplies on our lost blood.

3. Acedia is "an overwhelming sadness which produces such a depression in the human psyche that the person no longer has any desire to do anything whatsoever" (St. Thomas, *ST* 2-2, 35, 1c), especially in regard to what is the main concern of monastic life, the search for God. This lack of desire hinders the joy flowing from the charity that motivates the search. When the lack of desire is deliberately cultivated, it becomes a capital sin (ibid., 35, 3-4).

4. Plato, *Laws* 653a-c.

5. Ibid., 732c-733a.

6. Aristotle, *Nicomachean Ethics* 1104b9-12; cf. 1104b22, 1105a5, and St. Thomas' commentary on these passages.

7. Cf. this clear analysis by Anne Philipe in her *Le temps d'un soupir*, pp. 88-89: "The farther back I go into my childhood the stronger I find this taste for happiness, this idea that it was up to me to live, that I was in some way responsible for living. I remember long periods of darkness and cold when as a child, shrivelled up into myself and with teeth clenched, I felt sad and ashamed of it; I wanted healing as though I were ill, whereas the joys I felt seemed only right and beautiful. Later on I realized that a large part of ourselves is shaped by the meaning we give to the idea of happiness, which is not reducible simply to comfort of mind and body."

8. Aristotle, *Nicomachean Ethics* 1172a19.

9. Ibid., 1172a23.

10. Ibid., 1154b5.

11. Ibid., 1154b2-4. Cf. St. Thomas' commentary. Cf. also 1176b17-23 and *ST* 1-2, 31, 5, ad 1.

12. *Nicomachean Ethics* 1119b3-18.

13. Ibid, 1154b5-14, and *ST* 1-2, 48, 1c.

14. St. Thomas, *ST* 2-2, 168, 2c.

15. Aristotle, *Nicomachean Ethics* 1108a23-25. Cf. St. Thomas' commentary on this passage, and also *ST* 2-2, q. 168, where three articles are devoted to the virtue of eutrapelia.

16. *ST* 1-2, 48, 3, ad 2.

17. *Nicomachean Ethics* 1105a1.

18. Ibid., 1119a34, and St. Thomas' commentary on the passage, as well as *ST* 2-2, 142, 2c.

19. Charles Baudelaire, *My Heart Laid Bare*, no. XLII, in *My Heart Laid Bare, and Other Prose Writings*, p. 180.

20. Aristotle, *Nicomachean Ethics* 1152a23-25; 1176b17-20. St. Thomas, *ST* 2-2, 53, 4, ad 2.

21. Aristotle, ibid., 1166b7.

22. Ibid., 1176b17.

23. Ibid., 1166b10.

24. Ibid., 1109b1.

25. Ibid., 1109b7.

26. Sigmund Freud, *New Introductory Lectures on Psychoanalysis*, p. 149.

27. Françoise Dolto, "Au jeu du désir les dés sont pipés et les cartes truquées," *Bulletin de la Société Française de Philosophie*, 1972, no. 4, p. 132.

28. Vasse, *Le Temps du Désir*, p. 60.

29. St. Augustine, *Enarrationes in Psalmos* 102, 9 (*PL* 37:1523).

30. Françoise Dolto, "L'homme et son désir," *Christus*, no. 71 (June, 1971), 358.

31. Cf. Francis Pasche, *A Partir de Freud* (Paris: Payot, 1969), p. 196: "A private ethical ideal should not be allowed, if only because it is easier for many to bottle up their aggressivity, somehow or other, than to become a full person and because in the final analysis moral principles are less burdensome and less demanding than the dogma of success in a culture like ours."

32. This sclerosis is what the Bible calls "hardness of heart" (*sklērokardia*: Mt 19:8) or "sclerosis of the heart."

33. Daniel Wildocher, "Le Cours de l'Analyse et la Vie," *RFP*, September–December, 1971, p. 834.

34. Françoise Dolto, "L'Homme et son Désir," p. 365.

35. Cf. above, Chapter 9.

36. Dolto, art. cit., pp. 360–61.

37. Sigmund Freud, *The Future of an Illusion* [but I have not been able to find the cited words in the English translation—Tr.].

38. Aristotle, *Nicomachean Ethics* 1168b34.

39. Sigmund Freud, *New Introductory Lectures on Psychoanalysis*, p. 80.

40. Cf. Freud, "Instincts and Their Vicissitudes," *CP* 4:78; "Negation," *CP* 5:181–85; "Formulations Regarding the Two Principles in Mental Functioning," *CP* 4:13–21.

41. Sigmund Freud, *Beyond the Pleasure Principle*, p. 21.

42. Sigmund Freud, *The Ego and the Id*, p. 75.

43. Sigmund Freud, *Totem and Taboo*, p. 117.

44. Sigmund Freud, "The Loss of Reality in Neurosis and Psychosis," *CP* 2:277–82.

45. Sigmund Freud, "On Narcissism: An Introduction," *CP* 4:56–57.

46. Chasseguet-Smirgel, art. cit., p. 834.

47. Cf. above, [pp. 140–145 of French, pp. 121–25 of English trans.].

48. St. Thomas, *ST* 1-2, 89, 6c.

49. St. Thomas, *In Epistulam ad Philippenses*, cap. 4, lect. 1.

50. St. Thomas, *ST* 1-2, 90, 2c.

51. Ibid., 1-2, 102, 1c.

52. Aristotle, *Nicomachean Ethics* 1168a9.

53. Eph 6:4.

54. Aristotle, *Nicomachean Ethics* 1105a4–5.

55. Marcel Pagnol, *César* (Paris: Presses Pocket, 1976), p. 37.

56. St. Thomas, *ST* 1-2, 59, 3c; cf. 1-2, 107, 4c; etc.

57. Aristotle, *Nicomachean Ethics* 1169b29.

58. Ibid., 1114a31. St. Thomas often makes use of this principle.

59. St. Thomas, *ST* 2-2, 136, 3. Cf. Freud, *Civilization and Its Discontents*, p. 56: "My love is something valuable to me which I ought not to throw away without reflection. It imposes duties on me for whose fulfillment I must be ready to make sacrifices."

60. Cf. 1 Cor 7:31. Cf. above, [pp. 172-82 of French, pp. 150-61 of English trans.]. and St. Thomas, *Contra Gentiles* 3:134.

61. *Gustus bene dispositus* ("rightly ordered taste"), says St. Thomas, *ST* 1-2, 2, 1, ad 1.

62. Aristotle, *Nicomachean Ethics* 1172a21-25.

63. St. Augustine, *In Evangelium Joannis Tractatus* 73, 1 (*PL* 35:1824).

64. St. Thomas, *ST* 2-2, 45, 2, obj. 2.

65. Ibid., 2-2, 45, 2c.

66. Aristotle, *Eudemean Ethics* 1215a31.

67. Buffon, *Discours de Réception à l'Académie Française*, August 27, 1753.

68. Cf. Kierkegaard, *Either/Or* 2:240: "One must be careful how one lives, how one enjoys."

69. Cf. *Alain on Happiness*, no. LXXXIV (p. 226): "I spoke of an Art of Living that should be taught. As one of the rules I would set down the following: 'Give pleasure.' "

70. Cf. what Freud says about the "art of living" in "Psychanalyse et médicine," in *Ma Vie et la Psychanalyse* (Paris: Gallimard, 1949), pp. 151-52.

INDEX